Lessons In Money Management

Lorenzo L. Heard

Hope of Vision Publishing
Bridgeport, Connecticut

Lessons In Money Management
By: Lorenzo L. Heard

Copyright © 2010 by Lorenzo L. Heard

All rights reserved. No part of this book may be reproduced, copied, stored or transmitted in any form or by any means – graphic, electronic, or mechanical, including photocopying, recording, or information storage and retrieval systems without the prior written permission of Lorenzo L. Heard or Hope of Vision Publishing, except where permitted by law.

All scripture references and quotations in this book are taken from the King James Version of the Bible and The Amplified Bible Copyright © 1954, 1958, 1962, 1964, 1965, 1987 by The Lockman Foundation. All rights reserved. Used by permission. Holy Bible, New Living Translation, copyright 1996, 2004. Used by permission of Tyndale House Publishers, Inc., Wheaton, Illinois 60189. All rights reserved.

Hope of Vision Publishing
a division of HOV, LLC.
hopeofvision@gmail.com
www.HopeofvisionPublishing.com

Cover Design: Kaye Coleman

Editor: Elana Simms for Red Pen, LLC, Shawn Lewis and Kimberly K. Ward

Lorenzo L. Heard Photo Credit: Francine Caldwell

Lorenzo L. Heard Ministries
Greater 2nd Mt. Olive Baptist Church
302 Adkins Street
Albany, Georgia 31705
229-435-9961

Email: lessonsinmoney@gmail.com
www.lorenzolheardministries.com
www.lessonsinmoney.net
www.theoliveexperience.org

For more information about special discounts for bulk purchases, please contact Lorenzo L. Heard Ministries at (229) 435-9961, www.hopeofvisionpublishing.com or hopeofvision@gmail.com

For bookings and Lessons In Money Management Sessions contact (229) 435-9961 or email lessonsinmoney@gmail.com.

ISBN 978-0-9818253-4-2
Library of Congress Control Number: 2010940029

10 9 8 7 6 5 4 3 2 1

Printed in the United States of America

CONTENTS

Introduction		5
1	Is it Biblically Correct to Co-sign?	7
2	Financial Commitment on the Front End!	11
3	Giving that Gets God's Attention!	15
4	Mismanagement Can Mess Me up with My Master!	19
5	Wisdom to Make Money within the House!	25
6	God Wants Us to Know How We Got Our Wealth!	31
7	God Gives the Power to Get Wealth!	37
8	What to Do When the Much is Missing?	43
9	Giving That Recognizes God!	47
10	God Comes First in Our Finances!	51
11	No Longer Making God Second with My Money!	57
12	The Right Attitude about Giving to God!	63
13	The Secret to Getting More Seeds!	69
14	The Difference Sowing in Difficult Times Can Make!	73
15	The Cost of Getting God's Attention	79
16	The Sacrifice that Satisfies Must Cost Us Something	83
17	Giving unto God Was in Place from the Start!	89
18	When the Tenth is My Testimony of Thanks for Victory!	93
19	The Danger of Being Dishonest about Donations!	99
20	The Dangers and the Risks of Being Rich!	105
21	Don't Let Money Become Your Master!	109
22	Don't Make Too Much Out of Making Ends Meet!	113
23	God Has the Gift of Adding!	119
24	The Magnitude of My little, As a Righteous Man!	123
25	My Way is God's Way!	129
26	God's Strange Ways of Getting Me Money to Make the Ends Meet!	135
27	Good Money Management Matters!	139
28	Financial Faithfulness = Trust with More Kingdom Treasures	145
29	Exposing Wrong Attitudes about Wealth!	151
30	The Wisdom and Wealth Connection!	155
31	Doing Right by Those We've Done Wrong!	161
32	My Prosperity May Be Hidden in My Prayer!	165
33	Making It Through A Famine!	171
34	Giving That Comes Back When it Looks Like it's Only Going Out!	177
35	"Facing My Financial Failures!"	183
36	Don't Promise If We Aren't Willing to Pay!	189
37	A Wise Way to Look at Wealth!	195
38	Facing Financial Losses with Faith in Our Father!	201
39	Intentional Giving to an Interesting God!	207
Conclusion		211

INTRODUCTION

Our view of money can be derived from the Word, and taught in a way that honors God, or derived from the popular views of the surrounding culture. My personal testimony is that I was caught up in the world's estimation of money and money-management principles. Such was the case, even after I witnessed a beautiful legacy in the lives of my parents, grandparents and great-grandparents – that of the fruits and rewards that result from obedience to what the Bible teaches about money and money-management. The patriarchs and matriarchs of my family lived biblical money-management principles daily. I was taught these principles as these loved ones led by example in their giving to God. I saw them giving to God, and I saw their inability to out-give God as increase was returned into their lives.

Somewhere along the way, I strayed from what I was taught. So, the lessons of life had to take me to a financial cliff. It was at this place that God, and what He said about the money He gave me, became the rope in the cliffhanger moment of my life. This book is a very transparent account of how God did not let me go over the edge, and the lessons that I have learned along the way.

"Lessons in Money Management" explores the reality that we either learn about money subconsciously from the world around us, or make a conscious decision to learn what the Bible teaches about money. The Bible provides a wealth of opportunities to learn about anything we want to know. This includes Christian money-management principles. No matter how much or how little we are given in terms of money, the Lord expects us to make wise decisions and do what we can with what we have. The important thing to remember is that biblical financial principles boil down to one thing; being a good manager of what God has provided, whether that is a lot or a little.

Being a good manager has its foundation in the truth that God owns everything. He has merely blessed us with a portion of His bounty to manage. As God's managers, the size of the portion does not matter. Rather, it is the size of our responsibility that matters! The size of our responsibility is God-sized, and this is why it matters what we do with our portion. Do you use your portion to help others? Is your portion used to help your family obtain the things they need (as opposed to what your family wants)? Do you carefully consider the items for which you go into debt? Are you making plans for the future – for example, retirement – with your portion? These questions are essential to assessing the type of manager you are. Then, we are to make a plan to put what God has given us to better use.

Once I saw where my mismanagement took me – to the cliff's edge – I reached for the rope of hope, God and what He said about money management. I learned that if I would make wise decisions with the money God gives me, God would help me obtain what I need. We will receive our reward, either in this life or in the next.

LESSON 1

IS IT BIBLICALLY CORRECT TO CO-SIGN?
Proverbs 11:15; 17:18; 22:26

The Word declares we must live by every word that proceeds out of the mouth of God. We are challenged to open our ears, hearts, and spirit to hear the voice of God on every subject. Then, we must correctly respond to the Word that we have heard. To that end, this book sets before the Body of Christ biblical principles from my Money Management Series that will challenge us on how we handle money issues.

Every believer ought to want to prosper and to have more than just enough to meet needs. Just think of what churches could do if members had a heart for God and had the financial resources to fund any vision birthed in the house. Just imagine, if money wasn't an issue for the majority of members, or if money wasn't an issue for you. What great things could be done!

The first step in our financial recovery and prosperity is to admit to God that we have done what we wanted to do with the blessings He has bestowed upon us. Secondly, we must repent for not making hearing His voice and obeying His word a priority on all subjects, and that includes finances. When is the last time, we sought God or really begged God to guide us in making the right financial decisions on everything?

This first lesson is on co-signing for other people's loans. The Word has specific directions and instructions and we must decide if we are going to listen to the Lord or listen to the one who wants a loan.

The three passages in Proverbs make specific points to co-signing for another person's loan. Proverbs 11:15 says, *"He that is surety for a stranger shall smart for it; and he that hateth suretyship is sure."* So often, we meet people who are in need of our help. This lesson is not about not helping people, but rather knowing when we are going beyond the biblical boundaries for a believer. The first thing the King James Version says will happen when we guarantee a loan for someone who is a stranger, outsider (*Amplified Version*), or another (*New International Version*) is that we will smart for it, suffer for it (*New American Standard*), surely suffer (*NIV*), or be in danger (*New Living Translation*).

We see at least four negative things that potentially will happen when we co-sign or guarantee someone else's loan. Please list them:
  1. _____
  2. _____
  3. _____
  4. _____

The New Living Translation interprets Proverbs 11:15 this way: *"Guaranteeing a loan for a stranger is dangerous; it is better to refuse than to suffer later."* We must always remember the Word of God is not comprised of suggestions or good ideas, but directions and instructions that will save and make us wise, if we will only listen and obey. The Word says *it is better to refuse than to suffer later.* No matter how much we want to help, God's Word says to refuse to commit to such a binding responsibility. Sometimes, the enemy tries to trick us by raising questions like, "Haven't you known them for years?" Other times, he'll cause us to second guess ourselves, dropping sly statements like, "They are not strangers! The Bible clearly says '*strangers.*'" However, for the most part, we don't know people well, when it comes to financial responsibility. There are questions we can ask ourselves to help determine if a loan seeker is a stranger. We must be able to answer these questions before we are asked to co-sign:

1. How much money do they make an hour, week, month and year?
2. How much money do they normally have in their checking account during an average month?
3. Whose name is on their life insurance policy? How much life insurance do they have?
4. How much is their car and house note or rent each month?
5. Who do they owe and how much do they owe? Why haven't they paid these companies and individuals back?
6. When is the last time they received a raise? How much was it? What are they doing with it?
7. If you advised them to get rid of their cell phone and cable TV to pay back the loans, would they do it?
8. Do they pay their bills on time?
9. If they had the choice of paying a bill on time or getting an item they wanted but did not need, which would take priority?

If our answers are "I don't know" and "no," that means when it comes to their money, we really are strangers. With that knowledge, rest assured that they fit into the category of don't co-sign their loan.

People who want you to co-sign are normally people who want what people with good credit have or could have without waiting, working, paying and/or maturing to get it in their own time. Proverbs 17:18 says, *"It is poor judgment to co-sign a friend's note, to become responsible for a neighbor's debts."*

Just in case someone is still wrestling with whether to co-sign based on whether the loan seeker is a stranger, the Word says co-signing is not prudent, even for friends! There is no guessing this time. Even friends are not responsible enough for us to commit to standing for their loans. The Amplified Version of the Bible puts it this way: *"A man void of good sense gives a pledge and becomes security for another in the presence of his neighbor."* Please note what the Word calls the mental mindset of someone who guarantees the loans of someone else: poor in judgment void of good sense, and the New International Version says lacking in judgment. The Word is saying we are not very smart when we co-sign on another's loan. So, why do we co-sign for other people?

1. We feel pressured by the other person.
2. We hate to tell people "no!"
3. The person makes such great promises to repay.
4. If we don't help them, "What will they do?" is often times our question.
5. People suggest that they don't have anybody else to help but us.
6. The Lord told them to ask us, showed us to them or put us on their heart.
7. _____
8. _____
9. _____

We must always remember that when we co-sign on a note, we are responsible if the other person does not pay the loan. We must also remember that we are just as responsible for repaying the loan because the creditor never would have granted a loan or gave the person the product had we not made a promise. When we co-sign we are saying to the lender: "I am just as committed to paying you as the person who wants what you are selling." Co-signing signifies to the lender that you not only have the credit, but you also are commitment to making sure the lender gets every dime of his money. When we co-sign a loan, we are really saying that the lender doesn't need to worry about the irresponsibility of the other person because we are responsible. If you do not have the money to honor a debt, you should never co-sign a loan. If you are not going to be all right with paying off the debt, you should not co-sign for people. God holds us just as accountable for the repaying of the loan as we hold the person who uses our credit and our good name to obtain the loan. Co-signing is equal to commitment, and if we are not committed we should not mislead creditors into believing we are.

Proverbs 22:26-27 says, *"Do not co-sign another person's note or put up a guarantee for someone else's loan. If you can't pay it, even your bed will be snatched from under you."*

Here again, God warns us about co-signing on loans. It is a bad practice and it disobeys biblical principles. There has to be a reason God would use Solomon to speak on this issue three times in the book of Proverbs. It is a warning that all must heed or ultimately suffer because we chose to ignore the Word and went with our own will. Everyone is not as concerned about his or her credit as you are about yours. Some saints don't care to pay on time and even take the position that the creditor should just be glad that they paid!

Another issue co-signing brings up is over committing. We must always remember the difference between our credit limit and our paying limit. Sometimes, we have more credit than we have money to make ends meet. If a believer is already overextended but still has credit cards, lines of credit, or a good credit rating, he or she must take into consideration not whether the credit is there, but whether there is money to repay the loan. We must always remind ourselves that we cannot get blood from a turnip!

Anyone over the age of 30 who cannot borrow $500 from anyone but you is always a risky loan. Anyone over age 40 who cannot borrow $500 from anyone but you isn't likely to repay a loan.

We owe it to God to listen to Him and follow His path and plan for financial prosperity. If we neglect to hear Him and obey, destruction will be our destination. It is not that God does not want us to help; He does not want to see us hurt. As many old saints use to say, "Friendship and money don't mix."

The lender has the right to take what is rightfully ours when we over commit by co-signing. The lender has the right to take what we will really need because we made a promise to pay if the other person did not.

LESSON 2

FINANCIAL COMMITMENT ON THE FRONT END!
Luke 14:28-30

This lesson is again about gaining wisdom from the Word of God when it comes to making great financial-management decisions. So often the believer, who loves, knows and trusts God can find himself or herself in such a financial crisis that our finances seem to stretch, strip and sometimes strangle us of our faith. Not only do we not always know how we are going to get out of a financial mess, but we also don't always know how we got in the financial mess. If we had to explain step by step what happened or how we got to this place financially, most saints could not say. Those of us who are going through a financial storm, coming out of a financial storm, or about to go into a financial storm probably cannot say with great accuracy what happened. It is easy to blame one event or one situation, such as:

1. Someone did not pay me back.
2. The light bill jumped up an extra $100 this month.
3. The job messed up my money this week.
4. I got laid off yesterday so I can't pay my rent today.
5. _____
6. _____
7. _____

No one small event, circumstance, situation, or setback would mess us up financially if we stopped doing at least a few things: living on the edge; spending without counting the cost; living and spending without a plan and not working the plan before spending; and blaming someone else for our failure to properly plan. In this text, Jesus teaches us how we are expected to live by God's principles. In simple terms, Jesus teaches us to budget.

Verse 28. For which of you, intending to build a tower, sitteth not down first, and counteth the cost, whether he have sufficient to finish it?

No matter how much faith we have or how spiritual we believe ourselves to be, the Word of God says we should do first things first. So often, we set out to do a project without ever really developing a plan or seeking God for wisdom. Think of the last projects you spearheaded for your life, family, or future and see if there was ever a plan. If a person is considering purchasing a car, for example, there are some things he or she must consider:

1. How much car can I/we afford?
2. If I/we cannot afford to get four new tires on the old car, where are we going to find money now for a note for maybe five years?
3. Will the insurance go up on a new car? How much? Did I struggle to pay the insurance on the older car?

4. If the insurance goes up, where will I get the extra money?
5. If I can really come up with the money for the note for the new car and extra money for the insurance, why not see if I can do it for 6 to 12 months before getting the car? If I can, I'll buy the car. If not, why not reconsider my plan?
6. Do I need to get a car that's more fuel-efficient or will this gas mobile break me?
7. _____

Jesus says *sit down first and count the cost*. In other words, sit down and calculate not just your present income and expenses, but also the possibility of anything in your future that needs to be factored into the equation. Is the company about to begin layoffs? Are we about to have a child? Is there a child about to go to college? Are we already behind in our bills or about to be behind? Is the economy negatively affecting us already? If one bad thing happened to us financially right now, would it throw us into being broke immediately, or do we have emergency money saved? Is the whole house in one accord for the investment we are about to make? Are our credit cards already maxed out? Are we already financially stretched?

Sit down first suggests don't be too hasty to move without some deep thought and real consideration. Think about it and talk it over with someone who can offer wise financial counsel before making a big move that could negatively affect the family's finances, their future and faith. *Sit down first* denotes no financial decision should be rushed into without first being well prayed over, thought out and fasted about, if necessary. Jesus also says *count the cost,* which means we must calculate and see what we are getting into, and furthermore, know if we have enough for the task we are undertaking. Why? Why waste time calculating when we know what we want? The joy for many of us is getting it, but the joy of the Father for us is being able to get it and keep it without losing our heart or passion for the Kingdom in the process. Some people gain the world but lose their souls in the process. There are others who gain what they want just to lose it down the road – and that's not good for the testimony they had given that God helped them get it. Simply put, God does not want us to start but He wants us to finish.

Verse 29. Lest haply, after he hath laid the foundation, and is not able to finish it, all that behold it begin to mock him.

If the goal is to construct a building, we must not be satisfied with just pouring the foundation. For too long we have been content with the effort, good intent, or amazing start while God is saying, "That was never the goal; finish the job." Many Christians have wasted a lot of money because they were not committed to seeing their financial ventures and obligations through. To spend thousands on getting land, clearing the land, digging, acquiring concrete, paying to pour the concrete and then not complete the project is a waste of time, money, energy and resources – commodities you cannot get back. It's an offense to God when we buy furniture and pay on it for three years just to have the vendor pick it up the last year. When we buy a car with a five-year note, pay on it for four years and then let the car be repossessed, it's an offense to the Kingdom. Consider this scenario: You purchase a car with a five-year note and pay on it for four years. Then, because the transmission goes out on the car, you decide to stop paying on it, purchase another car (acquiring another note!) and allow the creditor to pick up the car that is not paid for and sue for the rest. This is totally against Kingdom principles. We would do better to get the transmission repaired and go back to driving the car than to stop paying on the car we have and start paying on a new car we did not need.

... And is not able to finish it, all that behold it begin to mock him.

God is concerned about what His children show the world. God never starts a project unless He is committed to completing it. This lesson stresses the importance of commitment to completing whatever we begin financially. If we are not financially committed to completing a project, we should not be financially committed to starting it. God is bothered when the world laughs at His people, no matter whether it is a group project or an individual's project. When the children of God do not complete their financial obligations and see a project through, satanic signals are sent to the world that suggest things about God and His people. This offends our God.

The Top 5 Things Incomplete Projects May Suggest:
1. To not finish a project may suggest we were never as committed to the project as we should have been;
2. To not finish a project suggests we did not think things through or as thoroughly as we should have;
3. To not finish a project suggests the project was bigger than us, and bigger than our commitment;
4. To not finish a project tarnishes the character of God because those who make light of God, the people of God and the things of God conclude the project is not complete because God is not big enough to make it happen, or that God does not have the resources to help His people and
5. To not finish a project suggests we are Counterfeit Kids and not Kingdom Kids. God's children ought to look like Him and finish what we start.

We must no longer allow people to laugh at us for not being committed to every financial endeavor we undertake. It infuriates God that the enemy to our faith is giggling that His children cannot be trusted to finish what we have started financially.

Verse 30. Saying, This man began to build, and was not able to finish.

The Word of God says the world begins talking about our inability. Most parents must know how God feels because we as parents do not like when people speak negatively about our children. People of God will always be criticized and scrutinized, but we must never give the unbeliever ammunition. One of the ways to discover how committed we are to a project is to see what we will sacrifice before we get started. Sometimes, we must test of our faith and our faithfulness by seeing if we will sacrifice for a season. If we are not willing to sacrifice before we get started, more than likely we will not be willing to sacrifice if we get in trouble after we have started. Before making your next big purchase, see how committed you are to buying it by paying off something first or saving several months of what that bill would be. Consider simply saving the money for that potential bill and purchasing the item flat-out rather than financing it with interest. The world loves negative things about the children of God, therefore we must not give the world fodder to say something negative about the way we handle our financial affairs. So, what do you do, if you are already beyond the point of pouring the foundation and have no means of constructing the building? The first thing is to stop laying foundations until you finish this one that has been poured. Take inventory of what you have and what it will take to finish what you have begun. Never be afraid to ask God for wisdom on how to finish a project, or even if it was a project you should have started and how to proceed from this point. We will find out that God is always willing, ready and able to help. We can only manage what we have and what we make, but the smaller the amount, the better the management must be.

There is nothing we are in that God cannot help us out of. There is nothing we have started that God cannot help us complete. There is no project for which our God does not have the resources to help us finish. However, it is always wise to start with what we have and trust God to provide the rest. We cannot really expect God to supply the rest if we waste what we already have. May God fulfill and complete every financial commitment and every project undertaken to His glory.

LESSON 3

GIVING THAT GETS GOD'S ATTENTION!
Mark 12:41-44

There are many things we know about God. One undeniable fact about God is that He is a giver. A person does not have to know God well or have been around Him long to find out God is a giver. Even if a person has just started walking with God and has never attended a Bible study, Church-In-Training, Sunday school, or a seminary, it is obvious God likes giving to us. In most instances, God gives even when we are not deserving of the good things He gives. As a matter of fact, every good gift and perfect gift comes from Him, the Father of Lights in whom there is no variableness, nor shadow of turning (James 1:17). Oftentimes, God gives to people who never say to Him, "Thank You." There are even times when God gives to people who do not know Him, recognize Him, acknowledgment Him, or honor Him.

This lesson is not about what God gets from us, or even what He expects from us. This lesson is about what God deserves from us. In this text, we encounter a lady at church during an offering. It's amazing that the Gospel writer does not spend time talking about how the lady listened during the sermon or what she experienced during praise and worship. God chose to let us look at her during the most private and personal part of the worship experience – the part that is hidden in our pockets or purses. This is the part of worship that is concealed in an envelope and then sealed shut. Only God has a right to reveal how much we have given or even to lift and then look at the amount in the envelope.

Verse 41. And Jesus sat over against the treasury, and beheld how the people cast money into the treasury: and many that were rich cast in much.

Though Jesus was not taking up an offering, He did sit near the collection plate and observe. He did have a right to see how much was given because it was His Father's money. This text reminds us that the Lord does take notice of our giving. The Lord watched each person as he or she came around and sowed into the Kingdom. The people were not giving to the church or temple, nor were they giving to the priest or to the preacher. Their gifts and our gifts are to be given unto God. God uses the gifts to help with the expenses of the church, the spreading of the Gospel and for relief to the poor, widows and orphans. These three things are the financial obligations of the Christian believer and the reason we support our local church. The Bible does not suggest they knew where every dime was going before they gave. The Word of God simply says they gave. *... And many that were rich cast in much.* There were some big gifts given that day in worship. Many gave that day and most gave according to their ability. Those who were rich cast in much, but this did not impress the Lord because these individuals had much, and even after giving they still had much left. We probably would have been impressed if Oprah had been there and had given. We would have walked around talking about the thousands Oprah donated that day. Just imagine Bill Gates being in the worship that day and how much he would have given in tithes and offerings. We would have walked away talking about how much money he gave and what we could do with that much money. But what impresses us does not always impress God. As a matter of fact, Jesus never even said how much the rich folks gave.

Verse 42. And there came a certain poor widow, and she threw in two mites, which make a farthing.

The phrase "and there came a certain poor widow" suggests this woman's husband is dead, and she has no one to depend upon but the Lord. The money counters are not nearly as excited about seeing her come around as they are when the rich come to give their gifts. Please don't miss this: Not only does she not have a man or someone to depend upon, but the Lord also says she is poor. Despite her poverty, she still comes to the House of the Lord and when it is offering time, she brings her gift to God. Real givers can look past what we have and give because of our need. Real givers know we need God's involvement in our affairs. Real givers know we have a need for God's mercy and that God's mercy goes farther than our money. Real givers know that God's goodness can not only get us groceries without money, but also a good appetite to eat! Make no mistake, there are people who have plenty of food but don't have a good appetite to eat it.

... And she threw in two mites, which make a farthing.

When she threw in the two mites, she was throwing herself at the mercy seat of God. There must be something this woman knows about God. Could she be saying to God, "If I keep the two mites there is only so far they can go, but if I put them in your hands – because You are God – You can do much more with it than I can." Perhaps she has heard about the widow woman in Elijah's day who was running out of meal and was about to gather sticks to make a fire and prepare her last meal but ran into the Man of God. When she chose to take care of not the man or the Man of God but the will of God, He did not let the meal in the barrel run out, and therefore she, the prophet and her son did eat many days (1 Kings 17: 8-16).

Verse 43. And he called unto him his disciples, and saith unto them, Verily I say unto you, That this poor widow hast cast more in, than all they which have cast into the treasury:

Her gift got God's attention. Her gift moved the Master to call over unto himself His disciples. Jesus wanted those who were His students or followers to take notice of the poor widow's giving. Selfish giving never gets His attention like this nor would it ever move the Master to say, "This is worth talking about with joy!" The Lord uses her giving as a lesson to teach those of us who maintain we are traveling with Him and that we trust Him. Have you ever given a gift to someone and the gift was so nice that it got others' attention? Have you ever given a gift to God that got His attention as well as that of the angels? God likes giving expensive gifts. God is not a cheap God and anything that He gives is priceless: air, love, life, health and strength, salvation, righteousness, peace, anointing, His Son – and the list goes on!

... That this poor widow hast cast more in, than all they which have cast into the treasury.

Jesus says this woman contributed the most during that worship. The very gift we are sometimes ashamed of or matters the least to most folks may be the gift that God, while counting the offering in heaven, says, "Here comes a large gift! We are going to need an angel to carry the return on this type investment into the Kingdom to my child. It's too large for this lady to carry home in her purse. The blessing the Father is going to give her for sowing into the Kingdom is too much for the men counting the offering around the table to handle." Jesus, upon finishing His calculations of the collection, says this woman gave more. God does not count in the same manner as most Christians. To us it appears rich people put more money in the basket as their form of worship. Christians count the size of the seed, but God counts the size of the sacrifice. While people are counting the amount of seeds, God is counting the amount of the sacrifice. Some gifts that we give do not cost us anything. During Christmas, many saints just re-gift the gifts that we do not like and give them to someone else (who really does not want that gift either). Consider our logic. Didn't He see what the others had given? Did He not count the rich folks' gifts correctly? He must not have counted correctly because He said the poor widow woman gave more than all the rest in the worship. The real truth is that God does not count the way we do. Just because others might be impressed with the size of our gift or the size of our seed, it does not mean God is impressed or moved at all. That gift you brought might be more show than seed. What may impress others at the offering table may not even get God's attention in heaven. Just remember, those who are counting at church take note of the size of the seed. But the size of our sacrifice is the only thing Christ counts in heaven.

Verse 44. For all they did cast in of their abundance; but she of her want did cast in all that she had, even all her living.

This lesson is not about asking people to give their money until there is none left. This lesson is about allowing God to see His reflection in us through our giving. God never gives to us grudgingly or unwilling. There has never been anything we have needed that He did not supply with His best. Anyone who is a good gift giver also loves to get good gifts. Anyone who is a great gift giver really loves being given great gifts, but will accept good gifts with grace. It is unacceptable to always be a poor gift giver while loving to be lavished with the best of gifts. This widow catches God's attention because she is a great gift giver.

... But she of her want did cast in all that she had, even all her living.

This woman gave out of her poverty while others gave out of their surplus. All the others had much more than what they gave. But when the poor widow woman gave, she let the Lord have all that she had. I would say we ought never to give God all that we have, but if I did I would be totally wrong because when we needed Him, He gave all He had. It would sound foolish to advise believers to be OK with giving all we have to God or to the Kingdom – but that's just what Christ did on the cross and that is just what Christ does all day when a new believer comes into salvation. Jesus shares His entire inheritance with us, and even at this very moment He is giving His inheritance away to someone who has confessed faith in Him as Lord and Savior.

God is not selfish and everything we have seen about Christ suggests the Father's children should not be selfish either. When we are not willing to give to God, it might mean we need to yield more to Him. The more of us He has, the less we will struggle to share with someone who has given us everything. Christ not only saw what the widow gave, but He also noticed what she had left. Can God count on us to look more like Him when it comes to giving – especially those of us who say we love the Lord? The widow will never be forgotten because what she did caused Christ to make His disciples take note of her and Mark to write about her so we would get to meet her. Surely, anyone that good to God will never be off His mind. I would have loved to have watched how God worked in her life from that day forward. If He made the example of her giving so important as to have her story recorded in the Holy Scripture, there must have been an angel dispatched to make sure her every need was met. God deserves the best and nothing less. God desires our best and nothing less. So, the next time the question of what will we give God pops up, hopefully, the answer will be OUR BEST!

LESSON 4

MISMANAGEMENT CAN MESS ME UP WITH MY MASTER!
Matthew 25:24-28

In this lesson, we continue to explore Jesus' explanation of what the Kingdom of Heaven is really like. Jesus likened the Kingdom to an owner of a company preparing to go out of town who, just before leaving, entrusts his possessions to his three employees. The owner of the company knows his employees' capabilities. Therefore, he does not give the three the same amount of responsibility. In this text, the word talent refers to money. The owner gives each employee a certain amount of money to handle until he returns. When the owner returns, he discovers the employee who was given the most – five talents – had gone out and worked until he doubled what he had been given. With great commendations, his boss congratulates him on the great work he's done.

The employee who was entrusted with two talents also was faithful and successfully doubled what had been given to him. This second employee was given the same type of commendations and applause for the excellent investment and management of what had been entrusted to him.

Not only does the owner of the company say "well done" to the two employees who had worked hard to make more of what was given them, but he also says, "I will make you rulers over many things." Good management of the things of God equals promotion. The employees never asked for a promotion but their performance merited promotion. Now, let's look at what the employee or servant with the least did with what was given to him.

Verse 24. Then he which had received the one talent came and said, 'Lord, I knew thee, that thou art a hard man, reaping where thou hast not sown, and gathering where thou hast not strewed.

I wish I could tell you that God does not care what we do with what has been given unto us, but that is not true. I wish I could tell you that any excuse will do for not being good managers of the money entrusted to us by the Master, but I can't. We all will have to explain what we did with what God gave us and why. The very thing that could have given this servant's life new meaning – mastering the money that his master left in his care – he frittered away and blew it. God gives to us what the King James Version calls talents, but it is more specifically money, financial resources, credit and money-making opportunities. But what do some folks do with it? BLOW IT! The man (employee, servant) cannot deny he was given an opportunity just like everyone else. Still, he was not given as much as everybody else. At first, it appears as though his boss may have been showing favoritism, but don't forget that verse 15 says the owner, boss, or master gave to each one "according to his several ability." Let's look at verse 15 again.

And unto one he gave five talents, to another two, and to another one; to every man according to his several ability; and straightway took his journey.

Please notice several major points:
1. The master gave, so it was his goods or possessions.
2. The master gave everyone something to work with.
3. The master gave to each servant according to the servant's ability, or what he could handle.
4. The master may have had more, but he only gave according to the ability of the servants.
5. The abilities of the servants could have been money-management skills, ambition, intuitiveness, willingness to work, commitment to making things happen, familiarity with finances, the ability to handle pressure, accountability and/or trustworthiness.
6. _____
7. _____
8. _____

Possession of – or the lack of – any of these characteristics could be the reason why we are or are not trusted with more from our Master. For those of us who want God to give us more, we must ask and answer the question about our several abilities. God does not normally give more for us to do less with it. If we want more, we must do more with the less.

... Lord, I knew thee, that thou art a hard man, reaping where thou hast not sown, and gathering where thou hast not strewed.

The question is still being raised: How well do we know God? Many who say they are saints see God in this same way. The man says in the text that the master is a hard man – hard to please, hard to satisfy, hard to settle with, hard to understand, and hard to work for. I have not always worked to the best of my ability, but I must admit that working with God and working for God has been great! God could have and should have fired me and a few other folks I know a long time ago. Even when I did not do my best, He still gave me the best pay. Many people in the church want the Master's money without any accountability. Many people in the church want the Master to give us enough to buy the best car, live in the most impressive house, wear the finest of clothes, eat the richest of foods and enjoy the best of life's entertainment. But when He asks us for one dime out of every dollar He gave us, we think He is too hard! Everything the servants in the text have to work with came from their master. Everything we have to work with came from our Master.

... Reaping where thou hast not sown, and gathering where thou hast not strewed.

This under-achieving servant sounds like a lot of us – ungrateful and uninformed. This unawareness is why many church folk will remain in the hood and misunderstood! If we change the way we think about God's money, God might change the amount of

CHANGE He allows us to manage. Whatever amount we have of God's money is change in comparison to the amount of wealth God has. God has a right to count and collect every penny He gives us, but in His goodness He gives us a dollar and then says if we are grateful, give Him back the dime. If we committed to do more with the 90 cents we are left with, we could give God, the church, charities and our children a lot more. Mismanagement causes everybody to be left out and then we end up wondering, "What did we do with our money?" Routinely, the Creator, the church, the children, and the charities are left lacking, and we still owe the rent and the rest (car note, insurance and light bill). Poor prioritizing is a telltale sign in most people who consistently mismanagement money.

Verse 25. And I was afraid, and went and hid thy talent in the earth. Lo, there thou hast what is thine.

The man claims he was afraid he might lose the master's money, so he went and dug a hole and put the money in the hole. Fear is a crippling emotion that leads many saints to making poor money decisions. Some people mismanage money because they are afraid. Often their rationale is:
1. If I miss this sale, there may never be another one.
2. If I don't buy now, I may be too old and never get it.
3. If I don't get it now, I'm afraid somebody else may get it.
4. If I don't buy something new, people may think I don't have it going on and I want to be impressive.
5. _____
6. _____

Excessive shopping is nothing more than putting the Master's money in a hole. Buying things we really don't need and cannot afford in an effort to impress people we really don't like is nothing more than putting the Master's money in a hole. The bottom line: The man did nothing with the money the Master had given to him. We must not be found guilty of not doing anything positive with the money that has been entrusted to us. The servant actually has what he was given.

... Lo, there thou hast what is thine.

This is the equivalent of someone borrowing a thousand dollars from you with the promise that they will repay you in three weeks. Three weeks turns into 30 years. Then, they finally repay you with no interest. The thousand dollars 30 years from now with no interest is not the same money as the thousand dollars being repaid three months from the point at which it was borrowed. The servant's attitude toward his master is that the master ought to just be glad he gave him back the money! People with poor money management skills usually have a poor attitude about repayment, accountability, financial responsibility, credit, saving, investing, and building financial wealth. If we pay our tithe but do not give God an offering, we are just giving God back the amount He gave us. Jesus says the Master really wants His back with some interest.

Verse 26. His Lord answered and said unto him, Thou wicked and slothful servant, thou knewest that I reap where I sowed not, and gather where I have not strewed:

Jesus says the master first addressed the fact that the servant did not know him. One of the reasons, we handle the Lord's money the way we do is we really do not know our Master. Everything we have is because of Him and came from Him. Nothing we have is ours. Everything we have belongs to the Master but is ours to use and enjoy at the His discretion. We do not have anything, because we worked for it; everything we have the Master graciously gave us. We can't go to work unless He gives us His health, strength, mercy and grace to get there and back. Before we can talk about the cars that we bought – with the money we made – we must first look at the materials from which our cars were constructed. All the materials our vehicles were made out of belong to Him! The streets and roads our cars ride on to get to work belong to the Lord. As a matter of fact, the ground the building sits on where we work really belongs to the Lord! The Master deserves not only what He gets, but also much more!

Verse 27. Thou oughtest therefore to have put my money to the exchangers, and then at my coming I should have received mine own with usury.

In essence, the master says to the man who mismanaged his money, "You should have taken advantage of the opportunities to make the money work for you." The Master is saying God is looking for more than what He gave us. Wealth comes with wisdom and poverty comes with poor financial priorities and poor financial perceptions. How we handle what we've received will greatly influence how much more we will get from God. Look for ways to better manage the money the Master has given you. We must do more than stretch it – the Master wants us to increase it. New businesses, new ventures and new opportunities pass our people by every day. If we don't want to lose it, we had better learn how to use it because the Master might just take it away (verses 28 and 29). The money the Lord allows us to make this week should grow. Have you ever wondered why men go to the barbershop? They go because hair grows. Our children grow. If our children do not grow, we begin taking them to the doctor because something is wrong. If our money is not growing, something is wrong. *Usury* is interest. At least a portion of the money we make ought to make some interest.

Verse 28. Take therefore the talent from him, and give it unto him which hath ten talents.

The reason the master takes from the servant with only one and gives unto the servant who has 10 is the one with 10 knows what to do with an opportunity. The one with 10 knows what to do with money and the one with only one does not know what to do with great opportunities. We must no longer dig holes to put the Lord's money into, such as:
- NSF checks;
- Quick loan companies;
- Title loans companies;

- Late payment fees;
- High interest payments and
- Clothes closets.
- _____
- _____

The Master is taking from poor investors and giving to the ones who know what to do with money. Notice, the Master is not taking from the poor but from the poor investors and giving it to the rich thinkers – those who are rich in ambition; the rich in will to make sure wealth works for them. We can posture ourselves for more from the Master by making the most of what we make or mastering the money the Master gave us. The servant ended up with less because he did less than he should have with the money that had been entrusted to him. It is my prayer that we receive the grace to grow in wisdom on how to handle wealth so we will have more to present to our Master.

LESSON 5

WISDOM TO MAKE MONEY WITHIN THE HOUSE!
2 Kings 4:1-7

As we continue in this Money Management Series, we discover the Word of God says a lot about how to get out of debt through better management of our money, financial resources, credit, spending, and financial obligations. This lesson deals with a family that is in bad shape financially and there appears to be no way out of their financial woes. The Word of God will show them and us that, though we may be drowning financially, there might be an answer to how to get out of debt, have enough to pay our debts and then have more than enough to live off the rest.

Verse 1. Now there cried a certain woman of the wives of the sons of the prophets unto Elisha, saying, Thy servant my husband is dead; and thou knowest that thy servant did fear the Lord: and the creditor is come to take unto him my two sons to be bondmen.

Please notice the emotional stress she is under from not being able to pay her bills. She cried unto the Man of God. This widow woman is like many of us; she is already under enough duress from the challenges and changes that life brings. She is a widow, which means that her husband – the bread winner in that day – is dead. Having to live without the love of her life had to be a difficult step. She is a single mother raising two sons all alone. Compounding that pain is her inability to pay bills, or to use an expression to which many saints can relate, she is unable to make ends meet. Before we finish adding to her problems, heap on the frustration caused by creditors aggravating her and threatening her to take her only property, her two sons, we must understand the times in which she lived. In Old Testament times, children were considered to be the property of their parents and if parents did not pay their bills, creditors could take the children as bondmen, or as we would say today, collateral. Even today, when we are unable to pay our creditors, they might take property belonging to us such as:
1. Houses in which we have raised our families;
2. Cars that we struggled to pay off;
3. Paychecks, which can be garnished;
4. Credit cards, which can be cancelled;
5. Checking accounts, which can be closed and the money therein withheld and
6. Income tax checks, which creditors also can withhold.

If any of these things have happened to you, you know how painful, embarrassing, depressing and challenging a situation it can be. This woman is about to lose her two sons to the creditors, who will make her sons work seven years of free – or slave – labor to pay off the debts of their parents.

Please notice that the widow woman's husband is one of the sons of the prophets. Here is a family that loves the Lord and has worked in the Kingdom. The deceased son of a prophet is believed to be Obadiah, who is written about in 1 Kings 18 and hid 100 prophets in caves when Queen Jezebel was killing off the prophets of God. With his own money Obadiah covered the cost of taking care of these 100 prophets. If we do not manage our money correctly, we too can turn our children over to the creditors. Parents who open accounts – for example, a light bill – in a child's name run the risk of ultimately turning their child over to the creditors. Parents who will not pay their light bills, allow the lights to be cut off, and then just put the light bill in their child's name run the risk of turning their child over to the creditors. We must stop putting bills in the names of our children. Our children are too young to pay the bill and too innocent to understand what we are doing to their credit. So, get those cell phones out of those kids' names!

The widow woman did not come to the Man of God for a donation. She came to him for direction. This point is paramount in the message to the widow woman, and to us, in getting what we need to get out of debt. We cannot borrow our way out of debt. We will not beg our way out of debt. We cannot cry our way out of debt. And we will not worry our way out of debt. So, if we are heads over heels in debt, we must no longer look for a donation. We must begin praying for direction. Most saints don't want direction to get out of debt; they just want a donation. Donations last only for a moment. Directions can last for a lifetime.

Verse 2. And Elisha said unto her, what shall I do unto thee? Tell me what hast thou in the house? And she said, Thine handmaid hast not anything in the house, save a pot of oil.

So often, we are in such a hurry to help that we ultimately become a hindrance. Many times in our haste to help, we hurt people, because we do not take the time to find out how they got into the financial trouble they are in. Without that key piece of information, we cannot help them find solutions so they do not end up at the same place again. It is not enough to funnel money to a person in a financial bind. There is only so much money you have to give or loan. We need to provide struggling individuals with the wisdom in correct money management. We cannot give enough or loan enough to compensate for the mismanagement of money. Our pockets are not deep enough and people who like mismanaging money will always come for more money. Money management skills can prevent a frequent flow from your purse or wallet.

... Tell me what hast thou in the house...

The Man of God makes the widow woman assess what she has in her own house. One of the first things we get out of his direction is to look in our own houses and see how we've spent our money. When evaluating our own homes, we are sometimes forced to look at waste and overspending. In our assessment, we see what we could possibly live without. We also see valuables in our houses that, if used correctly, could get us out of the jam that we are in. Every person reading this lesson, even if it appears you are broke, could find something of value in your home to pay the light bill, meet the mortgage or rent, pay to repair the broken plumbing and purchase groceries.

... and she said, Thine handmaid hath not anything in the house save a pot of oil.

One of the things we learn with divine direction is to stop minimizing what God has given us. We may not have what everybody else has, but we do have enough to make it, be successful and live comfortably at the level we are on – if we would stop trying to live like the fellow who is making more money than us. In bowling, they call it bowling in your own lane. In everyday life we say, "Learn how to live in your own lane." If we make hot dog money, we must learn to live a hot dog life until God moves us up. If you make hamburger money, learn to live and enjoy a hamburger life. We cannot lead a successful, stress-free existence trying to live the steak-and-lobster life on hot dog and hamburger money or a sardine salary.

... Thine hand maid hath not anything in the house, save a pot of oil.

We really do have enough to be successful and live comfortably, if we would just correctly assess what is in our houses, and then look at how to best handle what God has given us. Since you and the kids in the community like buying ice cream, why not open up an ice cream shop or snow cone shop at the house during the hot summer months. To the widow woman, it appears her sons are all but lost. She is unaware that she has enough to pay her bills and save her sons from the creditors. Obedience added to our faith, plus some thinking outside of the box, minus mismanagement will equal prosperity. It worked wonders for her and it can for us. The pot of oil will not look like much to the untrained entrepreneur, the person lacking in vision or the immature in financial management. The pot of oil you are about to waste or throw away may be just what you need to get out of the hole and put you back on top financially.

We must vow to never again minimize the blessings of God. We must not minimize the blessings of God in our minds, messages, or in our motives. We must begin praying: Lord, show me how to have much with what seems to be so little. God does not always give us the trees with full-grown limbs and branches, the fruit already ripe. But God will give us seed, which suggests to the saints that there is more than a piece of fruit, more than a bite, more than a snack, more than one meal. There is an orchard in that one seed, if it's properly planted, willfully worked and skillfully seen after! Just remember, the widow woman did not come to the Man of God for a donation. She came to the Man of God for direction. Donations can last for a day, but directions can last throughout our destiny.

Verse 3. Then he said, Go, borrow thee vessels abroad of all thy neighbors, even empty vessels, borrow not a few.

The Man of God is not trying to get the widow woman to borrow her way out of debt. The vessels she is to borrow have no value to any of her neighbors and the empty vessels are of no value to her. As a matter of fact, this is an act of faith and obedience because there is no reason to borrow empty vessel except to follow the directions of the Man of God. She will use the empty vessels to house the miracle of God that will lift her family out of debt. If there was anything the widow woman had in her house, it was empty vessels. Can you imagine the difficulty in following the Man of God's directions, especially when you know that the milk jug is empty, the soda bottle is empty, the flour canister is empty and every container in the house is empty? The widow is asked to amass empty vessels of no obvious value, though she cannot she how the vessels will help her situation get better. What God will do to get us out of debt may not be easily seen and may make no real sense, even to the intelligent mind.

Verse 4. And when thou art come in, thou shalt shut the door upon thee and upon thy sons, and shalt pour out into all those vessels, and thou shalt set aside that which is full.

This assignment takes a lot of faith to even attempt. Some things God tells us are best left with us. There will always be people who will talk us out of our blessing if we choose to heed their advice. We must always be mindful that God does not think like us and His ways are not our ways. God has a way to get us out of the mess that we are in – if we will seek Him. If we follow the path He puts before us, we will find success in every area.

Shut the door upon thee and thy sons ...

We must shut the world out of God's business. Close the door on closed-minded people who always miss the mind and the move of God.

Verse 5. So she went from him, and shut the door upon her and her sons, who brought the vessels to her, and she poured out.

The widow woman made up her mind that she was going to follow directions. She borrowed vessels from her neighbors, shut the door and began to pour. We must be honest and admit this does not seem like it will work or cause any noticeable change in the family's financial condition. If we were her friends before praying about it, we likely would have opened our mouths and told her what we thought about the idea before she and her sons had tried to work the plan. We all have been talked out of a miracle, and we have talked others out of their miracles. What helped the widow and what will surely help us see a breakthrough is learning how to shut the door on worldly opinions, feelings, family, friends and negative neighbors. This widow woman is too desperate *not* to do it. She has nothing to lose and everything to gain by just following divine directions.

... She poured out.

She poured from the same container that she minimized earlier. She poured out of the same oil that she thought was insufficient to help make a difference for her, her family and her finances. The answer for our inadequacies is already in the house; we just have to get with God and find out how to handle what appears to be insignificant. Possessions may seem unimportant in the wrong hands, but when the widow obeyed the voice of God she put the pot, the oil, the predicament and the power to get wealth in the Master's hand.

Verse 6. And it came to pass, when the vessels were full, that she said unto her son, Bring me yet a vessel. And he said unto her, There is not a vessel more. And the oil stayed.

The widow now has taken her eyes off the process and placed her focus on participating in the promise. In the midst of the miracle, she has not noticed the number of vessels that have been filled. Her job was not to count the vessels but to pour, and that's what she has been doing. While she has been pouring, God has been filling every empty container. When she asked her son for another vessel, he has to tell her, *"There is not a vessel more."* God did not run out of oil, the woman ran out of available containers.

Verse 7. ... Then she came and told the man of God. And he said, Go, sell the oil and pay thy debt and live thou and thy children of the rest.

The Man of God instructs the widow woman to become an entrepreneur. Get the oil out of the house, make money from the oil, pay the folks you owe and then learn to live from what you are making. Most Christians don't really know what to do with what they make, so they end up back in debt. This widow woman should never be broke again, because she received divine directions.

LESSON 6

GOD WANTS US TO KNOW HOW WE GOT OUR WEALTH
Deuteronomy 8:1-4 and 7-10

One of the worst types of people to deal with is people who are incredibly blessed but extremely ungrateful. These are people who never say thank you because they never see the sacrifices others made to get them to where they are. Though all who have confessed their faith in Jesus the Christ as Lord and Savior can assume the status of children of God, not all can assume that as children of God that they are grateful. The children of Israel, under the leadership of Moses, are no exception. Like us, they start off with nothing and end up in a better place because of the blessings and the goodness of God.

This text is an excellent illustration as to what God may be doing in His delay in getting us to a wealthy place. God took His time getting the children of Israel to the Promised Land. It was not that God could not get them there sooner. The children of Israel were not ready. He was preparing them to handle His blessings correctly.

Verse 1. All the commandments which I command thee this day shall ye observe to do, that ye may live, and multiply, and go in and possess the land which the Lord sware unto your fathers.

There are blessings God has in store for us, but the blessings are not because of us and are, in some cases, despite us. He promised our forefathers that He would do it. The text says God swore this land and these provisions to the forefathers, but it is this generation that is the beneficiary of the favor of God. The generation receiving the benefits of God's favor is the one responsible to God and obligated to observe and to do all that He has commanded. If this generation will observe and do what God commands, God says four things will happen for them and for us:
1. We shall live.
2. We shall multiply.
3. We shall go in.
4. We shall possess the land.

Many times we do not experience the fullness of what God has for us because we choose not to obey the commands of God, and we treat God's commands as if they are suggestions.

Verse 2. And thou shalt remember all the way which the Lord thy God led thee these forty years in the wilderness, to humble thee, and prove thee, to know what was in thine heart, whether thou wouldest keep his commandments, or no.

We are told not to forget God's way – the way He led us, the way He provided for us, the way He fed us, the way He protected us, and the way He proved to us that He was God. Never make the mistake of having a short memory. The old church used to pray that God would keep their minds. They did not want to forget God and what God had done for them, nor the ways of God. If we just paid more attention to the way and the ways of God, we would not be so intimidated when troubles come. If the children of God are not careful, we can go through this life and never notice or learn the way and ways of God, and thereby miss out on one of the greatest blessings of being born.

God does nothing haphazardly. He does everything with a specific purpose or meaning in mind. Every now and then, we are found guilty of doing something that lacks meaning or purpose. God took 40 years to get Israel to the Promised Land as a way to humble the Israelites, prove (test) them, and allow them to see what was in their hearts. So often, we think our hearts are pure. When in actuality, it is easy to be good when there appears to be no great advantages to being bad. When it seems we can get further ahead, have a lot more, make 10 times more money or have a lot more fun being bad than good, that's when the temptation becomes attractive.

Verse 3. And he humbled thee, and suffered thee to hunger, and fed thee with manna, which thou knewest not, neither did thy fathers know; that he might make thee know that man doth not live by bread only, but by every word that proceedeth out of the mouth of the Lord doth man live.

Before God gave them possessions, He first worked on the person. God never wants us to have more than what we know we are worth to Him. Some people think they are important because they have stuff, when the truth is God gives us stuff because we are important. So, it is not the possessions that make the person, it's the person who makes the possessions.

And He humbled thee ...

God never wants our things, jobs, cars, clothes, cash or whatever we may possess to fill us with pride. God wants us to be humble no matter how blessed we are, so sometimes He has to hold back on His blessings until we can handle them. So, some saints may have a driver's license long before they have a car to drive. This is not because we cannot drive, but rather God does not want what we have to drive us.

When the Israelites were in the wilderness and had no provisions of their own, God fed them manna each day from heaven. They were not allowed to store up any manna for the next day except on each Friday so they did not have to work or gather on the Jewish Sabbath, which is Saturday. For 40 years, this was the process for getting food. They had to totally depend upon the Lord. We sometimes worry today about what we are going to eat next week, while our doctors are trying to put some of us on diets. Some saint's worry about what they will eat, when there is food spoiling in their refrigerators. Please notice the way God fed them – day by day. No one lost any weight. If it is God's way for us to learn to trust Him through His providing day by day, then just learn to trust that He will show up every day. Just as we recognize that we must eat to stay alive on this side, we also must recognize that we must digest the Word of God to stay alive on this side, too.

Verse 4. Thy raiment waxed not old upon thee, neither did thy foot swell, these forty years.

Whether traveling out of town by car, train, bus or plane, don't forget to look out the window and enjoy the scenery. Every time God works on our behalf, we ought roll down the window or let up the shade to see the way God works. No one works things out like God. Israel should have learned to appreciate God just based on how He took care of their clothes when they were in the wilderness, or in transition. The clothes did not fade, go out of style, get too small, or tear up because God knew there were no malls or shopping plazas in the wilderness. This is important to remember so that when God finally gets us through the wilderness – or through the transition – we should not be guilty of staying all day at the mall and only having a few minutes for the church. Attitude is everything! Don't act like we cannot live without plenty of shoes, even if it means at the expense of paying our tithes or having something for our children's future. Remembering how God kept our feet when we were in transition, ought to cause us to give God a shoe offering even now. We should just think about where your feet have traveled and where God has brought you. We really ought to look down at our feet and ask ourselves: When is the last time I spent this type of money in the Kingdom trying to say thank you to God for where You have brought my family and I from?

Verse 7. For the Lord thy God bringeth thee into a good land, a land of brooks of water, of fountains and depths that spring out of valleys and hills;

As grateful believers, we must look at where we are, and then compare that to where we use to be. Then, we should ask ourselves: How did we get here? If you are living in a better place than where you grew up, or in a better place than when you first got married or first moved out on your own, pose this question: Who made the provisions to get to this place? If you got to where you are by yourself, then that is who you owe and your money should reflect that. But if it was the Lord who got us to where we are, then our spending and our giving ought to reflect that.

Water represents life. Here, the children of Israel are surrounded by it. Brooks, fountains and springs are flowing; this is a great place God has brought Israel to, and a great place God is bringing us to. He takes His time getting us there because we take our time recognizing it is He who is making us and not we ourselves. Oftentimes, we overspend trying to get our money to take us places. If we would just take the time to observe where we already are, we would find much fascination in the wonders of God all around us.

Verse 8. A land of wheat, and barley, and vines, and fig trees, and pomegranates; a land of oil olive, and honey.

God does not bring us to a place, unless we are better off there. Yet, when we get to a better place and forget God, we end up worse off. We must teach His ways in this new place of success. We must remember and respect His commands in this new place of prosperity, especially if we want to continue thriving. This is not all that God has for Israel, or for us. A healthy reverence for God causes us to discover more than what meets the eye when it comes to what He has for us. There is a spiritual secret to incredible success in the land flowing with wheat, barley, vines, fig trees, pomegranates, olive trees and honey. God often only shares this secret with those who have a will to work, a mind to envision, power to put things into action, and a heart to honor and obey His voice. If we are not careful, we will be standing in a field of abundance and manage to starve. The question is not whether we have the resources, but rather do we know we have them – and do we know what to do with them?

... a land of olive oil ...

Some people had the vision to realize what they had with the olive tree. They started crushing olives, bottling the oil and then selling it, while their neighbor just put an olive in their martini. It is not what we have, but what we do with what we have that makes the difference between the haves and the have-nots. Someone else took figs from the fig tree, made a preserve, started canning and selling them. Meanwhile, their neighbor ate as many figs as they wanted and left the rest to rot.

Verse 9. A land wherein thou shalt eat bread without scarceness, thou shalt not lack any thing in it; a land whose stones are iron, and out of whose hills thou mayest dig brass (copper – NIV).

It is amazing where God places us after taking us through so much. People who do not appreciate from whence God has brought them normally end back up in the same place where God brought them out of bondage! Indebtedness is no different than living in Egypt; we are just owned by a pharaoh of a different name. When we are sick and need to take a day off but can't because the credit cards are maxed out, the mortgage or rent is not only high but due and the car note is already behind, your pharaoh is called DEBT! BAD DEBT will have us making bricks without straw. In other words, debt will have us working like a slave, while having nothing to work with. Don't get lost in the eating without scarceness and enjoying. Always keep in the back (no, that's too far – always keep in the front) of your mind that it's essential to make something happen while you are here. Make the most of where God has you! Look at what was there before Israel arrived: iron and brass, or copper, as other translations call it. The copper is hidden and the only thing Israel will have to do is dig it out. With a little digging, we would discover we were not supposed to be broke. Without that effort, we miss the moment and the movement of God. The previous verse said there is richness we can see. This verse says there is richness we cannot see, but it's there and if we are willing to work – or dig – we can have it. This verse is saying there is potential in you and God has placed potential where you are standing. If we are willing to work and if we have an imagination that is above and beneath the surface, we are to move to a wealthy place.

Verse 10. When thou hast eaten and art full, then thou shalt bless the Lord thy God for the good land which he hath given thee.

God does not ask us to give Him anything first. He only asks us to give in response to what He has already given. Many saints are miserable because when they had eaten and were full, they were to have blessed the Lord our God and did not. We behave like our greedy family on Thanksgiving Day – belts loose, button open and pants unzipped, just trying to stuff as much as we can even though we are full. Oftentimes, people claim to have nothing to give to God, and it's not because God has not given unto us. It's because we are selfish and unsatisfied, until we have had everything for ourselves.

... Then thou shalt bless the Lord thy God for the good land which he hath given thee.

We must be good to God for being good to us. We owe Him – and a burped "thank you" is not adequate. God might show us more of what is hidden, if we are willing to bless Him back. God has given us more than enough to be successful, prosperous and financially secure. It's in our hands and under our feet. The question that still remains is: What will we do with it? Either use it or lose it! It is up to each of us to decide what we will do with what we have been given. Maximize the moment, maximize the mind and maximize the money.

LESSON 7

GOD GIVES THE POWER TO GET WEALTH!
Deuteronomy 8:11-18

Everyone should want to have all the blessings God wants to bestow. Lessons we all must learn are that not everyone wants to have something in life, not everyone wants to accomplish noble things in this life, and not everyone wants to go places in this life. We could imagine that one of the hardest things for God to do is bless people who do not want anything. Our God is gracious and He loves to give because giving is a part of His nature. We, the people of God, have not gotten all that God has in store for us. God wants to bless us and not burden us. When the people of God are immature with handling business, innocent when it comes to managing our credit, and ignorant when it comes to financial responsibility, every blessing from the Father has the potential to become a burden. How well we handle the blessings of God might determine how many blessings we are handed. The people of God should never be prideful, arrogant, high-minded, or puffed up because God has blessed us. We should be humbled, grateful and very thankful for every blessing the Father bestows upon us.

Verse 11. Beware that thou forget not the Lord thy God, in not keeping his commandments, and his judgments, and his statutes, which I command thee this day:

There is always a tendency to forget where we have come from and to forget who got us to where we are. It is my prayer that we see the warning sign at the front of this verse – BEWARE! Whenever we see this word as we approach a building or house, it should cause us to use caution. If an owner has in front of the house a sign advising "Beware of Dog," we should not go running through the gate and up to the house. Even though we may not see the dog, we see the sign. If we see the sign and honor the sign, it may help us out with the dog. Before we go into the goodness of God, there is an alarming sign that says BEWARE! The question raised by us is: What do I need to BEWARE of? An alarming answer comes back: Don't forget what God has said! God warns us to remember every command, every decision and every law He has made. With blessings and wealth comes responsibility. God gives us instructions on how to handle what He has given us.

Verse 12. Lest when thou hast eaten and art full, and hast built goodly houses, and dwelt therein;

Please notice, there is a potential shift in the posture and in the person, when an individual gets to his or her apparent destination and becomes comfortable. At this place, we would think that people are really grateful and appreciative to God for bringing them to a place of success and satisfaction. One of the main times we need the BEWARE sign in front of us is when we have gotten what we want from God. It is obvious that God not only knows where we are going, but He also knows us. After they've eaten too much, we've often heard people say, "I ain't good for nothing right now!" So often, this is a true statement about people just after God has tremendously blessed us. We should never live our lives so blessed of God that we are of no value to God. There should always be a hunger in the bosom of every believer. The people of God should always have a hunger and a thirst for righteousness. A hunger to please God and a hunger to know Christ should never be satisfied by people, places or things. The only one who can satisfy our hunger is God, and the more God gives us of Himself, the more we should want. The hunger of a child of God is never really satisfied because there is so much of God we have not gotten, and there is still so much of God to get.

...And hast built goodly houses, and dwelt therein.

God had promised to give the children of Israel houses that they did not build. This verse says they will have even greater success than that – some will get to build brand new homes. The picture is painted of a person who moves into a new house but moves farther from a passion to please God. We must never move into new houses and become more concerned about planting trees than paying tithes. We should never move into new houses and become more concerned about shrubbery than we are about our sacrifice to Him. The bottom line: When we are doing better, we ought to do better concerning God. With every blessing, there comes *respons*ibility. We must make a concerted effort to RESPOND correctly to every blessing that is bestowed upon us. When I was a child, every time my grandmother gave us a piece of chewing gum, we had to say, "thank you." At first, grandmother would say, "What do you say?" After a while, we knew what to say without her having to say, "What do you say?" Even when our grandmother split a stick of gum between the two of us, we had to say "thank you" with the same measure of gratitude we would show if we had been given our own stick of gum. Either way, it was her gum. She paid for it and she wanted us to be grateful for whatever we received from her.

Verse 13. And when thy herds and thy flocks multiply, and thy silver and thy gold is multiplied, and all that thou hast is multiplied;

God is speaking increase in their lives, which means God is not expecting them to remain the same or just have the same amount they started with. Notice that God is not talking about adding to their lives. God's plans are to multiply. We also must move into the mindset of God. We have to start talking multiplication and thinking multiplication, too. Everything Israel possessed had the potential to multiply – their herds, flocks, silver, gold and all that they had. God wants to do more than just add to our lives. The text says God wants to MULTIPLY!

Today's corporate America crowd would say their investments were diversified because they had herds, flocks, silver and gold. What do we have that has the potential to multiply?

1. _____
2. _____
3. _____

The people of God should have several streams of income. Remember, the reason for having more than one stream of income is that if one stream gets cut off or dries up, you can still live well off the other streams.

Verse 14. Then thine heart be lifted up, and thou forget the Lord thy God, which brought thee forth out of the land of Egypt, from the house of bondage.

The reason we must BEWARE is that it is so easy to forget it was God who helped us get where we are. It is easy to start thinking the herds and flocks in the previous verse increased because of something we did. The enemy of our destiny can be deceiving, and if we are not careful, we could begin thinking that it was the feed that we gave them or the field we put the animals in that helped them to multiply.

Then thine heart be lifted up...

The enemy always wants us to make the same mistake he made in heaven. The deceiver tries to trick us into believing we got to where we are without God's help. When he convinces us of that, we become filled with pride. It's always important to look back and remind ourselves how we got to this place. The Lord brought Israel so far from where they use to be – so far in fact that even they did not remember how far they had come. They and we were slaves and descendents of slaves. Now, they and we are buying and building new homes!

Verse 15. Who led thee through that great and terrible wilderness, wherein were fiery serpents, and scorpions, and drought, where there was no water, who brought thee forth water out of a rock of flint;

The Word of God reminds them and us that there are situations the Lord brought us through that would have killed us had God not been committed to bringing us through. There are many things that could have taken us out:
- The great and terrible wilderness,
- Fiery serpents,
- Scorpions and
- Drought and no water.

It is amazing what the Lord brings us through, and if there is anyone who should not forget the Lord when they get to where they are going, it's the believer! God has worked miracles for them and for us. He brought forth water out of the rock. If God could bring us through all of this, just imagine what He would take us to if we just remained faithful and loyal to Him.

Verse 16. Who fed thee in the wilderness with manna, which thou fathers knew not, that he might humble thee, and that he might prove thee, to do thee good at the latter end;

Another miracle that God performed for Israel is how He fed them. He fed them manna from heaven. There were no bakeries and nothing to buy. All they had was a belief in God to be faithful to feed everyone every day. The matured crowd had never had manna before, and they certainly had never experienced God providing like this before. They had to admit the bread was coming from heaven. Even when they arrived at their destination, they still forgot to give God the glory. Notice why God provided for them this way:

- That He might humble thee;
- That He might prove (test) thee and
- To do thee good at the latter end.

While we are frustrated with how the Father does things (because we want it today), God is working on our faith today and preparing our faith to handle our future. God wants us to have a great latter end.

Verse 17. And thou shalt say in thine heart, My power and the might of mine hand hath gotten me this wealth.

God hears our faintest whisper, but even the hidden or silent words that are only expressed in our hearts can be offensive to God. None of us really hear what another is saying in his or her heart, but God hears it. Many times, we would not dare say openly what we are saying softly in our hearts. There have been times we have suggested in our hearts that we do not owe God for any of that which we have. There have been times we have had a conversation with ourselves inside our hearts, and the bad news is not only were we wrong, but God heard it as well.

We did not get what we have through hard work. We did not get what we have because we deserve it. We have what we have because of the grace of God. There are some folks who worked just as hard and have much less. Do we really think it was our power, smarts, go-get-'em spirit, hard work or overtime that got us where we are? Can you honestly say it was that right-place, right-time hunch, luck, prayers, seized opportunity, right decision or parental prayers that got us where we are? Notice that God is not talking about being rich, yet in still He speaks of wealth. We can be rich in one thing and be poor in other areas. God wants us to have wealth – or prosper – in every area of existence. It is God who gives the flock and the herds the capacity of reproduce. It is God who gives us the wisdom concerning when to buy and sell silver and gold. It is God's gold and silver that we are selling. Most saints who play the lottery play because they want to be rich, but God wants us healthy in our bodies, whole in our spirit, single in our thoughts, complete in our souls, at peace with our Maker, and stable and secure in our finances. That's what we believe having wealth consists of. We can be rich today. With the wrong investment or losses, we can be poor before tomorrow. We cannot lose wealth in one day.

Verse 18. But thou shalt remember the Lord thy God: for it is he that giveth thee power to get wealth, that he may establish his covenant which he sware unto thy fathers, as it is this day.

The Word of God tells us to never forget God because He is the one who gives us power (access, potential, authority, wisdom, plans, ability, entrepreneurial skills, faith, adventurous spirit, insight, fortitude, guts, ideas, connections, resources, opportunities, and grace) to get wealth. It's amazing what God gives in order that we might come to our wealthy place. Still, many miss God because they do not have the mind of Christ. The mind of Christ keeps us from missing out on opportunities God is giving to get out of poverty. The saints must unwrap ideas, concepts and opportunities to see what God is giving to us. Everything that God gives is not for consumption. Some things are an idea for commercial expansion. We must stop stepping over God's opportunities and resources to get wealth.

... that He may establish His covenant ...

We must learn to be more like Mike – that is Michael Jordan, not Mike Tyson. Use your gifts to make room for you. We must look for ways to expand our gifts beyond what we can do right now because we probably won't always be able to do everything we can do right now. God wants His covenant people blessed, and He wants to bless us so we can represent Him in the earth. God is looking for people He can bless and turn around and use them to advertise the Kingdom. Kingdom people are a blessed people, and we should look like it. As kingdom people, we become a good advertisement for God by allowing God to give us all the skills needed to make wealth *and* by doing something with the opportunities God gives us. Jesus said the poor would be with us always – not because God does not want to give, but because we do not always know what to do with what God gives. This is why many people like the lottery. We don't want to do anything but scratch it to get it. God makes us work for it.

LESSON 8

WHAT TO DO WHEN THE MUCH IS MISSING?
Proverbs 13:11, 21-23

God does give His people the power to get wealth, and it's because He wants to establish His covenant with His children. Since this is the case with God, there has to be some reason or reasons that we are as broke as we oftentimes are. Let's examine some of the possibilities, as to what is causing us to struggle financially, when the Word talks about the children of God having much. In order to bring more insight to the text, we will start at the back portion and then move forward.

Verse 23. Much food is in the tillage of the poor: but there is that is destroyed for want of judgment.

This verse could be tough to wrap our minds around. On the surface, it presents a clear contradiction – much food belonging to the poor. It is difficult to imagine the poor having much, especially much food. We must ask ourselves: "How could much food be in the tillage of the poor and the poor still be poor?" This sounds like a great inconsistency. One would think that if someone possessed much food, the very thing that is needed all over the world and the very thing that will never go unneeded so long as people exist on the earth, that person would be greatly successful. The Word of God is saying people can have everything they need to be prosperous and still end up poor – lacking, in need, in bad shape, barely making it, without – and not really prosperous by most men's standards. To understand how we could have the very thing that everybody not only wants, but also needs, and still not live better, we must find out where this food belonging to the poor is.

Much food is in the tilled land of the poor (Amplified Version)...

The potential to prosper is there, but we must learn to work it. A person can have land, but there is a great difference in what land alone versus land that is tilled can do for a person. The much that is missing is missing because we have failed to till what we have. We will never have the much if we do not get busy and till the land. In agriculture, to till means to work by plowing, sowing, raising and then reaping the crops. In short, the people of God have the fields or the land; we just are not working what our Daddy gave us. If the poor would just work the land, the land would work for the poor and they would become prosperous.

The *tilled land* in the text is undeveloped territory, untapped talents, unexplored gifts and unused areas of anointing God has given each of His children so, we do not live in lack, or poverty. When we allow the Lord to shepherd us more than just on Sundays during worship and a few minutes during Bible Study, we learn that He leads us into ventures and exploring undeveloped areas of our lives. In allowing Him to lead, we

become recognized as His people, who have not only what the world wants, but also what the world needs to have for the best quality of life. There maybe someone saying, "I do not have land to till. Therefore, this text does not apply to me. That is why I am struggling financially." Please believe God has given to each of us land that we must learn to till. Our untilled land could be:
1. A sewing ability that you are allowing to lie dormant. Start your own sewing business on the side. Connect with clothing stores or cleaners to offer alteration services, or even connect with fabric stores to sew for their customers.
2. A great cooking ability evidenced by compliments and the fact that everyone in the house is overweight! Start your own catering service. Bake cakes, pies or desserts and sell them to restaurants, caterers, or to families during the holidays or any days!
3. The ability to detail cars with a spirit of excellence. Some people can wash the newness back into their cars. Expand the vision and start detailing for people in the neighborhood. Set up appointments with people on your job and let your detailed car do the advertising.
4. An affinity for childcare. If you love kids and enjoy taking care of kids, why not have a service on the side for kids? You don't have to quit your job right now. Why not offer a daycare service for the weekend?
5. An ability to take care of seniors. This could be an excellent opportunity to give a family a break and make some money.

The point the text is making is that the opportunity to prosper is out there, and it's readily available. We've just got to work it! Can you list some untilled land in you?
1. _____
2. _____
3. _____

... But there is that is destroyed for want of judgment.

There is always something or someone that tries to lessen our potential to prosper. When explaining this verse, some scholars talk about injustices that may hinder the poor from benefiting from the land that has been developed. Other scholars, when referencing this verse, suggest the poor person's potential is destroyed not only by the enemies without, but also the enemies within. The enemies without are those who try to take advantage of the struggling person. Conversely, the enemies within could be our lack of prudence in the management of what we have; unwillingness to work with what we have; a lack of knowledge about the business; and a lack of personal development. It is not enough to just have something. We must pray for the wisdom of God to know what to do with what we have. What's the difference between the person who has nothing and the person who has something but has no clue what to do with what he or she has? NOTHING! To not know what one has or to have no vision or ambition to do something with what we have will always lead us down the same path of ending up with NOTHING! We do not need something to do NOTHING with!

Verse 22. A good man leaveth an inheritance to his children's children; and the wealth of the sinner is laid up for the just.

By this standard, most people's departures from this life were not as good as they should have been. A good person who lives a good life does not burden others with the cost of a burial, but rather leaves an inheritance. Even if we leave just enough to bury ourselves so our children don't have to, we still missed how good God expected us to be. God wants us to live a life filled with such wealth that we cannot spend it all in one life span. The matured believer is challenged to think ahead and to make good business decisions that will last beyond his or her lifetime. Many of the old saints left acres of land and a house for their families. They did not have college degrees but they had vision and wisdom. Please notice that the Word says *a good man leaveth an inheritance*. With God's help, they left something. Let's leave something for our children, other than just our earthly remains.

LESSON 9

GIVING THAT RECOGNIZES GOD!
Malachi 3:7-11

Oftentimes, when the subject of repentance arises in the household of faith, we think of verbalizing an "I'm sorry" and the feeling of regret in our hearts. This lesson shows that there is at least one additional way to repent that meets God's standard. We will discover that sometimes repentance has to cost us.

Verse 7. Even from the days of your fathers ye have gone away from mine ordinances, and have not kept them, Return unto me, and I will return unto you, saith the Lord of hosts. But ye said, Wherein shall we return?

We must always remember that God cannot be separated from His Word. His Word is who He is and He lives up to every Word He says. When we go away from His Word, we are really going away from Him. Just as the Jews in the text, many of us have gone away from God, and have been gone so long that we do not realize that the space between God and us is abnormal, unhealthy and too distant. God is the one who invites us to close the gap. The children of God can do the things we have always done, such as going to church, working in ministry, putting money in the collection basket, and being helpful to others, and yet we are so far from God.

…Return unto me, and I will return unto you, saith the Lord of hosts…

God is saying that there is more than distance between us -- you have left me. Imagine a child accompanying his parents to a crowded place such as the mall, the fair, or a parade. Amid the bustle, you can almost hear the parents saying, "Stay close!" and "Keep up!" This is not what God is saying in this text today. God is saying that we are not even in the same place as Him. It is easy to get detached or lost from God and purpose, because there are so many things pulling on us and trying to divert our attention. When we were children, our parents made us hold their hands or at least one another's hands so that we would not get lost in a crowded place. When is the last time you felt God holding your hand? I remember that as I grew older, I really didn't want to hold my parents' hands. It is frightening that we would distance ourselves from God in any way. He is *the Lord of Hosts* – He is the One who wars for us – and it is He who has the armies to fight for us.

…But ye said, Wherein shall we return?

Do we really know how to come back to God? So often we do not realize we have walked away from God. God instructs the children of Israel – and us – on how to return to Him and come back with signs acceptable of repentance.

Verse 8. Will a man rob God? Yet ye have robbed me. But ye say, Wherein have we robbed thee? In tithes and offerings.

One of the ways we can move away from God is to rob Him of tithes and offerings – the percentage of the money we make or are given that is due to Him. Please notice what God says we did with the money – we robbed Him! He does not say borrowed and have not paid Him back. He does not say we stole the money from Him. He does not say we swindled or tricked Him out of the money. The criminal actions lie in the way He says we acquired His money. When He gets ready to give, the question is raised, "How does God see us?" I hope God does not see us as bold criminals, who are wicked enough to take what we want with no regards to the owner. There are church people and Christians who rob God every week and are not bothered about it. Sometimes, we see people on the news, who rob businesses, banks and others. Some of these criminals have the audacity to wear hats and shades, as a disguise. Those of us watching the news often think, "Don't they know somebody can recognize them?" That is what we ought to say to people who are robbing God and think they are getting away with it. The excuses we use to explain why we have not paid God His tithes are nothing more than the hat-and-shades disguise that does not adequately hide what we are doing – robbing God! Let's look at some of the hat-and-shades disguises Christians use to hide the truth that God and His Kingdom are not financial priorities to us:

- God knows my heart;
- I don't make enough to tithe;
- I would tithe if I had more to give and
- I don't know what they do with the money.

Verse 9. Ye are cursed with a curse: for ye have robbed me, even this whole nation.

People who rob God are cursed. God does not want them cursed, but that is the consequence of taking from God. Satan got in trouble because he tried to rob God of His glory. This should remind us of the danger of taking from God what He rightfully desires and deserves. Anyone who robs God never gets ALL that God has for them until he or she cancels the curse by willingly giving God what is due Him!

A people can live under a curse for so long that they begin thinking the way they are living is normal. As a matter of fact, we can live under a curse so long that we can birth people, businesses and careers in that inferior state. Therefore, a cursed way of life is all that everything and everyone birthed under the curse will know. A business birthed under a curse may make money, but somehow never enough to pay the owner or reach a level at which the family can become wealthy. A business birthed and operating under a curse can struggle just as much twenty years into the business, as it did the day it opened. A business birthed and operating under a curse may own no more equipment of value after twenty-five years in business than it did the week it opened. The painting contractor under a curse will not own a paintbrush, paint bucket, or even a drop cloth after twenty-five years of being in the business. All he'll own is a false belief that he has his own business.

...This whole nation. They were surrounded by evidence of the curse. It wasn't just a neighborhood or a certain section of the city. The whole nation had been cursed, because of how they had handled God's money.

Verse 10. Bring ye all the tithes into the storehouse, that there may be meat in mine house, and prove me now herewith, saith the Lord of hosts, if I will not open you the windows of heaven, and pour you out a blessing, that there shall not be room enough to receive it.

The prescription that God writes for rising above the curse is to bring His tithes and offerings to the storehouse. God's tithe is 10 percent of our income, which includes our paychecks, Supplemental Security Income, disability and whatever other income that comes into our lives. Just in case, you are not sure what income means. We will define it as anything that comes in. The tithe is owed to God. It is not a gift. It's what is owed. Offerings are gifts to God in appreciation of what He has given and what He has done.

...Into the storehouse, that there may be meat in mine house...

There are a lot of great nonprofit organizations in the world that are doing great things for people, but not one of them are His storehouse, unless it is a Church. This does not mean that we cannot support nonprofits and use our charitable donations as a tax deduction. What it does mean is that we cannot support these groups in the place of supporting our local church. The missions of most nonprofit organizations developed, because the Church has not been financially able to do what we ought. There was a lack of financial support from the people in the pews.

...And prove me now herewith saith the Lord of hosts...

God invites His people to put Him to the test. When we pay our tithe, we are proving that we believe God is faithful to His promise. Tithing is not a matter of money, but rather a matter of faith and obedience. When people tithe they are saying, "I believe, therefore I obey!" Individuals who tithe also are saying that they believe it was God who gave them what they have. If they are to get anything in the future, it will be God who gives it to them. Nothing truly says we trust God like paying His tithe. No matter how well we sing, singing does not say it like paying it. We can preach with power how much we trust God, but nothing says we trust God like trying Him by the paying the tithe. We can testify and talk all day about how much we believe in God, but money actions speak louder than words.

...If I will not open you the windows of heaven, and pour you out a blessing...

God has incredible ways of blessing the people, who believe Him enough to obey. We do not normally hand people things or blessings out of the windows of our houses –

we open the door. God has some abnormal ways of blessing people, who walk in financial obedience with Him. The enemy cannot block blessings belonging to the God's children, because the enemy can't tell how the Lord is going to bless His covenant people. There is no set or predictable way for the Lord to bless you when you obey His giving principles. God does not leave the blessing of his people up to chance. God commits to opening up the windows of Heaven. God can bless us from every direction when we become covenant kids to His financial plan. God is committed to pouring – not just giving a drop for a blessing. When we feel a raindrop, one swipe of the windshield wiper or brush of the hand can wipe it away. However, when the rain pours, we get drenched. God wants to do this with His blessings. He wants to pour them upon His people.

...That there shall not be room enough to receive it.

God has more blessings for us than we have room to receive. People who are stingy toward God never discover that God has more blessings than we have room. People who don't manage the blessings of God well never fully discover all that God has in store for them. We have not received all that God has our names on. Some things God has on layaway for us. He is just waiting for us to grow up so that we can receive them.

Verse 11. And I will rebuke the devourer for your sakes, and he shall not destroy the fruits of your ground; neither shall your vine cast her fruit before the time in the field, saith the Lord of hosts.

To the person who plants a garden, God commits to rebuking the insects, plagues or nuisances. God's promise goes farther than the farmer or the gardener. God is also speaking to those of us who pay tithes and sow seeds into the Kingdom and face the enemy's attempts to destroy our seeds or make what we are trying to grow a waste. Just as insects, bugs, droughts, excessive heat or cold, and too much rain can hinder a crop; there are enemies to whatever a child of God is trying to grow. We may be growing a family or trying to build a relationship, finances, a career, a business or any other positive endeavor, but experience something that tries to hinder its growth. God becomes to our enemies what pesticides are to the enemies of the farmer's crop – a defense that blocks anything that prevents it from growing. There are so many forces that rise against a great crop. There are many forces against us becoming successful in life. Moreover, insects are not always the potential enemy. Sometimes, strange things happen within nature and the seasons that can cause plants to blossom seemingly too soon. A cold frost can sweep through and kill a crop. The Word says God commits to handling anything that can kill our progress or interfere with our seed being productive.

Individuals who commit to tithing say to the Lord of Hosts, "We are counting on You to be our Protection, our Defense and The Blocker to anything that would hinder, bug or bother our blessings." A right relationship with the Lord, when it comes to His tithe and our offerings, illustrates that we recognize Him as the one, who has blessed us with what we have and with what we shall receive.

LESSON 10

GOD COMES FIRST IN OUR FINANCES!
Proverbs 3:9-10

The household of faith, whenever it deals with the issues of money, blessings, prosperity and success, then it must also address responsibility, accountability and priority. We, as people of God, must always keep this question before us: What do I owe God? It is easy to become self-centered and selfish. Therefore, we must ask this question and pray that our hearts receive the right answer from the Holy Spirit. Even in our best efforts, our hearts are not always pure and free of deceit and selfishness. The Spirit of God knows the heart of God and knows what God requires and desires of us.

In blessing His people, there is an amount that God requires. We call that the tithe. There is also an amount that God desires. We called that the offering. While the tithe is based on 10 percent of the income we get, the offering is based on the gratitude of the recipient, who is now in the position of the giver. Every wife wants her husband to help pay bills, but that is not all she wants from him. Every wife also wishes for a husband, who has a heart to give to her beyond the bills. In this text, God longs for a people with a heart to give back to Him beyond what is required. This lesson opens up for us another area in which God wants His children to give unto Him, and not only give, but also receive from Him.

Verse 9. Honor the Lord with thy substance, and with the first-fruits of all thine increase.

There is a responsibility to honor and esteem the Lord by giving of our substance. The New American Standard version of the Bible says honor the Lord from your wealth. We should raise the question every time we get a paycheck, disability check, SSI check, retirement check, child support check, unemployment check or any other type income. Remember the issue at hand: "Lord, what do I owe You and how do I show You I appreciate what You have given to me? We will never correctly honor the Lord with our substance, until we first correctly answer the question. We cannot honor the Lord with our substance without giving unto the Lord. The way to honor God is by giving Him what is right and not what is left.

The Word of God says to honor the Lord with thy substance *and with the first-fruits of all thine increase.* God should always come first. First-fruits offerings were established in the days of Moses, as a result of God delivering the children of Israel out of bondage through the death of the firstborn of the Egyptians. The Amplified version of the Bible says, "Honor the Lord with your capital and sufficiency (from righteous labors) and with the first-fruits of all your income." The first of a farmer's crops were not taken to the market or cooked in his kitchen, but were given unto the Lord. The first animals born in a farmer's flock were not taken and sold at the market or cooked in his kitchen, but were given unto the Lord. Before the farmers knew what they would make and take from the fields, they made it a priority in their hearts that God was going to get His first. Before the farmer got to taste the meat of the sheep and oxen he had raised, the priest at the House of the Lord had already received what belonged to the Lord. Before a farmer's family got to taste the sweetness of the fruits of the field, the man of God at the House of God had already received, in the name of the Lord, what belonged to the Lord.

We oftentimes are so busy wanting to be the first one to taste the labor of our hands that we do not realize we are setting ourselves up for the last supper. Giving in this kind of expression says to the Lord, "I am depending upon You and I recognize that it was You who has provided for me." When we take care of ourselves first, we are suggesting we believe we obtained what we have on our own. When we take care of ourselves first, we are suggesting in our own subtle way that we are more important than the King and the Kingdom. When God gets the first-fruits of our increase or income, we are saying God comes first in my heart, home and in my honor.

The church does not talk about it, but the first-fruits should always be given unto the Lord. Even though, the practice of first-fruits was established in the Old Testament, God never abolished it. There are Christians and Jews all over the world, which make it a practice to give God the first-fruits of all their labor. In modern times, first-fruits would be the first paycheck of the year. Many people live so close on the edge that most saints would suggest we could not give God the first paycheck of the year and make it, even though we just received 52 consecutive paychecks. God is challenging his people to begin preparing their hearts to honor God, when it comes to first-fruits. Let's manage our money and our lives to say to God, "We honor You with our first-fruits and we are totally depending upon You to bless us indeed!"

In modern times, first-fruits also would be the first raise, or increase in salary, we get. Whatever the amount of the new increase, it should always go unto the Lord. This is new way of thinking for some. In the Baptist church, for example, leaders labor just to get folks to give something other than dues. This is only "new age" thinking because we have not always operated with the mind of Christ when it comes to money and the Kingdom. This is not new to those who are totally open to paying the Master His money. The idea of first-fruits was about giving God our best, because He is the best and He gives us His best.

Verse 10. So shall thy barns be filled with plenty, and thy presses shall burst out with new wine.

There is a direct correlation between giving and receiving. God will never allow us to out-give Him. The old church use to sing a song that said:

You can't beat God giving no matter how you try.
And the more you give, the more He gives to you
so keep on giving because it's really true
that you can't beat God giving no matter how you try.

There were those of us, who sang it much better than we tried to prove it. It is much easier to sing it on key than to live it. Why? It doesn't take faith to sing it, but it will take faith and obedience to live it! This song is the truth and nothing but the truth. We cannot beat God's giving, and the more we give to Him, the more He gives to us. An empty barn is a sign that something is wrong. We can't always put our finger on the problem, but we must recognize there is a problem, especially when the barn is always empty. The Holy Spirit could have had Solomon simply say the barns will be filled, or just say the barns would have plenty. The Word of God says the barns shall be *filled with plenty*. We have a double guarantee from God that there will be a surplus for the saints who make giving to God what is right – and not what is left – a priority. No excuse is allowable and no excuse is acceptable. God must receive what belongs to Him and He must receive it FIRST! This text teaches that not only does God want to get what He is due first, but He also wants the FIRST-FRUITS! Most black Baptist pastors, who have held back from teaching about first fruits, have done so, because church folks get mad when a preacher starts talking about money. They begin to suspect an ulterior motive. Most pastors, if they are pure in heart, do have a motivation, and that is to see the people of God BLESSED beyond measure!

So shall thy barns be filled with plenty...

The questions that must be asked:
1. Why aren't our barns filled with plenty?
2. Why are the barns so empty?
3. Why are some of us so broke that we don't even have the barn or the need for a barn?
4. Does God have enough to fill our barns?
5. Does God want to fill our barns?
6. Could I be preventing my barns from being full?

One thing is for sure; God has enough to fill each barn until it overflows. Sometimes, we as saints must admit that we hinder our own barns from being full. Even if we wanted to blame the devil, God's desire to bless us is greater than the enemy's plot to stop it. If we are living in lack, we must admit it is not because our Heavenly Father does not have more than enough. It is not because our Father does not want to bless us. In Old Testament days, barns served as a type of storehouse. When we commit to giving to God's storehouse, God commits to filling our storehouses with plenty. There is a season in which we live in the land of not enough. Then, we move to a place of just enough. It is my prayer that this is our season to move into the land of more than enough.

This text shines a light on the children of God, who are now living in the land of more than enough. Some people are OK with living with just enough to pay the light bill and just enough to pay the mortgage or rent, but something in the lives of the saints ought to make them want to move. Some saints are OK with just enough to pay the bills but not enough to go on vacation. Others are satisfied with having just enough to go on vacation, but not enough to stay in a nice hotel. The people of God ought to want better. As a matter of fact, the children of God ought to want more. God has more in store for those who are called by His name.

So shall thy barns ...

If we are not careful in our reading, we might miss that God is talking about giving more than what fits in the hands. What God wants to give to us is too big to fit in the pockets of our pants or in our purses. We often have a problem understanding God, because He speaks a totally different language than us. Notice that God is talking about *barns*. What God has for us is too big for the hands, the pockets and the purse. It's too big for one barn! God wants to fill the barns with plenty. Before we can talk about what's in the barns, we need to see the blessing of the barns.

If we expand our view of God, we will automatically expand of our view of life. Any saint who can hold all of his or her money in a hand, pocket or purse is in trouble. Any saint who has all of his or her money on their person is in trouble. Before we can talk about the potential blessings in the barn, we must first talk about expanding our capacity. We need an expanded capacity to receive more of what God has in store for us. It is not that blessings are not available for us. Our biggest problem is our capacity is too limited! People of God with poor priorities have a little and limited capacity to receive the full blessings of God. This type of limited and little capacity will always keep you begging. People of God with no heart to give or bless God have little and limited capacity to receive from God. If we increase our heart and place for God, He will automatically increase our capacity to receive.

Oftentimes, we try to receive with a limited capacity and God can't help but to give us less than His best for us. When we increase in wisdom concerning how to honor and love God and how to honor and love people, we increase our capacity to have and handle more of what God has in store for us as His children. God is extremely gracious. He wants each of us to prosper and be blessed. Most saints' troubles are not the availability of the blessings, but the limited capacity to have and handle the blessings.

... and thy presses shalt burst out with new wine.

Those who do good with what they have shall have more to do more good with.[1] The text speaks of having more; not to just store, but to do good with. We will have more capacity to make great things happen. We won't get lost in the wine, but we will dive into the message that none of us should miss: The wine is bursting forth. There is an ample or abundant supply. The wine is flowing and success is steadily coming. There is no lack and there is no limit. Bursting forth suggests we can't contain all that God has coming forth for us. This is the life I want the saints to live – an uncontainable life, where the blessings of God are flowing forth.

The Amplified Version of the Bible says, "*So shall your storage places be filled with plenty, and your vats shall be overflowing with new wine.*" The vats or reservoirs

---
[1] Matthew Commentary

are the places, which the wine flowed after the grapes were pressed by those who sang and danced. We must take the limits off our lives by no longer limiting God through our lack of financial commitment to the Kingdom and King, who has made such an incredible commitment to the betterment of our lives. God has always shown His commitment to us and now it is time for us to show our commitment to Him. When we remove from our spirit the struggle to give to God, we open ourselves up a greater capacity to receive from God. What God has for us won't be used up in a day, when we expand our capacity to live for God and grow to desire to bless Him.

LESSON 11

NO LONGER MAKING GOD SECOND WITH MY MONEY!
Nehemiah 10:35-39

The idea of offering first-fruits may be ascribed to natural piety. The concept was well known to the Greeks and the Romans, but in the Mosaic Law, offering first-fruits was commanded.[2] Though little has been discussed about first-fruits in many Baptist settings, it was normal practice for those who were of Abraham's seed. During the times of Nehemiah, the people of God had gotten away from first-fruits offerings, because the nation had been invaded, the walls torn down, their faith shattered and their direction blurred. Nehemiah has come back to Judah and Jerusalem to restore the children of Israel to the place of grandeur they had once known. Part of Nehemiah's work is to restore their faith and religious obligation unto God. At the time of the text, Judah is a perfect picture of what the enemy wants to do with each of our lives: Invade us, strip us of our best, tear down our walls of values and leave us in a hopeless state. The Lord allowed this to happen to Judah, because as a nation they left the Lord and went after other gods. But now Judah is coming back to the Lord and Nehemiah is leading the way. The verses we will study are about a people, who are resolved to get back to God. This is evident in their commitment to give to God again.

Verse 35. And to bring the first fruits of our ground, and the firstfruits of all our fruit of all our trees, year by year, unto the house of the Lord.

So, you're asked the question "What is first-fruits?" The best way to explain is that the first-fruit is the farmer's first harvest of the season, whether it is from the ground, from a tree or from the vine. A farmer who plants crops does not see the fruits of his labor until the harvest. A farmer planting watermelons in Georgia would normally see a harvest in May or June. That first crop of watermelons would be what he owes to God as the first-fruits of that harvest.

God established in the Old Testament that He wanted the best of the fruit that came first. Because we get paid weekly, biweekly or monthly, we would give our first-fruits at the beginning of the year. This is when we get our initial harvest. Every pay period or paycheck is our harvest. First-fruits are not really the tithe. Though, we understand what people are trying to say when they call the tithe the first-fruits. Nehemiah is leading Judah as a nation to get back on their spiritual feet. The way he is doing it is by establishing God's place in their giving.

... And to bring the first fruits of our ground ...

---

[2] The Pulpit Commentary

To the immature person, this principle may seem unfair. Why must we bring to God the first fruits of the ground without a guarantee that the ground will produce as much as we will need to survive. The giving of first-fruits to God is a sign that the believer does not depend on the ground, but rather God to make the ground fertile and able to produce more than enough to meet our needs. The ground is too unpredictable for us to count on. We need someone, who has control over the rain, the wind and the sun. The ground has no control over the factors that help to bring about a great crop. When putting God first through our giving, we are saying to Him, "We need you to control more than nature (the sun, the rain, and the wind). We also need you to control the bugs, the worms, the ground, the grass, the weeds and anything else that could hinder us from having a bumper crop.

... And the firstfruits of all fruit of all our trees ...

There are those who will give the Lord the first of the fields – their corn, cotton and melons – but then struggle to give God the first-fruits of all the trees. Please notice that the children of Israel committed to giving God the first-fruit of ALL the trees. In doing so, they recognized every tree that buds, blossoms and produces fruit is a blessing from God. They are not going to just give God the first-fruits from some of the trees, but rather of ALL the trees.

As we talk about money management, please also notice that God blessed them to be diversified in their investments, as evidenced by grounds, trees and cattle that were producing (verse 35). They had several streams of income and so should we – just in case one stream of income dries up, we can still do well.

... year by year, unto the house of the Lord.

First-fruits are a yearly responsibility, because we expect yearly blessings from the Lord. How can we ask, pray or expect God to keep putting us first when we keep putting Him second, third and fourth? Sometimes, we discover we have not put Him anywhere. We are still trying to figure out where God "fits." However, some saints have discovered that God won't fit anywhere but first. If He is not first, He will never fit and we will never be fit for the best that God wants to give to those who are called by His name.

At the end of every year, parents and grandparents feel an obligation to get their children and grandchildren something for Christmas, even if the kids have not been good or done well in school or at home. First-fruits says that at the end of the year we should think more about showing our children a sign that we trust God rather than showing toys that will eventually break. So often, we think God understands. Who has heard Him say that? Has anyone really heard God say, "Oh, don't worry about me, just look out for yourself, your children, your boo, and your friends?" Are we just hoping He is looking at our lips when we say God matters the most and not at our actions, which express the truth of our hearts? Remember that, for the most part, the black Baptist church has not taught first-fruits, because we have not been able to get the "saints" to pay God His tithes.

There is normally a spirit of contempt, when the preacher starts talking about money. Coming to church every first Sunday is not enough to demonstrate that God is first in our lives. Our money also must say God is first and not second, third, or fourth. Are we going to fit Him in somewhere in the future?

Verse 36. Also the firstborn of our sons, and of our cattle, as it is written in the law, and the firstlings of our herds and of our flocks, to bring to the house of our God, unto the priests that minister in the house of our God.

There was no question that God wanted the first-fruits of all that they had – even the firstborn sons. Families were responsible for making an offering unto the Lord when the first son was born. Mary and Joseph honored the law when Jesus was born by taking Jesus to the temple and giving an offering unto God for His life (Luke 2:21-24). Though Jesus was God's son, Mary and Joseph understood God still expected the first-fruit offering for the life of a male child. When Hannah prayed to God for a male child and promised to give Him back unto the Lord, she was bowling right down God's alley. That is what God has always wanted – someone who willingly gives her child back to the Lord. To the immature eye, it seems as if we are getting less, because we just keep giving unto the Lord. However, the truth is giving to God benefits us, because God always gives back more than He gets. We always get back more than we gave.

The people of God gave back to God the firstborn of all clean male animals, and they gave an offering for those firstborn animals that were considered not clean. God's system is set up to be a blessing to the giver, not a burden. The enemy of our destiny tries to blind the saints, preventing them from seeing the blessing. Therefore, in our immaturity, we see it as a burden. One of the lessons that can help us come to terms with giving God the first-fruits is that whatever we have came from God. We would not have anything to give had God not given to us first. The real first-fruit came from God to us anyway – not from us to Him. As children of God, we must remind ourselves that we keep giving because we keep getting from God!

Verse 37. And that we should bring the firstfruits of our dough, and our offerings, and the fruit of all manner of trees, of wine and of oil, unto the priests, to the chambers of the house of our God; and the tithes of our ground unto the Levites, that same Levites might have the tithes in all the cities of our tillage.

The people of God are making a commitment to bring to the house of God the first-fruits of the dough (flour, ground meal and grain offerings). After they have planted the seed in the field, harvested the crop, and then ground up the meal, they honor their pledge to bring the best of the meal unto the Lord first. The only place where God is always a perfect fit is FIRST! It is obvious that whatever they make or whatever God bless them to get, they are committing to giving to God first.

... And that we should bring the firstfruits ...

God has a way of allowing trouble to come, in order to get it, if we will not bring it. It is always better to bring the first-fruit than to let trouble or tragedies come and take it because in that way we lose it. When we bring it, however, we really are investing or sowing it and we get a return on the investment. We lose it when trouble, tragedy and trials come and take it. The way to settle our hearts from always asking, "Will there be enough for us if we give God His first?" is to accept that it is not our jobs to look out for ourselves! We are never No. 1 – God is! When we make God No. 1, He turns around and makes us No. 1 on His list to bless.

... and the tithes of the ground unto the Levites, that same Levites might have the tithes in all the cities of our tillage.

This verse mentions first-fruits and tithes. Many Bible teachers will refer to the tithe as the first-fruits – and to some degree it is – but it is not the same as first-fruits. The tithe is the tenth that hallows the whole or represents the whole. When we pay God the tenth part or the 10 percent, God blesses the whole because of the portion that was surrendered back to Him. In tithes, we pay God the 10 percent. God allows us to keep the 90 percent and then blesses the 90 percent that we keep. When we pay God the 10, He blesses the 90 to go further. God helps us to do more with the 90 because we were honorable with the 10. Ultimately, God enlarges our 90 percent, because of how we handle His tenth. When we rob God of the tenth, we curse the whole amount.

... and the tithes of the ground unto the Levites ...

The tithes were a part of God's divine law that spoke of the people's responsibility to take care of the temple and those who worked in the temple. In Numbers 18:22-28, the law of God spelled out the responsibility of the tithe. Many saints today would rather not give the tithe. Therefore, the church cannot function as it should. It is the job of every member to make sure there is enough in the storehouse by being responsible with the tithe that belongs to the Lord. An offering says to the Lord, "I am grateful." First-fruits says God comes first and we are depending upon Him to take care of us throughout the year.

Verse 38. And the priest of the son of Aaron shall be with the Levites, when the Levites take tithes: and the Levites shall bring up the tithe of the tithes unto the house of our God, to the chambers, into the treasure house.

Though the tithe was used to carry out the work of the ministry, we must keep in mind that the ministry consisted of more than the people who worked in the temple. The ministry also consisted of the poor, the widows and the orphans. When we give unto the Lord, the body of Christ has a responsibility to use those resources to take care of every assignment God is giving to the local church body. This is only one of the reasons the children of God must manage what we make. We have an obligation to the support the work of the ministry that God has given to us. The old black Baptist church really did not hire or employ anyone except a part-time pastor, musician and janitor. The reason we did not employ staff was that the people did not always have a mind to give unto the Lord.

We were more concerned about raising money, and raising money meant asking folks who did not attend our church and sometimes did not go to church at all to support our church. The danger in having members who do not and will not support their church, Jesus says, is that their heart will never be with that church or with their God. Our money does not always follow our mouths, but our hearts always find a way to follow our money. Jesus says it this way: *"For where your treasure is, there will your heart be also"* (Mat. 6:21).

Verse 39. For the children of Israel and the children of Levi shall bring the offering of the corn, of the new wine, and the oil, unto the chambers, where are the vessels of the sanctuary, and the priests that minister, and the porters, and the singers: and we will not forsake the house of our God.

They know their nation has been weakened by the invasion; still they are committed to rebuilding Judah. They know it starts with a right relationship with God. Don't forsake God's house and God won't forsake your house. Treating God right and reverently must be a priority!

LESSON 12

THE RIGHT ATTITUDE ABOUT GIVING TO GOD!
2 Corinthians 9:1-8 (Amplified)

The Apostle Paul penned this text to the saints at the church in Corinth. The saints in Corinth had promised to give the Apostle gifts to carry on the work of the ministry for the saints in Jerusalem. Paul, thusly, sends some of his ministers ahead of him to make sure the gifts are ready. The Apostle had been doing ministry in Macedonia and told the saints in Macedonia of the generosity of the saints in Corinth.

There are many attributes or characteristics that should be seen in believers in Christ. Worship, a heart to forgive, love, joy, peace, meekness and kind-heartedness should be evident in the life of a believer. A follower of Christ should pray, exhibit righteousness, value the Word, be connected to a pastor and church, witness and testify of God. Though, there are many other characteristics, the last I will share is that a believer should be a GIVER! It is hard to be like Christ and have the love of God in us and simultaneously be stingy or selfish. The transforming power of Christ causes us to expand our focus to more than just ourselves. The transforming power of Christ causes us to be concerned about financing kingdom work, kingdom community, kingdom responsibilities (which include caring for the poor, widows and orphans) and kingdom citizens. Giving is a vast and significant part of God's nature, and it should become an integral part of the nature of the children of God as well.

Because of their faith in Jesus the Christ, Christians in the Apostle Paul's day suffered persecution and many fled their native land in hopes of finding a place with people, who would be friendly toward their new faith. Jews in Jerusalem, at the time of the text, who have now placed their faith in the death, burial, resurrection and ascension of Christ, find themselves in a very hostile environment. Some suffering lack and others must leave their homes, due to threats on their lives. In the midst of this duress, saints in other places such as Corinth and Macedonia made financial commitments to support their Christian brothers and sisters in Jerusalem.

Verse 1. Now about the offering that is [to be made] for the saints (God's people in Jerusalem), it is quite superfluous that I should write you.

The King James Version calls the giving to the saints in Jerusalem "the ministering to the saints," while the New Living Translation calls it "ministry of giving." What is important to recognize here is that giving is a ministry in itself. Oftentimes, we think we are ministering only when we sing, preach, pray, teach or testify. The Word says giving is also ministry. People in nursing homes, those sick in hospitals or sick and out of work at home, and the sick who have no money to pay for their prescriptions, often will tell us there is more than one way to minister to them. As a matter of fact, they tell us that they appreciate the prayers and the visits. Sometimes, money would help them a great deal, too.

The saints in Corinth made a commitment to help their fellow saints in trouble in Jerusalem. Paul is saying to them that he knows he really does not need to write to them about the gifts because of the Corinthian saints' willingness to give. Still, he is writing as a reminder that the saints in Macedonia have heard about the Corinthians' heart to give. Paul does not want to arrive with gifts unequal to what he has been saying about them.

Verse 2. For I am well acquainted with your willingness (your readiness and your eagerness to promote it) and I have proudly told about you to the people in Macedonia, saying that Achaia (most of Greece) has been prepared since last year for this contribution; and [consequently] your enthusiasm has stimulated the majority of them.

The truth is the saints, or household of faith, should have a great attitude about giving and helping others. One of the worst atmospheres is when it is time to give and the people of God start to say, "I need too ...", or defiantly declare, "I ain't giving nothing" or "Let them get theirs the way I got mine" or "I ain't giving them, him or Rev. all my money!" It is this type of satanic spirit that can catch hold of the immature in the worship and cause them to start acting like those individuals with the negative spirit. When we see or hear this negative spirit in the Lord's house, we must rebuke it, because it comes from the pit of hell. This spirit speaks in a whisper so only those who are not in authority hear its rebellious words. It is at that moment we must take authority over the atmosphere and not let the enemy get the victory.

Apostle Paul says he is well acquainted with their willingness, readiness and eagerness to give. That should be the heart, spirit and attitude of every child of God, especially when it is the Lord who is leading the effort in giving. If we are in tune with God, He will let us know when a giving assignment is His!

... has prepared since last year for this contribution ...

One of the reasons many saints don't want to give is that they never really prepare to do so. When it comes to giving a great offering, a large offering or an offering beyond the norm, preparation is usually required. When we fail to prepare, we can never give beyond what is comfortable, convenient or common. The Apostle says these saints prepared a year beforehand to give this special offering unto the Lord and help the saints in Jerusalem. The believer should have several pots into which they can distribute money:
- Retirement;
- Emergency;
- Vacation;
- Regular bills and
- Entertainment/fun money.

Never dip into your emergency money for entertainment or fun, but you can dip into your entertainment/fun money for emergencies. Never use your regular bill money for vacation, but you can dip into vacation money to pay your bills. When you dip into the various pots, just know that you have to build them back up to meet various needs, desires, or future expectations. Considering a getaway? Planning a vacation does not just mean making reservations at a hotel or calling kinfolk to arrange to stay with them. Effective preparation means planning out the total cost of the trip and budgeting before the trip, so money for the rent, mortgage, light bill and car note are not spent on the vacation. As responsible stewards, we also should plan out our spending on a weekly or monthly basis. So, we know how much money we can spend eating out or going to the movies. This practice is a surefire way to keep from being over budget and broke at the end of the month.

When we prepare to give unto the Lord, we must first look at how much we owe God and give what rightfully belongs to Him. Only then can we start picking a house, car, clothes or whatever other desires we can afford. Never buy the house, the car, and the clothes and then, look at what is left for the Lord. The saints' most important bill is the one we owe the Lord. Everything else centers on that.

Verse 3. Still, I am sending the brethren [on to you], lest our pride in you should be made an empty boast in this particular case, and so that you may be all ready, as I told them you would be.

Paul is sending Titus and the brethren before he arrives to make sure all is ready. There are times that we need someone to help us prepare so we are ready to meet life's challenges and responsibilities. It is better to have Titus and the brethren help than to be embarrassed among those of unlike or no faith. Maybe, you need to talk with someone about managing what you make because your money pots are empty. Maybe, you have no need for pots at all because there is never any money left over. Maybe you routinely face this scenario: You got paid last Friday and will get paid again this Friday. Yet, the rent/mortgage, car note, insurance, credit card, student loans and medical bills are unpaid. The shame is not in not having enough. The shame is in not getting help to do something about it.

Verse 4. Lest, if [any] Macedonians should come with me and find you unprepared [for this generosity], we, to say nothing of yourselves, being humiliated for our being so confident.

It is always embarrassing to not meet financial obligations. That is why preparation is so important. Have you ever written a check and it bounced? Do you remember how embarrassed you were the first time it happened? Maybe you lied or offered a weak excuse: "I wrote it from the old account by accident," or "The bank messed up my money." Being ill prepared and unwise in money management can indeed be embarrassing. It is humiliating for people to think we have it going on. Then, one day see our car being towed from work, knowing that it is not broken down. Avoid humiliating moments by managing what you make. If money is tight, it's a sure sign that we must be better managers of what we make. For the next 21 days, track every penny you spend – every penny! Beginning tomorrow, each time money is released from your hands, record it. If you give a person on the street a dollar, record it! At the end of each day and at the end of each week, look at where your money is going. We are not going to get wealth being lucky. We must plan to prosper.

Verse 5. That is why I thought it necessary to urge these brethren to go to you before I do and make arrangements in advance for this bountiful, promised gift of yours, so that it may be ready, not as an extortion [wrung out of you] but as a generous and willing gift.

When we do not prepare to give unto the Lord and to the causes of Christ, it seems like we are being pulled apart in order to get us to give. This should never be. Always prepare for the revivals, conferences, anniversaries and special events your church may have. No church should have any of these events for the sole purpose of raising money, but rather they should be for fellowship and enrichment, to honor or to express love and appreciation. Getting the body to support a cause should not be like pulling teeth. Paul is sending his team of ministers in early to help prepare the people of God to be ready to give as they had promised.

Verse 6. [Remember] this: he who sows sparingly and grudgingly will also reap sparingly and grudgingly, and he who sows generously [that blessings may come to someone] will also reap generously and with blessings.

The old law of sowing and reaping is always in effect. The person who plants tomatoes reaps tomatoes, no matter how much he prays for peaches. We don't get peaches except we plant peach seeds, and then, pray in faith for the harvest we want. We must plant peach seeds. Though the good we sow sometimes takes time to come back to us, we must trust that if the seed we've sown is good seed, then good eventually will sprout up. We may not get the harvest of good when we want it, but it will surely come up within the time that God knows we need it!

The verse goes further, as if to say the issue of giving is already settled in the hearts of the believers: They will reap the good they have sown. The underlying issue in this verse is: How much? How – not if – is the point of this text. How much do you and I want to reap? For the person who is wondering how much he or she will reap, the Word says our reaping is in direct proportion to how much we are sowing. The New Living Translation says the farmer who plants only a few seeds will get a small crop. It is not the size of the prayer, but the size of the sacrifice that determines the size of the harvest. If we plant only a few seeds, we can only realistically expect a small harvest. If we want a large harvest, we must begin planting a lot of seeds.

The amazing mystery in the text is really saying we must sow what we want to end up with. If we want a lot, then we should sow a lot. Every time we get ready to sow we should get excited! It is hard to get excited about giving if we do not have faith to see our future. When we have the right attitude about giving and the faith to see our future, we will have an excitement about giving. Our giving announces our harvest. A bucket brimming with seeds on planting day testifies of the child of God, who possesses a good attitude. The bucket reminds us that we will need more than a bucket when we return for the harvest. The bucket reminds us to make sure the wagon is ready, because a bucket cannot handle what the Lord has in store for the planter. On the day we plant or sow, we are already saying what we want for our harvest. If we plant little, our action says all we want is a little, and that becomes all we can expect.

Most of us have lived with little. Now, it is time to start learning and planning to live with much. We cannot say that everyone who has a lot planted a lot, but we can say the Word says we have an assurance that we will never have a lot if we keep giving God little. Some people acquired what we think is a lot through dishonest living. When that happens the person doesn't have a lot – the lot has them. God wants us to have a lot and have joy testifying about how we obtained it. So, don't eat your seed – SOW it! So, it will GROW!

LESSON 13

THE SECRET TO GETTING MORE SEEDS!
2 Corinthians 9:7-10 (Amplified)

Most believers would agree that we love to receive and have blessings bestowed upon us without boundaries or limitations. Not every child of God wants to be a millionaire or Bill Gates' rich, but I'd venture to say all of us want to have more than enough to meet our needs and have the resources to obtain the desires of our hearts. Most people are really not interested in struggling financially, and if we're honest with ourselves, we would rather have the wealth to tithe and not tip, pay all of our bills, live in the house and neighborhood of our choice, drive the car of our dreams, wear the clothes we want, and still have more money than we would ever spend in a few months. This text shows us there is a heart that God loves, and the heart that God loves becomes the heart He loves to bless.

Verse 7. Let each one [give] as he has made up his own mind and purposed in his heart, not reluctantly or sorrowfully or under compulsion, for God loves (He takes pleasure in, prizes above other things, and is unwilling to abandon or to do without) a cheerful (joyous, "prompt to do it") giver [whose heart is in his giving].

The Word of God not only tells us the amount we are to pay, but the Word also instructs us concerning the spirit in which God wants us to give. The children of God are to pay 10 percent to God in tithes. The tithe is definite, but the amount we are to give is not. The spirit in which God takes pleasure in our giving is definite: willingly, cheerfully, generously, bountifully and purposely. We must always remember that tithing is not giving to God – it is paying God what He is owed. The offering is giving to God out of a spirit of gratitude. The Jews had two chests in the temple for alms. One was for what the law required and the other was for free-will offerings. This text does not suggest God did away with tithes because the Apostle Paul says, *"Every man according as he purposeth in his heart, so let him give; not grudgingly, or of necessity: for God loveth a cheerful giver (KJV)."* Paul is not doing away with the tithe, because his emphasis is on tithing not being about GIVING, but rather about PAYING! He admonishes the people to give what is in their hearts. Conversely, we know the offering is not about PAYING but rather GIVING. So when it comes to tithing, we cannot just pay what is in our hearts. If we are to be right with God, we must pay Him what we owe, and even that must be done with a good spirit if we are going to get the best from the seeds we have sown. When we have a benevolent heart and we give from that type of heart, we will always give gifts that get God's attention and His approval.

Let each one [give] as he has made up his own mind and purposed in his heart ...

Giving is a personal conviction that should not be influenced by the person sitting on the pew with you. No one really knows how good the Lord has been to you but you.

We should, therefore, make up our own minds concerning how much we want give to express gratitude to God. The old preacher used to say, "If the Lord has not done anything for you, you don't have to say anything. But if the Lord has been good to you, you ought to say something!" Our giving always says something about how we feel heaven has handled our affairs. Giving should be a heart decision – not a hard decision. It should not be difficult to give to God, when in our hearts we know all that we have has graciously been given to us by God.

... not reluctantly or sorrowfully or under compulsion ...

When it comes to giving, we are normally at our best as we follow our first instinct or the first feeling of our hearts. When we start listening to outside forces, such as debts, bills, needs, selfishness and even a stingy spirit, we are about to get in trouble with God, as it pertains to the best way to give. Giving is not at its best, when it is done under pressure. Sometimes, we feel pressured to give, because we don't want the preacher to be angry with us for not giving. Sometimes, we give in full view of others, in response to a call for a certain amount. So, we don't appear stingy or as if we don't have it going on. When we give and then return home with a sense of regret, it may mean our giving did not give God the greatest glory. An individual's struggle to give does not mean he or she should not give. It may mean that a spirit needs dealing with. Just because a person struggles to give does not mean anything is wrong with the offering, or the person who is asking for the offering. This inner battle may simply point to a struggle to give, though there is likely no struggle with receiving.

... for God loveth a cheerful giver.

We should want to be a part of whatever God loves. The Amplified Version says God loves *"a giver whose heart is in his giving."* God wants us to get great joy out of being able to give. Joy should radiate on our end. Because we have received and have something to give, we should rejoice. We could have been in need, but God has so prospered us that we can be the giver — that should be good news. We should be glad to give, because giving enables us to sow more seeds, and sowing more seeds translates into a bigger harvest.

We should never be bothered about giving to Christ or the cause of Christ. Giving is an indicator that we are not in utter lack or broke. We will lack nothing, because we are making an investment in Kingdom things. The text does not just suggest God loves the way the cheerful giver gives, but it states God loves the GIVER who is CHEERFUL. There is a deeper meaning and revelation here. Consider what God did in His boundless love: He gave His only begotten Son, because He loves everyone and does not want anyone to perish. God gave His Son for a crowd of people who were at odds with Him and as sinners had not yet accepted him. So, what does God do? He gives. What more would God give to the people He loves who are cheerful givers? We may not discover all that God gives to those who are givers and glad about it. There must be MORE!

Verse 8. And God is able to make all grace (every favor and earthly blessing) come to you in abundance, so that you may always and under all circumstances and whatever the need be self-sufficient [possessing enough to require no aid or support and furnished in abundance for every good work and charitable donation].

Here, Apostle Paul begins to explain what God gives to those He loves because of the manner in which they give. One of the benefits glad givers receive is **ALL GRACE**. God gives glad givers limitless grace. We know it was grace that saved us, grace that brought us safe thus far, and grace that will lead us home. God's unlimited grace is available to those who have the right attitude about giving toward the things that matter the most to Him. When we have the right attitude about giving toward the plans and the purposes of God, God turns around and gives to us that which money can't buy, time can't end, thieves can't steal, winds can't blow away, death can't kill and the cheerful giver can't lose! That gift is ALL GRACE! God makes sure the cheerful giver is on the receiving end of every favor and earthly blessing. When we will not give willingly, please notice not what we are living with but rather what we are living without: grace in every area. No wonder some of us didn't get caught! No wonder some of us did not end up with AIDS! No wonder some of us got out just in the nick of time! No wonder others got fired for doing once what we had been doing for years! No wonder God let us live when we should have died! God makes ALL GRACE available to the givers who are cheerful and – please notice the amount – in abundance! Don't cheat yourselves by missing out on what you could receive because you refuse to let go of what you have.

... so that you may always and under all circumstances and whatever the need be self-sufficient ...

There is too much to lose being stingy and too much to gain in being freehearted toward God. God has ALL GRACE available for all circumstances to those who possess the right heart and attitude about giving. No matter what the circumstance, God has grace ready to fit the occasion. I'm sure you have some impressive clothes, but diamonds and silk don't fit all occasions. God's grace does. It fits every circumstance of our lives and He is willing to give it when we are willing to give. There is nothing we have that fits our life challenges like the ALL GRACE our Heavenly Father willingly gives to those who willingly give to Him. There is a sufficiency available to us not just for the asking, but also just for the giving to accomplish every good deed.

Verse 9. As it is written, He [the benevolent person] scatters abroad; He gives to the poor; His deeds of justice and goodness and kindness and benevolence will go on and endure forever.

The cheerful giver does not just give at home and to those he or she knows. The cheerful giver also shares with strangers from afar and with those whom he or she does not know. Bottom line: People with generous hearts do not need to know the persons in need in order to give. With the heart of Christ, benevolent people give without expecting to receive in return. With there being so many scam artists in the world today, it can be a challenge to determine who indeed is in need. Nonetheless, even if we are taken advantage of because of a helpful heart, God will reward not based on the legitimacy of the need, but on the sincerity and generosity of the giver. This means that even if we are scammed, the Lord will still bless us. Either way, we won't lose.

... His deeds of justice and goodness and kindness and benevolence will go on and endure forever.

Another benefit of being a cheerful giver is that believers with this type of heart will be REMEMBERED! Giving will keep us from being forgotten. It keeps us on God's mind, especially when He is passing out blessings and grace. Being on God's mind is an awesome thing, and the good we have done will not remain on His mind without there being a great reward for it. We all know what happens when we are on the minds of people who love us. We also know what happens when people we love are on our minds; gifts are given, love is shared and blessings are bestowed. What happens when people who love you go on vacation? They bring you back something! Good deeds will go on even when the gift is used up. No matter how good a gift, a deed lasts longer. Paul says it lasts forever. The goodness of our gifts lasts, as long as, the memory of the gifts. God is saying He does not forget when we give to others out of agape love.

Verse 10. And [God] Who provides seed for the sower and bread for eating will also provide and multiply your [resources for] sowing and increase the fruits of your righteousness [which manifest itself in active goodness, kindness, and charity].

The Word of God declares that the person who is committed to sowing unto the Lord will always be provided with seeds. God does not always provide seeds to those who routinely sow at the mall, but He will make sure we have seed if, we make it our purpose to sow unto Him. The graciousness of God teaches us that if He gives us seed to sow, He also will give us much more. Inside of every harvest, we call a paycheck, is seed to sow. When we learn to take seed out of the harvest and graciously sow back to God, we position ourselves to ultimately be blessed with more seed. More seed means more income and more income means more seed. The imbalance that occurs within most immature Christian seed-sowers is that they stop wanting to graciously sow in proportion to the harvest they have received. The person who struggles to give struggles because he or she looks at the seed and not at the harvest. We never give more than what we get from God to God, so stop acting as if we are giving God all. We are giving God a portion, not the sum total. God blesses the all, because we willingly gave Him a portion of the sum total. Not only are we given *ALL GRACE* and are *REMEMBERED,* but we also get *MORE SEED!* If you want more seed, SOW! God always gives us more for simply being willing givers toward the things that matter the most to Him. God promises to provide and to increase our resources because of our willingness to share. Those who have an excuse for not giving unto the Lord just might be excusing themselves from the blessings that come only from Him. God has ways of rewarding us, and God will reward you for being a blessing. Sometimes, He does it in goodness, kindness and charity (love). Let us live and give so the blessings of God overflow and overtake us. The truth is we really can't beat God's giving.

LESSON 14

THE DIFFERENCE SOWING IN DIFFICULT TIMES CAN MAKE!
Genesis 26:12–14

At the time of this text, a famine is in the land. The Word lets us know this is not the first famine the patriarchs have endured. The first famine transpired during the days of Abraham. It happened at a time in Abraham's life, when he was learning to trust God, even though he did not know where the Lord was leading him. God allowed Jacob, Abraham's grandson, to go through a famine in Genesis chapters 43 through 47. Isaac was not born to his father, Abraham, during a time of famine. Here, in the 26th chapter of Genesis, we see Isaac having to experience one himself.

When Abraham went through a famine, he left the place he knew God had promised and went down into Egypt, because the Egyptians had plenty. God allowed Abraham to go to Egypt. There, he almost lost his wife trying to make a living. God was teaching Abraham that a child of God has to have faith that is greater than the famine, and that God allows us to go *through*. Abraham learned the hard way that there was a famine in the land, but not a famine in the Lord. Abraham, therefore, got back to the place, because it was never about the place, but rather God's promise that gives us the assurance we are going to be all right. When Isaac went through his famine, the first thing God told him was not to go to Egypt. When Jacob and his family were in the midst of famine, the Lord sent them to Egypt and there Jacob discovered that not only was Joseph, his son, alive, but God had made him a leader. In biblical times, famines normally constituted a shortage of food and water, and often were caused by a lack of rain or, sometimes, sin. In this text, we will see how Isaac was successful, when going through the season of lack in his day.

Verse 12. Then Isaac sowed in that land, and received in the same year a hundredfold: and the Lord blessed him.

Whenever we go through a season of famine or shortage, there is always a tendency to hold on to all we have and be intimidated by the idea of sowing. Sometimes, the only way to get out of a famine, or to at least cancel the conditions of the famine, is to do what Isaac did – sow! Isaac does not wait until things get better to start sowing.

Many times, we hear believers suggest to God that He allow us to wait until things get better – or at least until we come out of tough times – before He requires us to sow. That might be the reason we remain in famines much longer than necessary. In the life of a believer, the most critical time, as it pertains to handling seeds, is that moment in which we have nothing to waste and everything to lose. When we are at the poorest points in our lives, those are the times to be wise and act judiciously with the seeds God has given. The most dangerous time in the life of a believer, when it comes to the issue of blessings and being blessed abundantly, is that season in which he or she has an abundance of seeds – but little substance – and is not sure what to do with what God has given.

Any farmer who eats seeds rather than planting them will not reap a harvest. As most economists will tell you, America is in a time of famine. What you do with your seeds will determine how you fair during tough times. This is not the time for excuses to justify why we are mismanaging or throwing away our seeds. I often hear parents say they had to help a child in financial trouble. Grown children with no children to support, who either will not work, or will not manage the money they make, should not be allowed to have seeds intended to be sown into good ground and harvested. It is one thing to give of ourselves out of love or to meet a need, but it's a totally different matter to give away God's seeds. Inside every paycheck is a seed. We must make sure we do not overspend and use the seed for something else other than sowing.

Then Isaac sowed in that land ...

Please remember that not only is Isaac in a famine, but he is in transition as well. This is a temporary place for Isaac and his family. Isaac sowed in a season in which he was not stable, but he knew he needed to sow if he ever were to become stable. Stability is not a necessity or a requirement for sowing. Inherent to having seeds is a requirement for sowing, and needing a harvest necessitates sowing! Isaac planted during an unpredictable season in his life and so must we.

... and received in the same year a hundredfold ...

This was a rare or unusual blessing and rate of return on an investment. To receive a thirty-fold or sixty-fold return was remarkable, but the Word says the child of God who planted in faith in this season of uncertainty received a hundredfold! The children of God must not shrink from expecting to receive after seeds are sown. No farmer would sow without having some expectations. Every time the people of God sow into the Kingdom, we ought to expect a return on our investment. A believer's expectancy of the rate of return on a Kingdom investment depends upon the level or dimension of his or her faith. Our faith influences our rate of return, because God always matches or exceeds the faith. He never goes below the rate of faith with which we sow. We cannot increase the rate of the return on Kingdom investments with a false faith. You cannot trick the Master. God knows real faith. He knows the quality of faith we are working with and the quality of faith that is working in us.

Delving further, please notice a hundredfold is not a 100 percent return on Isaac's investment, but rather a 10,000 percent rate of return! A hundredfold is 100 multiplied by 100, which is 10,000. It is evident that Isaac had to have an incredible level of faith to plant seed during a drought; in the midst of a famine; during a period of transition; on land he is leasing but does not own; around a people he is not perfectly at peace with; in the midst of a people who have problems with his prospering; and at a point, where he has just proven, he is not perfect by being caught living with a lie! We cannot forget that it was when Isaac was just a boy that his daddy received one of God's new names –

Jehovah Jireh. I am sure Isaac never forgot that God does provide. He is the living proof that God will make a way.

... and the Lord blessed him.

The hundredfold return is what God gave Isaac through the sowing of seeds in the land, but that is not all Isaac received from God. The verse says, *"and the Lord blessed him."* All of the blessings did not come from the land. God has many, more ways of blessing people, who live by a lifestyle of faith. Sometimes, God blesses us directly from His hand to ours, but then there are times God blesses us indirectly (such as through the ground, the job, co-workers, supervisors, the owner of a company, raises, promotions, neighbors, biological family, church family, the stranger on the street, the salesman, governments, etc.). We must thank God for the roundabout ways He blesses us, but then also thank Him for blessing us directly. When God blesses us directly, He moves the middleman. So, there is no guessing regarding who gave us the blessing. We must always and at all times be grateful and recognize the hand of God blessing our lives because *every good and perfect gift does come from God* (James 1:17).

Verse 13. And the man waxed great, and went forward, and grew until he became great.

The term "great" in this verse can be somewhat tricky. To fully understand the text, we must see both meanings of "greatness" in the verse. The first mention of great speaks to what the child of God had or the possessions that he accumulated. The second reference does not deal with what the child of God has, but rather who Isaac has become. This reference turns our focus to the person. It is one thing to have a lot of great stuff, but it is *more* impressive to be a great person, who can be trusted with a lot of great stuff. While Isaac is growing in material wealth, he is also growing in personality, character, faith and conviction. Some saints act as if believers can grow only in one area at a time. However, the truth is we should be growing in all areas. Isaac's money is growing, but as his money is growing, Isaac is growing as a man, a master, a husband, a businessman, an entrepreneur, a thinker, a citizen, a believer, a neighbor, an investor, and as a person, who can be trusted with prosperity. Remember, this is all happening in a time of famine. When there is real growth in us, famine does not matter. Our growth overshadows the famine.

... And the man waxed great ...

This portion of the verse raises a question each of us must answer honestly. And that question is: "How much can each of us be trusted with?" How much can we handle and still keep our sights on what heaven has for us? There is a certain amount that the immature believer can receive and still be grateful, give God glory, and give to God what's owed to Him. Above that blessing, we become arrogant, prideful, and self-centered – and that is when the blessing becomes a burden!

... and went forward ...

Real success is a forward progression. It is not the appearance that we are going forward just to find out later that we have actually moved backward. There are moments in which real success can seem to be a backward motion, when in reality the process does move us forward. Only God and time can reveal, if what we are experiencing is truly success. We must not remain stagnant in our thinking or in our practices. Earlier in the chapter, Isaac makes a great mistake. Even in that error, we can reason that he moved forward. Sometimes, we make bad decisions about God, life, people, opportunities, and money. There must be documented proof that we are not still stuck in yesterday's mistakes. We must get up, get busy, get involved and get back to God. Time is ticking and it is already late in the day. Isaac teaches us that we never know what God is going to do with the seeds we are sowing. One thing we do know is what will happen if the seeds are not sown at all – NOTHING! The direction each of us must go – even through bad decisions, tough times and difficult days – is forward.

... and grew until he became very great.

What a great testimony it would be for the record to show the person we became after coming out of the famine. For those who are in a financial famine and seemingly cannot make the ends meet, what greater testimony is there than for you to come out financially wiser, investment savvy, corporate clever, entrepreneur ingenious and Kingdom committed.

Verse 14. For he had possessions of flocks, and possessions of herds, and great store of servants: and the Philistines envied him.

Isaac is an Old Testament patriarch. Yet, he possesses an exemplary and modern concept about business and diversifying his finances that would make him successful even today. Every believer should have more than one stream of income. Some suggest that people should have seven streams of income. The purpose of having more than one stream of income is so if one stream is blocked or cut off, the person can still fulfill his or her responsibilities, live comfortably and not go bankrupt.

We saw in verse 12 that the seeds Isaac planted became one stream of income. The land he leased was a second stream of income. The favor of God over his family was a third stream. In verse 14, we see three other streams of income: the flocks, the herds and the servants. If for some reason the flocks of sheep or goats stopped producing, Isaac would still not be cut off financially because he has potential revenue in his herds of cattle. His servants, who are essentially employees, are a stream of income. Though Isaac has to pay them, they work to make him money. Isaac's seventh stream of income takes the shape of wells, which increased the potential production of his crops through irrigation and the productivity of his flocks and herds. The wells provided an ample supply of water. The wells also could generate income through the leasing out of water rights to other farmers and shepherds who needed water, especially during times of a famine.

To "diversify" means to make diverse; to give variety to; and to balance (as in investment portfolio) defensively by dividing funds among securities of different industries or of different classes.[3] We are called to not only diversify our investments, but also to diversify our income. Simply put, we must have more than one way to make money and we must have more than one way for our money to make us more money. If our money is not making us money, something is wrong with our thinking. If we are not thinking of more than one way to make more money, we are missing out on some great God-given opportunities! Our problems are not that there is a lack of opportunities to make money – our problems stem from not looking!

---

[3] Merriam-Webster's Collegiate Dictionary

LESSON 15

THE COST OF GETTING GOD'S ATTENTION!
II Samuel 24:14-20

Oftentimes, we as believers err in our relationships with God. The mistakes we make cause great personal pain, as well as, pain to others. An apology does not always make amends, and though Christ has paid the ultimate cost for our sins, we must always be mindful of the fact that there are consequences when we miss the mark.

As chapter 24 of 2 Samuel unfolds, we see that David has made a great sin in counting the fighting men of Israel, when he should have been counting upon the Lord. God wants His people to walk in confidence – not because of the number of people who are with us, but based upon who we are in Him, who He is in us and what His Word says about us. King David's lack of trust in the Lord and listening to Satan resulted in his taking of a census, which offended the Lord. In verses 12 and 13, God gives David three punishment options: Seven years of famine; three months of being pursued by his enemies; or three days of pestilence in the land. David knows that if he picks the seven years of famine, he will more than likely fall into the hands of nature, and nature can be cruel, merciless and unpredictable. If David chooses to be chased by his enemies, he knows that he will be in the hands of men, and neither can he, nor we truly know what people will do, when we are defenseless and need their mercy the most. David picks the three days of pestilence, at the hands of God. Though David knows that God can be severe in punishment, God is always full of mercy, in spite of our mess. He will give us grace to get us through the gloom.

Remember now, David gets a whole nation in trouble because he fails to rely on God. We must never underestimate the offensiveness of the sin of not trusting, relying upon, and having a deep dependence upon God. The lack of trust in God cost David and Israel, and as quietly as it is kept, that lack of trust is costing us and all those who are connected to us. As we look into the text, we will see that David will have to pay for not trusting in God, and so will we.

Verse 14. And David said unto Gad, I am in a great strait: let us fall now into the hand of the Lord; for his mercies are great: and let me not fall into the hand of man.

David is in a mess and he admits it. The New Living Translation says that David declares, *"I am in a desperate situation…"*

Sometimes, it seems as though saints do not know when they are in bad situations, or what constitutes a bad situation. A bad situation is not a spike in gas prices, because high gas prices do not affect everyone. The person who purchases a vehicle with forethought of the gas mileage rather than forethought concerning whether the neighbor, family, friends or enemies will be impressed with what he or she drives is not devastated by high gas prices. The person who does not live on the financial edge and then, hopes that nothing breaks is not prone to desperation. Those who spend all that they make and even what they don't make are desperate without financial forethought.

Israel found itself in trouble, because of David's bad decision. This misstep affected everyone, not just a few. Some bad decisions hurt only us, while others hurt the people who love us or are around us. The consequences of our lack of trust in God are far-reaching and really affect much more than we could ever imagine. It is costly when we choose not to live by faith, and that sin hurts many more people than the overt sins saints deem most important.

Verse 15. So the Lord sent a pestilence upon Israel from the morning even to the time appointed: and there died of the people from Dan even to Beer-sheba seventy thousand men.

All of David's troubles, in this text, stem from his failure to trust in the Lord. David is not in trouble this time because of Bathsheba, and though the Church likes to talk about David's Bathsheba trouble, only two people died because of his adulterous act (Though arguably two deaths are too many). The text says the result of David's counting people and not counting on God is the death of 70,000 men. Though we consider adultery the graver sin, the sin that spurs the greatest punishment is not living by faith.

Most saints would agree that not trusting God is offensive. However, most believers would never suppose that trusting God is so vital that the failure to do so would result in the deaths of so many innocent people, at the hands of a man who should have believed but did not. Stop minimizing the doubt and disbelief that we are operating in when we do not fully give God what is due unto Him. Are we killing communities, the ignorant and the innocent weekly, as we walk around the offering table or pass offering baskets? With cell phones on our hips, cable in our view, rims that don't improve the car's ride, expensive clothes and a pension to eat out as though we aren't already overweight, are we sending a conflicting message? We can no longer dismiss the importance of counting on God. The way we handle our money indicates in whom or what we put our trust. If God does not get what He requires from us financially, it's a sure sign that we are counting on someone or something else. Are we counting on ourselves, our jobs, our parents, our sweethearts, on luck, or our God? The way we handle our money should testify to the fact that we are totally depending upon God. Big trouble lies in wait, when we count on anyone or anything other than God. Tithing is evidence of trust in God.

Verse 16. And when the angel stretched out his hand upon Jerusalem to destroy it, the Lord repented him of the evil, and said to the angel that destroyed the people, It is enough: stay now thine hand. And the angel of the Lord was by the threshing place of Araunah the Jebusite.

The angel was on the verge of pouring out the wrath of God upon Jerusalem, but God's goodness and mercy stopped him. In spite of whatever happens to us, we had better learn to thank God for the situations He did not allow. It could have been much worse – and it would have been much worse – had God not stepped in with grace. We have grown into an ungrateful people who do not handle God's money correctly, because we think we deserve so much. If we could peer behind the scenes of history, we would see how each and every decision not to trust God could have gone from bad to worse, but for His grace. How many times in a week or even in a day do we decide not to count on God? Without God's mercy, I fear that all of us would be wiped out – not because of anyone else's decisions, but our own unwillingness to rely solely on God. This text not only suggests that we need mercy, but it also suggests that we need to pray that God let us *see* mercy. We may already have done enough today to warrant the wiping out of our church or community, but God showed us mercy when He could have poured out His wrath.

Verse 17. And David spake unto the Lord when he saw the angel that smote the people, and said, Lo, I have sinned, and I have done wickedly: but these sheep, what have they done? Let thine hand I pray thee, be against me, and against my father's house.

David saw the angel of death and he began to pray. We need to pray that God allows us to see how our decision not to trust Him hurts everyone, even the people we are giving God's money to in the name of offering help. We cannot help our children with God's money – we can only hurt them and ourselves. David took responsibility for his decision not to count on his Creator!

Verse 18. And Gad came that day to David, and said unto him, Go up, rear an altar unto the Lord in the threshing floor of Araunah the Jebusite.

Please note who is speaking to David about his need to build a special place to meet with God. Gad is the prophet and David is the king. David is large and in charge. Yet, he needs direction on how to move the heart of God and get back into His good graces. Gad has been talking to God about the mess David made, and God has been speaking to the prophet about the king. If David listens to Gad, it will be as if he is listening to God, because Gad's instruction to David is from God. Gad tells David where to go and what he needs to build. Essentially, Gad tells David, the only thing that will alter his situation is an altar! David cannot go to an old altar or return to a familiar place. God is requiring that David pay to have a special place to meet with Him and inquire of His mercy. Many saints do not hear from God as they should, because they have paid little to nothing. Building an altar for God is costly. Some of that cost is paid with our time, our talent and our treasure. Cheap donations are insolent, when it comes to erecting a place to meet with the God, who has the power to alter any situation at any time.

...Go up, rear an altar unto the Lord in the threshing floor of Araunah the Jebusite.

Building an altar is expensive. It's going to cost valuable time, not idle time, available when you have nothing to do. The prophet tells David to "go up," and that means time. Time designated for God is a priceless commodity that most Christians don't have or really don't want to give. The reason going to church, getting on our knees and praying, and reading the Word are so tiresome is because through these acts we are going somewhere – up! Whenever, there is a real pursuit of God, it is an upward progression. Israel and David are at an all-time low. When David (and we) listen to the voice of God through the prophet and set our hearts on connecting with God and disconnecting from our sins, Gad is right, we are headed up! When Gad tells him to rear an altar, David knows it will take time, talent, and treasure. David does not grumble, because he also knows that Israel's predicament was his doing. If Israel is to emerge victorious, David knows he must get out of the way and allow God to move by His mercy.

Why is this place so important? Why can't David just make a sacrifice anywhere? Isn't the sacrifice what's most important? The answer is an emphatic NO! What is most important is following God's instructions and giving Him what He wants and requires? We miss out on so many blessings, because we never get to the place in life where we readily and willingly give God what he requires. After arriving at that altar, where God's will is all that matters, we find peace, prosperity, power and position. David cannot get to the issue of what to give, until he first arrives at the place where God is calling him. We must get to the place of the altar before we can offer an acceptable sacrifice.

Still, the question must be raised: "What is so important about where we construct the altar?" Araunah is the place, where God stopped the angel from killing any more Israelites, because of David's sin. Araunah is the place, where the wrath of God toward Jerusalem was held back. Araunah is the place where God's mercy made justice take a break. Araunah is the place where if God had not spoken to our situation, though it was bad, it was about to be worse. Araunah is the place where beloved gospel singer CeCe Winans says, "Mercy said, No! I am not going to let you go!" Araunah is the place where we see God working things out for us. So what better place to build an ALTAR but the place where we see God ALTERING things for us – even before we completely get it right with Him.

Verse 19. And David, according to the saying of Gad, went up as the Lord commanded.

By obeying Gad's instructions, David followed the command of God. His obedience begs the question: "How badly do we want the curse lifted from us?"

Verse 20. And Araunah looked, and saw the King and his servants coming on towards him: and Araunah went out, and bowed himself before the King on his face upon the ground.

A blessing lies in David's meeting Araunah. Araunah shows David – and us – what we need to do to get right with God. Araunah comes, he bows and he gets as low as he can go, the proper posture for a person who needs mercy.

LESSON 16

THE SACRIFICE THAT SATISFIES MUST COST US SOMETHING!
II Samuel 24:18-25

Let's continue in our study of the trouble that ensued when David counted the fighting men of Israel instead of counting on the God of Israel. Seventy thousand men have died as a result of David's blunder, and the prophet Gad has come to King David to tell him what to do to get out of the mess they're in.

Verse 18. And Gad came that day to David, and said unto him, Go up, rear an altar unto the Lord in the threshing-floor of Araunah the Jebusite.

The prophet, providing instruction directly from God, tells David exactly where to go and what to do. He must go to the threshing floor owned by Araunah and build an altar. You may ask, "Why is the king listening to the prophet and following his direction?" Verse 11 says the Prophet Gad is King David's seer. A prophet is a person, who is divinely inspired to communicate God's will to His people and to disclose the future to them.[4] Prophets also were called seers, which means they were able to see into the future, into the mysteries of God, into the hidden truths of God, into the heart of God, and into the strategies and plans of God, as well as get understanding of the will of God. That is why you can sit in a pew on a Sunday morning and hear the man or woman of God provide an answer to the very thing you have been praying about, talking to people about, or silently wondering about in your heart. The man or woman authentically called by God uses the gifts of God, as he or she preaches and teaches.

The Prophet Gad knows where King David has to go, because God has shown him. David's destination is Araunah's threshing floor, where grain is ground. Many times, our deliverance is delayed, because we do not hear the prophet, or we fail to accept that what the seer is showing us is what he or she received from God. This threshing floor was not an established place for an altar. There were established places for altars back home. Remember, if we want an ALTAR that will ALTER our bad situations, we must find out where God wants an altar and build it there. Why is this threshing floor so important as it pertains to building the altar? It was at this place that God told the destroying angel in verse 16, *"It is enough."* It is at this place that God showed Israel mercy. It is at this place that the destroying angel turned his attention toward Jerusalem, and even though 70,000 men already had died, the angel stood ready to claim the lives of more men. It is here that mercy overruled justice. Mercy took over the driver's seat and made justice sit in the passenger's seat. Israel does not know what has happened at Araunah, but they must trust and follow their leader, King David, who trusts and follows his prophet, Gad, who is listening to and following God.

---

[4] New Unger's Bible Dictionary

Verse 19. And David, according to the saying of Gad, went up as the Lord commanded.

This verse clearly tells us that going to the threshing floor is not a Gad idea, but rather a God idea. If David had not listened to Gad, he would essentially have been turning a deaf ear to the voice of God. How many times do we ignore the Gads in our lives, neglecting to see it is not Gad, who we are ignoring, but God Himself? Sometimes, we are not in the right place – literally or figuratively – to get God's attention. Other times, we are in the wrong place to hear his response. Position, in the Kingdom, must be a priority.

Verse 20. And Araunah looked, and saw the king and his servants coming on toward him: and Araunah went out, and bowed himself before the king on his face upon the ground.

The way Araunah postures himself, toward David is the way to get to the heart of the King. Araunah gives the king his attention, draws nearer to the king, and then bows before the king as to surrender in worship. Araunah demonstrates the proper way to approach the king, and shows us that a right heart can turn any place into a throne or altar. Please remember that David is a king, but he desperately needs a meeting with the King. If Araunah could bow to a king without knowing what he wanted, certainly David could bow to what he knows is the desire of the King. Araunah's humble manner moves David, and that example will aid in his approach to God.

Verse 21. And Araunah said, Wherefore is my lord the king come to thy servant? And David said, To buy the threshing-floor of thee, to build an altar unto the Lord, that the plague may be stayed from the people.

David wants to buy Araunah's threshing floor. Many saints would question why he would choose to buy the property, when he could simply borrow it. One would think David's sacrifice here would be a one-time affair and he'd have no reason to return to sacrifice again. However, David wants to buy the threshing floor. He wants ownership. We should take ownership of the altar to prevent ourselves from making the same mistakes over and over again. Taking ownership of the altar reminds us of where we met with God, and where God met with us and showed us mercy.

Consider the text's modern implication. These days, church foreclosures are becoming more and more prevalent. Much of that has more to do with saints not being committed to the cost of the vision than the economic difficulty of the times. Every church that is living out vision is at risk. The vision of the church is much larger than the commitment of those who attend and say they are members. Many in the Body are guilty of haphazardly siphoning off money that belongs to the Lord for the work of ministry to anything and anyone. Cable, cars, clothes, conventions, clubs, carnivals and children – anything can take priority over giving the Lord what is due him. Your church, the local body to which you belong, is a congregational altar. It is the place where God has altered many lives, and countless more would be changed, if there were a sense of ownership, a real commitment to making the altar open and accessible to the people. Had David borrowed the threshing floor and not took ownership of it, people would not have been able to use it when needed. Their access would be up to Araunah, who, again, used the threshing floor to grind grain.

Verse 22. And Araunah said unto David, Let my Lord the king take and offer up what seemeth good unto him: behold, here be oxen for burnt sacrifice, and threshing instruments and other instruments of oxen for wood.

Araunah has a great heart for the king, but he could hurt David by trying to help him make a sacrifice that requires no sacrifice! Without sacrifice, there is no sacrifice! If Araunah gives David everything to make the sacrifice, then there would be no sacrifice on David's part. God was not calling for a sacrifice from Araunah. God was demanding a sacrifice from David! We can no longer accept excuses for not tithing and giving an offering unto the Lord. Excuses are not acceptable sacrifices. Araunah was willing to give David the place, the wood for the altar and the fire, and the oxen for the sacrifice. If David accepts Araunah's offer, the sacrifice costs him nothing. Some saints are fine with that approach. They give nothing to the Lord. If that is your practice, don't be surprised to receive little of the fullness of God's grace and mercy.

Verse 23. All these things did Araunah, as a king, give unto the king. And Araunah said unto the king, The Lord thy God accept thee.

Nothing but our best is ever acceptable to the Lord. We must give our God our best faith, our best life, our best efforts, our best praise, our best worship, and our best love. Only our best is worth giving. Furthermore, our gifts to Him must be the best by His standards, not ours. Are you doubtful that God will reject a gift? Ask Cain! He will tell you that God demands the best!

Verse 24. And the king said unto Araunah, Nay; but I will surely buy it of thee at a price: neither will I offer burnt offerings unto the Lord my God of that which doth cost me nothing. So David bought the threshing-floor and the oxen for fifty shekels of silver.

It is only when we as believers get to that place where we want to spend money on God, spend time with God and expend our talents for God that we will see our hearts in the right place toward God. Without hesitating, David says, *"Nay!"* This is a satanic set-up and the enemy ensnared David one time by tricking him to number the people (1 Chronicles 21:1). David is not going to be tricked this time. We, as David did, must know what God wants, how God wants it and where God wants it. If we are not sure how to please God, we had better get us a seer. David absolutely rejects the idea of erecting an altar and giving an offering that is totally detached from his pocket and from him personally. How much does worship cost us on Sunday? When is the last time we began to pray for Sunday's worship during the week? When is the last time we stayed up late Saturday night praying for Sunday morning? Worship that gets God's attention and gets us in God's presence has to cost somebody something. God is a rewarder of those who diligently seek Him (Hebrews 11:6). We could all get more out of worship, if we were willing to pay a lot more for it. We must stop letting the choir sing for us, the preacher do all the praying for us, and other members pay to keep the church lights on for us. We get the best results from our sacrifice, when we resolve to always give our best sacrifice to the Lord.

... but I will surely buy it of thee at a price...

In our immaturity, most of us would have been glad to accept the gift and then call it a sacrifice unto the Lord. We may have smiled to ourselves, knowing it didn't cost us anything. During the Christmas season, there is a practice of giving called re-gifting. When a person re-gifts, he or she takes a gift that was given to him or her and presents it as a gift to another. We do a lot of re-gifting to God. Giving God anything that cost us nothing has no lasting value to us. David does not need a place to grind grain, but he needs this threshing-floor, because this is where God wants him to make a sacrifice. David realizes he must take ownership of this place, before he can make a sacrifice. Buying the threshing-floor itself is not the sacrifice. The sacrifice comes in the purchase of a permanent place – an altar – where a sacrifice is made to draw God's attention, God's mercy and God's grace. The tithe helps pay for the place, where we make our sacrifice, but the tithe is not the sacrifice. The tithe helps us to buy and maintain the place, where we bring our sacrifice, or the ALTAR.

... So David bought the threshing-floor and the oxen for fifty shekels of silver.

Not only does David buy the place to make a sacrifice, but he also buys the oxen he will use as a sacrifice. He also purchases the materials he will use to construct the altar.

Verse 25. And David built there an altar unto the Lord, and offered burnt offerings and peace offerings. So the Lord was entreated for the land, and the plague was stayed from Israel.

An altar not only will cost us money, but it also will cost us time. David offered burnt offerings unto to the Lord in an act of repentance for his sin of not counting on God. It cost David financially to sacrifice and show God that he was sorry. David also offered peace offerings unto the Lord. No one can be forgiven and still not have peace with God. David wants to know that he and God are all right again. Notice, the two types of offerings: burnt offerings to pay for the sin and peace offerings to restore his joy and peace. Christ is our sacrifice. He paid for all of our sins, and He gives us peace with God again. Though Christ is our complete sacrifice, who covers us for all eternity, His sacrifice does not exempt us from making the personal, costly sacrifices the Father at times requires.

... So the Lord was entreated for the land, and the plague was stayed from Israel.

Other translations say the Lord heard David's prayers. There are moments in our walk that we want reassurance that our mistakes will not keep us from getting in touch with God. That reassurance just might cost us. When we make mistakes and God's mercy keeps us from being wiped out, we should remember to place a sacrifice on the altar in an act of gratitude. When our souls are uneasy, we might need to present an offering to say to God that we need His peace, which surpasses all understanding.

LESSON 17

GIVING UNTO GOD WAS IN PLACE FROM THE START!
Genesis 4:3-7

This lesson deals with the first offering mentioned in the Bible. That offering is made by the children of the first family. Questions are often raised about the offerings of Cain and Abel. Many of those questions will not have an absolute answer, but they are worth pondering nonetheless. Were offerings a requirement from God at this time or were they an expression of the nature of a spirit of gratitude? Where did Cain and Abel get the idea to present offerings unto the Lord? Had they seen their parents, Adam and Eve, make sacrifices unto the Lord? Though we do not have the answers, we do know people have presented offerings to the Lord since the beginning of creation. There appears to be an expectation – a requirement – from the Lord. Otherwise, there would be no basis upon which to accept or reject an offering. As we delve into the story, we will see that even from the start, God reserved the right to not accept all gifts given unto Him.

Verse 3. And in the process of time it came to pass, that Cain brought of the fruit of the ground an offering unto the Lord.

"In the process of time," or as other translations say it, *"at the end of days,"* is believed by some scholars to be the end of a year, and a time for the ingathering of a harvest that is given to the Lord. Even in primitive days, there was a place for God in the lives of the first family. Their acknowledgment of God is evidenced by offerings made unto Him.

Every gift presented to the Lord has a message inside. Every beautifully wrapped gift we give carries a message inside. Some gifts let the recipients know they matter. Other gifts say a simple "I love you." Some gifts carry a message of "You're important to me." Other gifts let the recipient know you appreciate having him or her in your life.

Gifts can just as easily carry negative messages. Gifts can convey "I (the giver) am cheap! I felt I had to give you something, so I'm giving you a gift that cost me very little." That kind of gift silently tells the recipient that you put no real thought or heart into the gesture. Recipients hear negative messages loud and clear, though givers rarely intend for that to be so. Giving should not be reduced to the amount or size of a gift. The message is important, too. No, I'm not speaking of the notes we write and gingerly place beside a bow. It is the silent message inside that speaks to the heart of the recipient. Have you ever wondered what your gifts say to God, or what He says when He receives your gift? We do not always get to see God's expression as He receives our gifts, but we should want them to put a smile on His face! We should also want our gifts to God to communicate how important He is to us. Think about the last gift you gave to the Lord. What message did it have inside? Many saints know the Lord hears prayers. But make no mistake, He also hears gifts!

Verse 4. And Abel, he also brought of the firstlings of his flock and of the fat thereof. And the Lord had respect unto Abel and to his offering.

We see that both sons are viewed as givers. For certain, giving to the Lord has to be taught. It is worth noting these two men are not givers, because they are good. They are givers, because they have been taught. Either, they were taught by their parents or they were taught by the Lord. It is clear that someone taught them to make God a priority. For the most part, it is not in the nature of man to be good to God. Someone has to teach us. It is important that parents teach children to love God and to express their love and adoration to Him through giving. How unfortunate to grow up in a household in which parents do not make God a priority when it comes to time, talent and treasure! Parents should set the example of how heaven ought to be handled. Yet, in many cases, it is not the parents who teach children how to love the Lord. In those situations, the Lord will send someone or create circumstances to provide invaluable instruction on how to love and honor Him with possessions.

Please notice what Abel brought to the Lord – the FIRST born of his flock and the fat thereof. God wants His FIRST, not SECOND! I can remember sitting with my granddaddy and grandmother, at their dinner table as a child. My grandfather always picked up the first dish and then passed it around to everybody else. Granddaddy got the FIRST serving, because he was the one working to bring food into the house. In most cases, families that had a working man in charge more adequately prepared us to handle spiritual responsibility to the Lord. The true order of dishing out anything is to make sure the one responsible for the blessings is blessed FIRST – not SECOND! Families that switched the order of dishing out the food not only sent a bad signal in the house, but also throughout the kingdom. The children became the main focus, the priority and the head. The old meal-time tradition taught children to honor their father and mother.

... And the Lord had respect unto Abel and to his offering.

There is no absolute answer as to how God showed that He accepted or had respect for Abel's offering, but one thing is for sure – everybody knew God did. Giving to the Lord is essential, but what's most important is His acceptance. The last thing we should want to do is waste time giving God something He will not accept. Every believer should want his or her gift to be accepted by God. Take these gift-giving rules into account:
1. Give God our BEST!
2. Give God His FIRST!
3. Give to God with a grateful heart!
4. Give to God willingly!
5. Give God what's RIGHT and not what's LEFT!

We should never EXPECT God to ACCEPT any gift from us that does not RESPECT who He is. The Lord had respect for Abel's offering, because Abel's offering respected the Lord.

Verse 5. But unto Cain and to his offering he had not respect. And Cain was wroth, and his countenance fell.

This is the difficult part of the text, because this side of God is not familiar to us. Many of us do not know there is a side of God that will reject us and our offering. He will literally not accept either one, because of the heart in which the gift was given. One of the things, we must know about God is that He is not cheap. God is not stingy, and whenever we deal with God we must never be stingy or cheap toward Him. We cannot give God just anything and expect Him to be all right with it, especially when God gives us His best. *God gives us His best* is a truth that is much deeper than we can fully comprehend or explain in one lesson. Our best will never match up to His. Though our best is impressive to some and not others, God's best satisfies kings and the commoner; the rich and the poor; the haves and the have-nots; the illiterate and the educated; the well-traveled and the homebody. Our best may not satisfy the Oprahs, the Bill Gates, the Donald Trumps, and the Kennedys, but God's best leaves no one dissatisfied and everyone in awe. While our best is not always impressive to others, we shy from even attempting to give our best to God.

There are many theological theories, as to why Cain incurred God's rejection. A common thought is that Cain should have offered a blood sacrifice to represent the need for forgiveness of his sins. We can't be sure of God's reason for rejecting Cain's offering, but we can be sure Cain knew what God wanted before he gave. We must no longer buy into the fallacy that God will accept anything we give. On Father's Day, many dads happily accept gifts they really will never use. However, I'd venture to say most fathers would never tell their children they wished more thought was put into the gift. Well, God was honest with Cain and told him that He did not accept the gift. God is honest with us – we are just not listening sometimes! Even if scholars are correct and God did call for a blood sacrifice, Cain should have given God what He wanted and required.

The text teaches that not only did God turn down the gift, but He also turned down the giver. Our gifts are given as a reflection of who we are and how we really feel. So when God turned down Cain's gift, He turned down the heart Cain had toward Him. Our gifts are an expression of the heart. The least expensive gift – when given with the right heart – can say to the recipient, "I wanted to give you more, but I did give the best of what I have for where I am right now." Furthermore, we should never be satisfied with the gifts we give to God, because He deserves much more. Even our best gifts are inadequate, but they will be accepted by God when we follow the rules of good gift-giving.

... And Cain was wroth and his countenance fell.

Cain became angry, because God did not accept his gift. Cain's rage was permissible – even understandable – but he got angry with the wrong person. Cain should have gotten angry with himself. We should never get angry with others for giving God their best, especially when it becomes obvious that they and their gifts make God smile. Your best can incense others, but never let anyone talk you out of giving God the best you can give. God's approval of our best should compel us to make a promise that should He keep blessing us, we will do even better with what we give! People who withhold their best from God do not want others to give God what He is due. That act of obedience and love shows them up!

Verse 6. And the Lord said unto Cain, Why art thou wroth? And why is thy countenance fallen?

God speaks to Cain and God will speak with us. Here, we have support that before God rejects our gifts, we already know what is acceptable to Him. When we give great gifts – or even nice gifts – not only does the recipient feel good, but we feel good, too! People who crumple up their money and throw it in the offering tray are usually not proud of the gift they are giving, because they know it is not a gift to be proud of. The amplified version says God asked Cain, *"Why do you look sad and depressed and dejected?"* Cain knows the truth. God is not going to accept just anything, and what he has just given is ANYTHING! It's a dreadful feeling to be rejected by God, but we must always remember our gift is what brought about that rejection. The NIV version of the Bible says, *"Why is your face downcast?"* No one and nothing can make us feel better when we know we are not accepted by the very one who's approval is final. No one can make God change His mind. People may not appreciate what you do for God and what you give to God, but the good news is God is doing the grading! Make sure that whatever you give is acceptable to Him!

Verse 7. If thou doest well, shalt thou not be accepted? And if thou doest not well, sin lieth at the door. And unto thee shall be his desire, and thou shalt rule over him.

To deny God your best is a sin. To not give God your best is a trap of sin. The temptation to refuse God your best is a test of sin. If you allow sin to get the best of your gift-giving, you and you alone will feel the failure of it. There is nothing like the acceptance of God. The devil in hell and our enemies know it. We must master the sin to shortchange God in every area of our lives. We must give God all that belongs to Him, and after that give Him much more. God deserves ALL!

Lesson 18

When the Tenth is My Testimony of Thanks for Victory!
Genesis 14:16-23

There are times in life, when we pause to look back on the struggle – the conflicts, confrontations and battles we've come through. While it may seem things just "turned out" great, we know it was the Lord, who intervened and granted us victory. This lesson is about deciding how to express our gratitude to the Lord for life's victories. Though we are not always sure of the perfect way to express our appreciation, it would certainly be robbery not to declare in a special way that our successes belong to the Lord.

Here, we find Abram, or Abraham as he is called after God gives him a new name in Genesis chapter 17. He and the 318 men born in his house have gone to war against four nations that had overtaken Sodom and Gomorrah, and in the process swept up his nephew, Lot. Against the odds, Abraham and his men were victorious. Lot and a multitude of others were freed, because Abraham got involved. Now, Abraham is on his way back bearing the spoils of victory.

It is always a great feeling to return from battle having attained great victory, despite overwhelming odds. Amid the swells of pride and feelings of success a question must be raised: "Do we owe God anything for causing us to be successful?" If your answer is "No, God does not deserve anything," that's a telltale sign that you feel no obligation to give anything to the Lord. If your answer is, "Absolutely yes! God is the one responsible for giving us the victory," giving God over and above what He asks will be no problem!

We have all been in a battle. At some point, you will engage in war before you leave this earth. For some, the battle has been a child on drugs; a child who struggled academically; or a child who was tempted to join a gang, and then challenged with how to break free of that life. For others, the struggle was rooted in a marriage in jeopardy because of immaturity, infidelity, financial frustration or the inability to communicate. For some, the war is waged in the workplace. Many people have jobs they almost lost, because of company downsizing, co-workers' undermining efforts, controlling bosses, or their own incompetence. Others wrestle with bad or failing health. There's either not enough money to see a doctor, or not enough money to purchase medicine. Perhaps the doctor does not know how to handle a sickness. Maybe the medicine is not working.

For those of us to whom God has given grace to get through troublesome times and come out a VICTOR and not a VICTIM, there should be a sense of indebtedness. How do we express our thanks? This is the question that Abraham – and we – must answer.

Verse 16. And he brought back all the goods, and also brought again his brother Lot, and his goods, and the women also, and the people.

The war is over and we clearly see that Abraham and his 318 men have been successful. The text says, *And he brought back all the goods,* which means they left or lost nothing. Lot, who has been soundly defeated by the enemy, lost everything in battle. Yet, Abraham and his men reclaimed everything that the enemy had taken from Lot and his neighbors. Not one of Abraham's relatives (his nephew Lot, Lot's wife, and Lot's daughters or Lot's servants) was lost in battle. As a matter of fact, Abraham took the enemy's stuff! Furthermore, though Lot's neighbors were not necessarily a blessing to him, he ended up being a blessing to them. When Abraham came to the rescue, Lot's neighbors were saved as well.

Verse 17. And the king of Sodom went out to meet him after his return from the slaughter of Chedorlaomer, and of the kings that were with him, at the valley of Shaveh, which is the king's dale.

As is often the case with us, the first thing Abraham meets after his victory is Satan in disguise. This time the enemy is in the form of the king of Sodom. We must watch for the spirit of the enemy when God has granted us victory, because the enemy's goal is to distract us from giving God the fullest glory. The king of Sodom meets Abraham in the low place, which is where the enemy also meets us. In this text, the place is called the king's dale, or the king's valley. It is at the low place of the valley, where pride sometimes resides, over-ambition rules, or greed gets the best of us. Our enemy meets us there in an effort to distract us from offering the right response to God, after such a glorious victory.

Verse 18. And Melchizedek king of Salem brought forth bread and wine: and he was the priest of the most high God.

Though the king of Sodom represents the spirit of the enemy, who shows up after each victory, we see the representation of what is right also appearing on the scene. In this text, God can be seen through the kingly priest Melchizedek. We must remember that the spirit of righteousness and the spirit of wickedness always show up after each of our victories. Just like Abraham, we must decide which one we will honor. If we choose to honor the spirit of righteousness, we also will see that what he brings with him – bread and wine – will nourish and replenish us. God always comes to give us more than He will get from us. The enemy comes with a beguiling promise of gifts, when it is his true goal to take much more than he could ever give.

Verse 19. And he blessed him, and said, Blessed be Abram of the most high God, possessor of heaven and earth.

The Spirit of God reveals to us the favor that rests upon our lives. The Spirit even brings overflowing joy, as He reveals God's awareness and commitment toward us. It is a blessing to know that the Possessor, Creator and Sustainer of heaven and earth has us on

His mind. He is looking over us, and He has great plans for us! What a wonderful revelation that only the Spirit of the Father could give to Melchizedek, who then passes it on to Abraham and to us. The revelation comes at the most opportune time – just after a fight! We are successful in our struggles because God went in with us. He is the One who brought us out with the victory. No credit belongs to us. The person is blessed that knows God and that it is God, who grants victory!

Verse 20. And blessed be the most high God, which hath delivered thine enemies into thy hand. And he gave him tithes of all.

In the previous verse, Abraham, or Abram as he is called at this time, is reminded that he is blessed. However, in this verse, Abraham is reminded that God is to be blessed, praised and glorified for the victory that he has given into our hands.

... which hath delivered thine enemies into thy hand ...

Notice whose hands our enemies are in before they are shrunken to fit into our hands – HIS hands! God handles them and when He has dealt with our enemies so they will not overwhelm us, He delivers them into our hands. If our enemies reached us first, they would be too big! God meets them head-on. When He has body-slammed our enemies to the canvas, where they can no longer hurt us, God tags our hands and allows us to share His victory. When Abram hears this from the priest, he has to do something to show God his gratitude!

... And he gave him tithes of all.

Please notice that the priest never passed the plate. Abraham just knew that giving was the right thing, the reasonable thing, the responsible thing and the righteous thing to do in response to the overcoming and victorious power of God. Abraham knows it is El Elyon (the Most High God), who supplies His people with strategy, strength and success over the enemy's tactics to derail our destiny. Without hesitancy, Abraham pays tithes of ALL!

It is so sad that even today the people of God are trying to figure out if we tithe on the gross or the net. Will El Elyon, the Most High God, understand if we subtract our payments to the United Way or the Cancer Society from the tithe? Will He understand, if we choose to pay for overpriced houses we bought, cable with hundreds of channels, cellular phones with run-over minutes and two cars for one driver? The priest meets Abram as he is returning from victory. There is no church building, no deacons, and no trustees, yet he pays the tithes of ALL! When giving God what is His becomes most important, we will be like Abram and pay our tithes even if we work on Sunday, before we go out of town, before we leave for vacation; in essence, regardless of what comes our way.

Verse 21. And the king of Sodom said unto Abram, give me the persons, and take the goods to thyself.

Be careful of the spirit of the enemy that entices and urges you to always look out for yourself. It is God's job to look out for His children. It is our job as the children of God to look for ways that please the Father. The king of Sodom tells Abram to take the goods for himself and let him have back the citizens and the soldiers of Sodom. If Abram kept goods, the king of Sodom is right – it would be TAKE THE GOODS TO THYSELF! We must remember that some things are not ours to take, and to keep them without permission is thievery!

Verse 22. And Abram said to the king of Sodom, I have lift up mine hand unto the Lord, the most high God, the possessor of heaven and earth.

Abram has made a commitment to God. He made the commitment before going into battle, therefore, he knows coming out of the battle what belongs to him. We must spend more time with the Most High God, so we will know what God wants us to have. Oftentimes, we are not successful in our personal battles, because we do not know what to keep from the spoils. It would be much more injurious to look as if we have won the war and end up defeated, because we were overtaken by the demons of pride, greed and selfishness. What promise did you make to God regarding that job? What did you promise to get that promotion or pay off that bill? We must learn to live up to the promises we made after we have gotten the victory. It is easy to make a promise in the heat of battle. The real struggle lies within ourselves after we have come out of the war.

Verse 23. That I will not take from a thread even to a shoe-latchet, and that I will not take any thing that is thine, lest thou shouldest say, I have made Abram rich.

Abram's promise to God is that he will not accept anything from the wicked hands of the king of Sodom. We must never be in such a rush to obtain things that we are indifferent about where we get them or what it will cost us to acquire them. Wisdom says wait until the Lord wants to bless us. Many foreclosures, repossessions, closed accounts and low credit scores happen, because people do not have the heart of Abram – the heart to wait for what God has. Just because you have the job and the income, does not mean it is your season to have some things. Just because you have the credit, does not mean it is your season to buy some things. After emerging from a major struggle, we often want to get something for it, but God is intending that we get something out of it – in His timing!

Abram wants nothing from the king of Sodom, not even a piece of thread or the lace of a shoe! Now, this brother wants *nothing* from a relationship with Sodom! Abram knows taking that from Sodom will cost him later, and normally that cost is greater than the value of what is taken. Abram knows he will be rich. That is a settled issue in his heart. Also, Abram knows his wealth will come through God. God wants to bring His people to a wealthy place, so He can establish His covenant with us. It has to be God's way. We must give up on the wicked get-rich-quick schemes and satanic strategies that drive us to "get it at any cost." The greatest riches are the riches that come from a right relationship with God: peace, joy, faith, love, righteousness, being forgiven, power and fellowship.

Every promise that God made to Abraham, He also makes to us as the seed of Abraham. It is only when we live by faith and trust the faithfulness of God that we will see those promises coming to pass much sooner in our lives. We must appreciate Abram for not trying to advance through wicked gains. We must follow his example of being willing to turn down any ill-gotten opportunity to come closer to the wealth that the Father had promised him. Abram's actions illustrate that he trusts God. What do our actions say?

LESSON 19

THE DANGER OF BEING DISHONEST ABOUT DONATIONS!
Acts 4:37 and 5:1-7

This lesson takes a look at giving in the early church, whose members lived at a time when the saints were persecuted for their newfound faith in Christ Jesus. In a tangible expression of their love for Christ and the community of faith, many early believers sold their property and possessions and gave what they had to apostles assigned to meet the needs of others. It was not a requirement to sell one's property and donate the proceeds, but many willingly shared all they had with other saints.

So often, we find ourselves tempted to give more in appearances, than we do in reality. Giving might clearly be the right thing to do, but many would prefer to hold onto what they have and present themselves as gracious givers. The couple in this study found themselves in trouble, because they were not honest about their giving.

Verse 37. Having land, sold it, and brought the money, and laid it at the apostles' feet.

Barnabas was not compelled, forced or coerced to sell his property and lay it at the apostles' feet. The Holy Spirit led him and many others to give in this manner. There are times that the Holy Spirit moves upon us to be benevolent, and we must know when it is God, who is prompting us to give and not a desire to impress others or fit in. This lesson is not about the paying of tithes and giving of offerings, but rather being led of the Holy Spirit to give a sacrificial seed that is beyond the norm. Notice that Barnabas was not the first one to be led to sell land and houses and bring the money from the sale to the apostles (Acts 4:32-35). The purpose of the saints' sacrifice was so the apostles would have more than enough to take care of the needs of every individual in the household of faith.

Verse 1. But a certain man named Ananias, with Sapphira his wife, sold a possession.

Just as it is in the church today, there are people who seek some of the spotlight that seemingly comes with being a major player, but do not want to pay the full price of what it costs to do ministry. Ananias and Sapphira sell some of their land just as other saints did, but they are not quite committed to giving all that they receive from the sale of the land. There is a danger in wanting to do what everybody else does, or wanting to be perceived as doing what everyone else is doing. We applaud these individuals for being in church. We applaud them for their awareness and outward support of the church's vision. On the surface, Ananias and Sapphira appear to be a normal couple, who are connected with the church and the vision of the house.

Verse 2. And kept back part of the price, his wife also being privy to it, and brought a certain part, and laid it at the apostles' feet.

In the text, we must not fail to point out that there was nothing wrong with Ananais and Sapphira not giving all from the sale of their land. That was not the problem or the sin. Please note that their trouble started, when they decided to lie to the Lord and pretend they were bringing their all. In fact, they were bringing only a part. This couple would have avoided trouble, if they had simply been honest and said, "Our faith is not ready to give it all" or "Our bills are too big to give it all, but we sold some land and we want to give a portion of it for ministry."

And kept back part of the price ...

The Word does not tell us why Ananias and Sapphira withheld part of the money, and it really does not matter. What matters is they were dishonest about the money. Being dishonest with God about our blessings conveys to Him that we cannot be trusted. No one should ever lie to the Lord, when it comes to what each of us has, because He already knows. He gave the blessings to us! This couple wants to look as charitable as everyone else. Ananias and Sapphira wanted the applause and praise that everyone else received, when they publicly and graciously gave.

In modern-day terms, what Ananias and Sapphira did is no different from what we do when we write a bad check to the church, and then refuse to pay the charge to set things right. As a matter of fact, writing bad checks to the church and to others is worse! Not only are we not paying the Lord or another individual, but we also are costing the house of the Lord or that individual money. Imagine this couple in a worship service, all the while pretending to have made such a great sacrifice in support of the church and the Kingdom.

... his wife also being privy to it and brought a certain part ...

Ananias' wife had full knowledge of the dishonest practice of her husband. Moreover, she agreed with it. The deception may have been Ananias' idea, but together they will suffer the consequences of such a wicked scheme. Let's look at another deceptive practice, similar to the one committed by Ananias and Sapphira. When a request is made for a particular offering – say, $100 – it is unquestionably dishonest for anyone to respond with $5 balled up in his or her hand or in an envelope, and pretend in front of God and man to have given the desired amount.

Verse 3. But Peter said, Ananias, why hath Satan filled thine heart to lie to the Holy Ghost, and to keep back part of the price of the land.

Ananias and Sapphira are like so many of us. They thought they were tricking others, when in truth they were toying with the Holy Spirit. Each of us needs a Simon Peter in our lives to make sure we are honest with ourselves and with God. We cannot treat God the same way we treat Uncle Sam. So often, we try to give Uncle Sam, as little as possible, with the pretense that we are giving all that should be given. We can get in trouble with Uncle Sam – and with God – if we are caught! Satan was behind this couple's attempt to deceive the apostles and God's people. Satan never wants us to give God what He desires and deserves. There has to be a stronger conviction in our spirits, and an ability to discern, when the enemy is trying to lead us astray. Satan persuaded them to give a portion, while feigning to give their all. The manner in which they gave resulted in trouble, and their giving was not even required! If Ananias and Sapphira paid a woeful price for deceptive giving in an offering that wasn't required, what happens to those whose hearts are not right toward offerings that are required?

Verse 4. Whiles it remained, was it not thine own? And if it was sold, was it not in thine own power? Why hast thou conceived this thing in thine heart? Thou hast not lied unto men, but unto God.

The property belonged to Ananias and Sapphira, and the money obtained from its sale was theirs, too. It seems God was not asking or requiring that they give it. They gave, because they wanted to appear as though they were cheerful givers, especially with other saints around them giving so generously. It would have been better for Ananias and Sapphira to appear stingy than to have been dishonest about what they were giving. Peter's point is that no one made them give. If they did not want to give, they should have withheld the money and not given under false pretenses.

In another deceptive practice, people often "tithe" on the salary of one person in the household, while pretending to give 10 percent of the two salaries actually in the household. If a genuine tithe is not being given, don't check the box on the envelope, and don't confess to be tithers, when that isn't the truth.

... Why hast thou conceived this thing in thine heart?

There are some practices that we can stop by putting a stop to them in our hearts. Some issues must be handled in the heart, because they are matters of the heart. As previously mentioned, sometimes couples are tempted to be dishonest and tithe on one job in the household, rather than the two they are blessed to have. That is not true tithing and we must admit that. It is better to offer something to God and not call it a tithe than to incur His wrath for robbing and lying. Ananias and Sapphira did not get in trouble for robbery. They invited trouble for lying about their giving. God honors a contrite heart and He would rather we tell the truth and admit we are not tithing than pretend to tithe; knowing God's due is going to the cable company, the car note or the children's summer trip.

... thou hast not lied unto men, but unto God.

It is not outside of the realm of possibility that Ananias and Sapphira never thought they were doing anything more than fooling the apostles and the saints. They probably thought as some do today: It's no big deal to lie about giving! They probably missed, just as we do, the spiritual implications and consequences of their actions. They were not deceiving men, because the money did not belong to anyone else. At the moment, Ananias and Sapphira proclaimed they were selling the land to give the proceeds to the Lord; the money was set apart unto the Lord. Perhaps, God moved someone to buy the land, which never would have done so. Because that person wanted to follow the example of the other saints, the Lord allowed the land to be sold. Perhaps, God impressed upon someone to buy the land at a higher price, because he or she desired to present it unto the Lord. We never know what God is doing behind the scenes to bring about our success and provide us with seed to sow. Therefore, we cannot play with the offering that we have purposed to give unto the Lord.

Verse 5. And Ananias hearing these words fell down, and gave up the ghost: and great fear came on all them that heard these things.

What a tragic price for pretending to give unto the Lord. Like Ananias, many of us would have fallen down dead long ago had God tended to our lies about giving to the Kingdom. We cannot say what God is going to do in the future, but we do know that when we know better, we should do better. Do not play with money that you have purposed unto God. Many of us have made promises to God and to others about what we would do when we "get back on our feet." When that day came, many of us did not honor the commitment. Ananias fell down and died, because of his deception. Maybe God isn't striking down individuals for lying, but consider the reason why everything some people touch falls down and dies; income, credit scores, careers, dreams, goals, hopes – the list goes on. We cannot definitively say what consequences God has in store for those, who are pretending, when it comes to giving. We should be careful, because consequences are certain.

... and great fear came on all them that heard these things.

Just in case God is about to make an example out of those who pretend in their giving, do not lie about giving in this season. Everyone in the fellowship became afraid and realized it is not wise to play with God when it comes to giving.

Verse 6. And the young men arose, wound him up, and carried him out, and buried him.

Ananias died at that moment and was buried immediately. What an awful way to die – lying to the Lord! The text paints the picture that he would still have been alive and working in the church, if he had just been honest about his giving. The sad truth is he didn't have to give a thing. Ananias did not die, because he did not give. He died, because he lied about how much he gave, and God judged him on the spot. If your congregation is not tithing, go ahead and admit it. Then, with God's grace, do something about it! In the book of Malachi, we hear God talking about cursing a people who rob him. Yet, in this passage in Acts, we see God killing a couple who lie about giving. We should not want either consequence to happen to us, so don't mess with the Master's money!

Verse 7. And it was about the space of three hours after, when his wife, not knowing what was done, came in.

Ananias' wife returns without knowing what has transpired, and it's a sad commentary that she upholds the same lie. Sapphira could have saved her own life had she just told the truth. Verse 8 says that when questioned by Peter, she offers the same lie her husband told. Sapphira dies the same day and is buried next to her husband, because she would not break the bond of deception about their donation to the Lord! Let's make a pledge to never toy with the Lord's money or take part in any deception hatched, by those who dare to not take giving seriously.

LESSON 20

THE DANGERS AND THE RISKS OF BEING RICH!
1 Timothy 6:6-10 (The Amplified Version)

This lesson deals with the importance of having the right perspective and the right attitude about money. When dealing with people's affections, especially the affections of those who are immature, it is essential to emphasize why we should be careful of what we are exposed to, and why we should not become overly attached to the wrong people, the wrong places and the wrong things. In our childish or immature state, the easiest things and people to get attached to are things that are not best for us and people who were never meant to have a permanent place in our lives.

For example, some single parents are taught — while others learn the hard way — not to be hasty in bringing a person they have just begun dating around their children. If a single parent fails to exercise this precaution, children could become attached to a person, who might not be a part of their lives in the long term. Many children have been left hurting, longing for a relationship that was never meant to be.

We also can see how easily the young at heart become attached to friends, and not as much to family, especially in the teenage years. For the most part, teenagers, in their immaturity, only want to talk on the phone and text their peers, and rarely have time for their parents. At this young age, their affections have not been shaped fully by reason and wisdom. Therefore, mature individuals in their lives have the great responsibility of helping them become focused on family, the future, education and their need for faith in God.

In this lesson, the mature apostle helps immature believers to understand money's proper function, and that saints must be careful to not fall in love with money, material things and the acquisition of wealth. The mature apostle charges and challenges us to check our affections about money. Through the power of the Holy Spirit, the Apostle Paul admonishes us to never fall in love with money. As Christians living in the world today, we know we need money, we use money and we spend money – but we don't love money! As Christians, we love God, we love people and we love ourselves.

Verse 5. And protracted wrangling and wearing discussion and perpetual friction among men who are corrupted in mind and bereft of truth, who imagine that godliness or righteousness is a source of profit [moneymaking business, a means of livelihood]. From such withdraw.

This verse calls to mind the back-and-forth motion that causes something to wear thin. Consider how continuous walking on a tract of carpet can wear it thin, or how the continued bending of the knee would wear out the knee area on a pair of jeans. This is what happens when people go back and forward with the notion that "If it's not gain, then it cannot be God." Not every career will net great wealth, and going back and forward about what we could be doing based on the money that we could potentially make is not wisdom, nor is it the will of God.

Some people believe wealth – the size of the house one lives in or the steep price one is able to pay for things – is the only sign that a person is "right with God." The lofty price one is able to pay for things is in no way an indication of the purity of a person. Never allow anyone to lure you into a profession based solely on salary. That job must first pass the litmus test: Is it in line with the purpose and the plan of God for your life? Answer that question, and then you can deal with the issue of pay. Some people only deal with the payment aspect and neglect the importance of purpose and God's divine plan. Yet, our reason for existing is that God has a divine assignment for us! Some people's sole reason for hanging around God is to see what they can get out of Him. No one should ever be in a relationship simply for what he or she can get out of it! We must stop the back-and-forth warring that goes on in our minds as to why we are in church. Saints, we must settle in our souls and spirits that we are in church, because we love the Lord and not because we love what we can get out of God.

... From such withdraw.

The Word says to "leave alone" people whose only concern is money, and people who would rather have money than a relationship with the Master. They should not have to walk away from us, but we should distance ourselves from them. People, who try to help us feel good about being unfaithful to God with our money, are not the best people to be around, especially when they possess the ability to influence our thinking. People, who believe that making a dollar is much more important than being a disciple, and moreover, have no problem expressing that idiotic ideology on a frequent basis, truly have the capability to wear out our convictions. We need to step away from those people and that type of thinking.

Verse 6. [And it is, indeed, a source of immense profit, for] godliness accompanied with contentment (that commitment which is a sense of inward sufficiency) is great and abundant gain.

The real gain in life is a right relationship with God. If we as Christians do not receive anything other than the right to be called His children, we should praise Him eternally because that distinction is a privilege. The Christian does not rise early on Sunday to worship, because of what he or she has that can be spent in the mall or at the movies. We gather in His name to give Him a greater glory, a collective and sweeping glory for giving us such a redemptive story. It is not about what we wear or where we work. Our praise is rooted in the knowledge that He is working on us and has committed to completing the work He has begun in us, before we leave the earth. Please remember, no one wants to be in a relationship with someone who only seeks to receive – not even God. People, as well as God, want us to be in a relationship with them because we love them. The things we receive from them are just perks that come from the pleasure of loving them. We cannot love God and be in a relationship with Him and not benefit from that relationship. Even if we do not get all the things that we want out of this life, there are no regrets for walking with God.

... Godliness accompanied with contentment (that commitment which is a sense of inward sufficiency) is great and abundant gain.

As quietly as it is kept, material things never fully and consistently satisfy. No matter what things we have, sooner or later, we want something new or some modification to the old to make it like new again. There is something special about saints, who have a level of contentment in their relationship with God, and are not trying to find satisfaction in the things God gives or things that can be bought or sold. A relationship with God produces the peace that comes from being able to pray and know the Father hears us; the inward joy of knowing that we, His children, are forgiven. Therefore, we can freely forgive; and the rest that comes from the reassurance of His Spirit residing in us. A relationship with God ignites the power He has deposited within us to complete every task and overcome any attack of the enemy. Communion with Him also stirs up the faith He has given us to believe that all things are possible. These blessings are worth more than any amount of money. The treasures God gives are not sold at the mall or the flea market. Wal-Mart and Kmart will never have them on the shelves. These gifts are priceless and they automatically come with a relationship with the Lord! Now that's great gain! Our problem is we don't know what we have. These great gifts will never need to be traded in, repainted, repaired, upgraded or thrown out. El Shaddai – God Almighty, the All-Sufficient God, the God who gives good gifts, the Pourer out of gifts – gives them freely! Real contentment comes, when we are happy just having Him. He wills to give us gifts, because we belong to Him!

Verse 7. For we brought nothing into this world, and obviously we cannot take anything out of the world.

No matter what we accumulate on this earth, we will not be able to take one item when we depart. We entered the earth devoid of possessions. Not one person entered the world with HDTV, cable, cars, cash or clothes. The Apostle Paul and Job are correct – we came from our mothers' wombs naked and we are going to return to the unknown world naked. While we can take no earthly possessions with us, we will be able to take spiritual blessings, such as our right relationship with God, our spiritual inheritance with Christ, the love that we have received from the Father, as well as, the works we did for God.

The unfortunate fact is that the blessings we will take into eternity, most people do not have. We will leave behind what most people spend their lives trying to get. If earthly things were that important to our existence, God would have given them to us before we got here. Newborns would arrive with rims for the car, gold grills in their mouths, a cell phone for texting and designer outfits in tow. None of those things have eternal value. The only possession we leave the womb with is divine purpose and destiny! Take notice of what the Lord allows us to come into the world with, and what He allows us to leave with. That alone ought to indicate what the priority should be for people who want to please Him.

Verse 8. But if we have food and clothing, with these we shall be content (satisfied).

If we are looking for things to satisfy us, we are going to be disappointed. Things were never intended to satisfy, but rather pacify and add a little flavor to life. Do not expect things to do what only a right relationship with God can do. Oftentimes, we rob God to buy food for the month, when we cannot be sure that we will live throughout the month. Then, there are times we have more than enough to enjoy the day. Yet, we worry about what we don't have for tomorrow. This text lets us know that God has provided all the basics we need to make it through today, enjoy today and be blessed today. Therefore, we should learn to be satisfied and no longer complain. The truth is we already have more than what we can use.

Verse 9. But those who crave to be rich fall into temptation and a snare and into many foolish (useless, godless) and hurtful desires that plunge men into ruin and destruction and miserable perishing.

We must be careful what we pray for and crave. It should be our desire to be right with God rather than to be rich.

LESSON 21

DON'T LET MONEY BECOME YOUR MASTER!
Matthew 6:19-24

This lesson deals with the teachings of Jesus on the issues of money, money management and investment. Many wish they knew the mind of God, as it pertains to how we should pursue wealth and how to handle money in such a way that pleases Him. Money is a powerful medium of exchange. Though money is the most prevalent method of purchasing goods and services, it can become the master of many, if it is not submitted to Christ, the Master.

Verse 19. Lay not up for yourselves treasures upon the earth, where moth and rust doth corrupt, and where thieves break through and steal.

In the day in which Jesus was speaking, many of the houses people lived in were made of clay, dried hard by the sun. The people of the day fully understood how unsafe their investments were because, generally, there were three enemies to their treasures: moths, rust and thieves.

Moths were tiny insects that could eat through and destroy clothing and other materials. Moths represent the small things in life that can eat away at our investments and treasures. Moths are the small things in life that go undetected, and by the time they are noticed, treasure is taken, eaten or destroyed. The second enemy to investments mentioned in the text is rust. Rust represents the corroding process in nature and life that, with great assistance from time, destroys one's investments. Rust represents anything that eats away at or consumes one's property. The third enemy Jesus mentions is thieves. These are individuals, who want what another person has, but do not want to pay the price the other person paid to acquire it. Thieves were known to dig through the clay walls of homes, in order to steal people's possessions.

These three foes of our treasures can leave us with nothing, if we are not careful, and even caution does not guarantee that our treasures will not be taken away.

Lay not up for yourselves treasures upon the earth ...

Please do not read this verse and conclude Jesus was against investments, financial achievement, or owning property and possessions. Christ's intent was to make sure earthly investments are not our principal and only investments. Christ does not want us to make treasures on the earth our best and only investment, because He knows there are forces working all the time to take treasures and investments away from us. He also knows that even if the forces trying to rob us of our treasures do not succeed the possibility remains that we could die and leave those treasures behind.

During the time of the New Testament, treasures often consisted of clothes, changes of raiment, gold, silver, land, houses and other goods that made life comfortable. Jesus is not discouraging believers – past and present – from having investments or treasures. His intent is to let the children of God know there is a safer investment that will not to be stolen, nor destroyed by moths or rust.

Verse 20. But lay up for yourselves treasures in heaven, where neither moth nor rust doth corrupt, and where thieves do not break through nor steal.

Christ offers a place to store treasure that is, as the hymn says, safe and secure from all alarm. No matter how safe we think our earthly investments are there is always news that warns of scam artists, investment fraud, plummeting stock markets, thieving corporate leaders, inflation, tax increases, rate hikes and rising gas prices. These and other troubling scenarios remind us that what money we would have saved we often cannot, because there is always a reason to go into our pockets and take out some of our treasure. According to Christ, our treasure is safe in heaven, because in that place, nothing will eat away at our investment. Nothing will corrode our treasure over time. No thieves will break in and steal what we have worked so hard to save.

All that we do with a pure heart to advance the kingdom of God, exalt the Savior and build up the body of believers is an investment in the kingdom. Walking by faith; the worship we render; the praise we offer; the tithe we sow; the offerings we give; the love we share; the kindness we extend; the testimony we tell; the prayers we offer; and the ministry we build – these are all a part of the treasure that we are storing up in heaven. We should never become so discouraged that we stop doing the very things that cannot be taken from us when we arrive in glory to be with our God. The total treasure we have invested, with God-sized interest, will be given to those of us who have laid up treasure in heaven.

Verse 21. For where your treasure is, there will your heart be also.

If you want to know where a person's heart is, the Word of God says to follow that person's treasure. Our Father in heaven follows where we put our money, and that is why we cannot "fool" God into thinking the kingdom and the church are what is most important to us. I remember a Fruit Loops cereal commercial from my youth. The Fruit Loops mascot, Toucan Sam, would say, "Just follow your nose!" A lot of saints talk about how much they love the Lord, but their treasure does not match their testimony. The church would close down, while some people's boyfriends or girlfriends (who they just met five months ago) would be sharp as a tack, if it were left up to many in the church! Testimony can be a faulty indicator of where a person's treasure lies. Therefore, God says we must search the heart. If you desire a greater heart for God and the church, begin to give God more by increasing your giving to the church.

What's more, if we as believers want to change our hearts' attachment, we must change where we are spending or sowing our money. The heart does not follow the prayer, nor does it follow talk. The heart always follows the treasure. Some people will never love the Lord the way they should, because they will never love giving to the Lord the way they should. We gripe about giving to the Lord. Yet, we call our friends excited to tell them about something we bought that was *only* X amount of dollars. We never hear people say that they were asked for *only* $1,000, as a seed offering. We will chat about the car we purchased for just $5,000, or the whole outfit that we paid only $600 for – including the shoes! We have the nerve to ask, "Can you believe that's all I paid for that?"

Our hearts are too far from God, and that is the reason our treasures are too far from God. It is only when we place our interest, our attachment, our treasure in God that we will see our hearts move closer to the Creator. Many saints give money excitedly everywhere, but in the House of the Lord. Isn't it amazing how many saints can go to the fair or the mall and have no problem opening their pockets or purses, but the same individuals go to church and act as if they're in the midst of a robbery or hold-up, hiding away money, as though someone was trying to take it. We have no problem "super-sizing" our orders at the drive-through window, but we get to church and want to "kid's meal" the kingdom! Remember, giving is a HEART thing, not a HARD thing. Giving only becomes a hard thing, when the heart does not react with gratefulness, as we reflect on how good God has been to each of us. We should want our hearts to be in the right place. The only way to move our hearts into the right place is for our treasures to be in the right place.

Verse 22. The light of the body is the eye: if therefore thine eye be single, thy whole body shall be full of light.

When the eye is focused, the whole body becomes steady. A person being taught to walk on a log in a moving stream is told to focus on one steady object, such as the other side of the stream. A good instructor advises a student not look down at the rushing water, which can affect equilibrium. Through this verse, Jesus is telling us to stay focused on the rewards in heaven, so we don't become unbalanced by the cares of the world. When a person cannot look at a single object and stay focused on that object, the journey is sure to be tough. Many saints who are frustrated in life are usually discouraged, because they are focusing on things that are not stable or steady. On this side, possessions come and go, and negative factors are always at work to take them away. Nothing and no one can rob us of the treasures we have in Christ Jesus. The journey is so much easier, when the eye of faith is fixed on things that are eternal. When we see through eyes of desire and flesh, the enemy can distract us and, sometimes, overwhelm us.

Verse 23. But if thine eye be evil, thy whole body shall be full of darkness. If therefore the light that is in thee be darkness, how great is that darkness!

I'm sure that people, who deal with diseases of the eyes, will better appreciate this verse. Many saints know the value of having healthy eyes, but do not fully understand the eyes' importance, until their eyes are under attack. Life is dark when light and sight are gone. The enemy wants to blind us, obscuring our healthy view of how to handle treasure the Lord's way. When the mind or the principles of the soul are darkened by the pursuit of wealth, an individual cannot always see that not all wealth, and ways of getting wealth, is good for the child of God. As a matter of fact, some wealth and some pursuits of wealth can cost more than the individual would ever want to pay. Wealth gained dishonestly, immorally, mean spiritedly, destructively, or violently normally does not last. No matter how long ill-gotten wealth lasts, it does not bring the joy of wealth that comes from right living, or the wealth that God graciously gives. An over attachment to the idea or desire to have wealth is a dark view that comes from the enemy, whose goal is to destroy our souls. God has more than we will ever need, but He always wants us to attain it the right way – His way!

Verse 24. No man can serve two masters: for either he will hate the one, and love the other, or else he will hold to the one, and despise the other. Ye cannot serve God and mammon.

A right attitude about wealth is very important to the spiritual life of every believer. We can serve only one master. Both God and money desire to be master of every individual. Many saints already have become slaves to needs, slaves to wants and slaves to desires. Money drives our need to work, but work was intended to be a pipeline through which saints could obtain seeds to sow into the kingdom. Today, because many have not learned to bring money under the subjection and authority of Christ, money manipulates and destroys believers. Money has become our master, if we will do anything to get it. We live in a culture in which people will sell anything to anyone at anytime, if it means a dollar can be made. The Ojai's recorded a song in the late '70s titled *For the Love of Money*. Though it is not a Christian song, its message is still true today. People will do anything for the love of money.

Looking again at the text, mammon is a name given to an idol worshipped as the god of riches, wealth and prosperity. We cannot submit to the true and living God and at the same time submit to the idol god of wealth. When we submit our wealth and our wealth-generating opportunities to the Lord, we learn how to master our money. This is possible only when we've allowed Christ to master us. When we do not submit our money to Christ's rule, our money begins to rule us! This principle has been eternally declared by our Christ, who is Master. When money is master of a life, money does not just rule. It dominates and dictates, until it ultimately destroys.

... for either he will hate the one and love the other, or else he will hold to the one and despise the other...

Our affections will not allow us to be loyal to both God and mammon. We must pick one to rule our lives. This is a choice we must make – not just a chance we can take. To not make a choice is to allow mammon, money, wealth and prosperity to rule, which will result in disaster. Trying to love the two is not easy. As a matter of fact, Christ says loving the two is impossible to do! Make the choice and don't take the chance of settling the issue down the road. Use money, but let the Lord lead!

LESSON 22

DON'T MAKE TOO MUCH OUT OF MAKING ENDS MEET!
Matthew 6:25-32

As we continue in a study of Matthew chapter 6, we will see that anxiety arises when we try to make ends meet in our own power, rather than leaning on the Lord to supply all of our needs. Just about every adult we know has been in a tight spot, and many of us have been there more than once. Though things do not always work out when we want them to – or the way we want them to – through divine intervention, the Lord always makes a way.

Verse 25. Therefore I say unto you, Take no thought for your life, what ye shall eat, or what ye shall drink; nor yet for your body, what ye shall put on. Is not the life more than meat, and the body than raiment?

The things that are of greatest importance to most people are the very things Jesus instructs us not to concern ourselves with. In essence, Jesus tells us not to let the necessity of food, drink, clothing and shelter bring us to an emotional state of anxiety or perpetual uneasiness. For many, these issues are the main topic of discussion. They consume the lives of many of God's children. According to Jesus, food, drink and clothing are not the main concerns of mature children of God. Do not let these necessities trip you up and keep you from focusing on the more important issues in life. If the enemy blinds us to the real issues by keeping our attention on temporary things, we will miss the real questions, and therefore, never ascertain the most important answers in this life.

... Is not the life more than meat, and the body than raiment?

Jesus says there is more to life than the stuff we can get from a store. This may sound strange because, for the most part, acquiring things is what we think makes life worth living. Though this absolutely is not a lesson about being content with having no material possessions, remember, Jesus never owned an earthly house, never owned a boat, a wagon or a mule, and He never had a retirement account. Jesus was fine with that, because He put His life in the Father's hands and trusted Him to provide all that He would need in His earthly life and in the world to come. Many people will never see the faithfulness of the Father, because their attention is focused on how they are going to make it in their own strength.

Verse 26. Behold the fowls of the air: for they sow not, neither do they reap, nor gather into barns; yet your heavenly Father feuded them. Are you not much better than they?

Jesus tells us the source of the birds' provisions – our Father! The birds have to depend totally upon the providence of God to take care of them and supply all of their needs. The word "behold" means to look, and Jesus is saying to us, "Look at the birds!" The next time you are afraid and filled with anxiety about how you're going to make it, hold your head out the window and look up at the birds. Birds have no union membership or union cards and yet, they sing! Birds have no barns in which to store goods and yet, they sing! Birds have no ulcers and no health coverage plan and yet, they sing! It indeed appears that the Lord is taking care of them.

Many of us are sick, because we don't have health insurance in the event that we get sick! In an ideal world, everyone would have a medical insurance plan. As that is not the case, we have to develop healthier lifestyles and partner with God, trusting Him to be our healer.

... Are you not much better than they?

Jesus says that on God's chain of priority, we – His human creation – are more important than the birds. If the Father shows an unwavering commitment to something of lesser importance, it is clear that His commitment to people must be out of this world! A part of our problem is we do not know how important we are to the Father. Many are not sure that they can be counted among His children. No intelligent parent would feed the pet and starve the children. We are much more important than the birds to the Father.

Verse 27. Which of you by taking thought can add one cubit unto his stature?

Anxiety and worry will not lengthen a person's height nor lengthen a person's life. Worrying also will not help resolve anything. We put too much thought, time and attention into material possessions. Sometimes, worry is the result of trying to live beyond your means. Don't buy more house than you are willing to work and pay for. Don't rent more apartment than you can realistically afford. People like to acquire things that are above their means. Then, after finding themselves in a mess, they worry and blame God for the ensuing problems.

An elderly gentleman once told me that he and his wife lived on his salary and banked her salary. He said that he and his wife did not want to buy more house than they could afford on his salary, just in case she fell ill and could not work. The children of God would avoid a lot of anxiety by not spending to the max in light of their respective salaries. If you are single, try living on three paychecks a month instead of four. That may mean sharing an apartment and splitting the bills (not shacking up!), until you can do better by yourself. A married couple should either discipline themselves to live off of one person's salary or learn to live on only three weeks of both salaries. Couples should then, take the fourth week of both of their salaries and invest that money. For individuals or couples who are financially beyond that point, set a goal to begin working toward. For many, this might mean no new financial commitments, until spending is brought under control. Through this method, one can begin investing for the future without major frustrations. Worrying will not get the bills paid and worrying will not free up your finances!

Verse 28. And why take ye thought of raiment? Consider the lilies of the field, how they grow; they toil not, neither do they spin.

As He continues His message on the providence of the Father, Jesus turns our attention toward the lilies of the field. The lilies are not at the top of God's creation. Still, they get the attention they need from Him to survive and to thrive. Jesus, in essence, is saying to us, "Look! You are the crown of the Father's creation, and yet, you are filled with anxiety about what you have to wear!" Clothing is a necessity, but we have turned the issue of clothing into a need to distinguish our identity. We *must* have something that says we are different. There are certain outfits we do not want anybody else to have, and as a matter of fact, we'd rather not see anyone with the same colors on! When we run into that type of thinking, we are moving in the direction of anxiety. We are more concerned about the shoes we wear and making sure no one else has those shoes, than we are about whether our feet are on the path to purpose and headed in the direction of destiny.

The beauty of the lily is that it looks to the Lord to clothe it. It knows the color the Lord selects will look amazing, even if another lily is adorned the same way. Simply put, we are perplexed, overly consumed and stressed about the wrong things. When our attention is placed on the right issues of life, stress begins to fade away.

There is a greater issue than clothing for the body: Is the Lord clothing us in His righteousness? We look better no matter what our outer garment when we are clothed in His righteousness! Nothing looks the same, when Christ clothes us in right standing with the Father. Old outfits will appear new to those who cross our paths, because a new life in Christ always grabs the attention of those who are looking for people with substance.

Verse 29. And yet I say unto you, that even Solomon in all of his glory was not arrayed like one of these.

Kings of the day were known to wear purple and, at times, white robes. Jesus tells us that no matter how sharply Solomon dressed, his raiment could never hold a candle to the lilies of the field. Even with the designer suits and dresses of today, neither we nor modern kings and queens can match the beauty with which the Father arrays the lily. We have got to stop trying to use clothing to make a statement that can only be made when a life is right with Christ. We spend too much money on clothes, in an effort to convey that we are impressive or that we've got it going on. Anxiety results, because we buy what we cannot afford to convey what people already know - we want to be more important than we feel we are!

Verse 30. Wherefore, if God so clothe the grass of the field, which today is, and tomorrow is cast into the oven, shall he not much more clothe you, O ye of little faith?

Christ says the very flowers in the field can show us how far the providence of God reaches. God's care stoops low to make sure the flowers and grass of the field are taken care of. We all at some point in our walks with God are tempted to worry and be filled with anxiety. We must remind ourselves that if God's providence flows to the grass of the field, surely He will take care of us. Nothing goes unnoticed with God and His hand of provision is not short. God provides down to the smallest detail for the smallest of creatures. The grass in the field is gone so soon, but despite its short life, the Heavenly Father makes sure the grass has what it needs to live to its fullest potential.

... O ye of little faith?

One of our biggest challenges is having the courage to fully depend upon the Lord. We should stand firmly on the fact that God in His goodness can be trusted to provide for His people. It is an insult to the character and the faithfulness of God for the saints to be so frantic, when we are called to depend upon the Lord.

Verse 31. Therefore take no thought, saying, What shall we eat? Or, what shall we drink? Or, wherewithal shall we be clothed?

None of these things should be an issue to mature children of God. We are supposed to do our part and then trust God to do His part. Though we do not always do our part – or do it well – we can trust God to do His part, and do it well! According to Christ, we should not be confessing, "Lord, I don't know how I am going to make it?" or asking, "Lord, how am I going to make it" or "Lord, what am I going to do?" Those questions should already be settled in our hearts, minds, souls and spirits. With the same certainty that we answer the question "What's one plus one?", we should know how we are going to eat, drink and clothe ourselves. We are going to do what we have always done, depend upon the Lord to meet all of our needs. Some answers to questions ought to be automatic by now.

Verse 32. (For after all these things do the Gentiles seek:) for your heavenly Father knoweth that ye have need of all these things.

We look just like Gentiles, when we worry about provisions and place too much emphasis upon necessities and making ends meet. Gentiles are those who are disconnected from the faith and from the promises of God, and have no rights to the covenant privileges of Kingdom Kids! We are not supposed to seek things. We are supposed to seek the King and the kingdom. The purpose of necessities is to help us to recognize the need for Christ to be King in our lives. We have got to stop pursuing things and start pursuing Christ the King. If God knows we have need of these things, wisdom suggests we go after the One who knows our needs and also knows how to supply those needs. We can be so busy pursuing things that we never address our true need, which is to know Him and to be known by Him. Let's no longer be like the Gentiles, those who are disconnected from the faith and the inheritance of the King and the kingdom.

God is known for blessing those who go after Him and make Him a priority – not those who make the pursuit of Him a problem. We must declare our dependence upon Him by the way we ask for His help, pursue His purpose, seek His salvation and chase His character. We demonstrate that our trust is in Him, when we worship without wanting material things and fast to fight the good fight of faith. We honor Him, when we take the time to better know Him and meditate on His Word. So, we may clearly know His will, and learn to love Him by enduring experiences that force us to lean on his promises and lift us by His power. Our Heavenly Father knows what we need, and a peace that surpasses our understanding will rest upon our lives and guard our hearts, when we rest in the fact that He also knows the best time to bless us with the things that we need and desire.

LESSON 23

GOD HAS THE GIFT OF ADDING!
Matthew 6:31-34

This lesson addresses the importance of setting proper priorities. When we as children of God correctly establish what is most important, we position ourselves for the outpouring of God's blessings in our lives. This lesson also addresses what happens when the children of God, acting in accordance with their misplaced priorities, spend too much time and energy focusing on and pursuing the wrong things. Amassing things should never be the goal of this life. Our trust in God, as the source of our supply, should always be supreme.

Verse 31. Therefore take no thought, saying, What shall we eat? Or, What shall we drink? Or, Wherewithal shall we be clothed?

Jesus Christ instructs us not to worry or be anxious about having things. It is evident, however, that many today deem food and clothing the most important issues of life. A great percentage of our daily conversation and mental consideration revolves around the abundance or the lack of having things. Food, clothing and shelter are basic provisions that are covered by the Heavenly Father. Jesus is stressing that the Heavenly Father handles all of that for His children. That's His department. So often, we do not focus on the Lord, because we are focusing on these necessities. We should never justify working so much that we never have time for Bible study, worship or spiritual fellowship.

Many times believers get into trouble, because they try to obtain what others have instead of waiting on the Father to provide it. There are times when our Heavenly Father takes His time giving certain things to us. When blessings are given in His timing, we do not have to worry about the tow truck picking it up, while we are sleeping, or the mortgage company foreclosing on us, while we are wide awake.

Verse 32. (For after these things do the Gentiles seek:) for your heavenly Father knoweth that ye have need of all these things.

The Christian should never want to look like the identical twin of the Gentile or the sinner. When we are completely engrossed in the pursuit of things, we appear to be the world's twin. We should never want to be confused with people in the world. At one time or another we've all heard someone say, "You look like someone I know." We should never want people to equate our emotional, spiritual or directional behavior to that of the world. Putting a stop to wastefulness, bad money management, unwise spending, and shopping out of envy could help a lot of saints fare better financially. It is not the job of the children of God to seek things. Our job is to seek to know Him, seek to please

Him, seek to walk with Him and seek to serve Him. If we do our job, we will discover that He has already done His.

It is because we have not sought Him that we as believers are unaware that His work for us is already complete. He already has given us all things to enjoy. Most people can attest to the fact that during our youth our parents and grandparents provided all that we needed. We didn't get up early to go to work – we got up early to go to school. The "providers" took care of the necessities of the house. Our problem is that, as adults, we think our role has shifted. To the Heavenly Father, we are still children! And God provides for all children who allow Him to do so.

... for your heavenly Father knoweth that ye have need of all these things.

Jesus does not negate the fact that food, drink and clothing are necessities. He simply says it is not our job to focus on them – it's the Father's responsibility. At times, we receive more than we are mature enough to handle. If the saints would lay aside their anxiety, they would discover there are some things the Father will give if they would just wait on Him. Many people want everything they see the very moment they see it, but it might not be their season for those things. You may need to drive your car a little longer, instead of buying a new or slightly used car. Change the oil in your car. Rotate the tires. Furthermore, we must learn to precede spending with the same action that we offer before meals – prayer! Rather than praying that God bless our spending, we should pray for wise and disciplined spending. Some of the things we buy are not only bad for our budgets, but also bad for our health!

... for your heavenly Father knoweth that ye have need of all these things.

God already knows everything that we need. He knew it way before we found out about it! Have you ever spent money that you needed later? I'd venture to say that if you knew about that breakdown or urgent situation, you never would have spent the money. Well, God knows the beginning, the middle and the end of each of our stories, and He knows them in complete detail! God usually does not reimburse us when we move too fast and buy what He had intended to give us. Many saints never discover that He already knows their needs and He is committed to supplying them. Oftentimes, we are like the kid pushing the buggy in the grocery store. We want full control and NO parental hands on the buggy! God would fill our buggies, if we would just remove our hands and allow Him to take control.

Verse 33. But seek ye first the kingdom of God, and his righteousness; and all these things shall be added unto you.

Jesus solves the mystery of how to obtain what we need and what we want from God. We are to seek the kingdom of God – not things – if we want our needs and wants met. We must pursue the kingdom of God. We must desire Christ's authority, Christ's control and Christ's rule in our lives. Because wherever Christ is Lord, there *is* the kingdom of God. The kingdom of heaven best depicts the place, where we are going to be with God. The kingdom of God, however, is the realm or region over which Christ reigns. Those of us who have surrendered our lives to Jesus the Christ as Lord and Savior are in the kingdom of God. We are headed to live eternally in the kingdom of heaven! We have made Him Lord over our souls. We are therefore confident that we are going to heaven. However, anything that is not surrendered to His lordship has but one other place to go, and by now we know, it's hell. When we allow Christ to be Lord over our spending and our finances, our financial forecast will look like a foretaste of heaven. Until that time, most people's financial outlook will look like hell. We must seek the Kingdom of God completely. We must make Christ King – even in our finances! In a kingdom, the king rules! Right now, many of us are running our own finances. We must surrender all that we make, all that we have and all that we spend unto Christ our King.

As believers, we also must pray for God's perfect will, when it comes to shopping and spending. We must surrender our spending completely to Him. That means praying about the candy bar, the chips and the soda you picked up at the counter as you were paying for gas! This sounds silly to the person who is spiritually blinded by the deception of the enemy, who does not want us to flourish as kingdom kids are supposed to. At the very least, collective prayer should come before the purchase of a big-ticket item, or in other words, something that would cost a week's worth of pay. Anything that we would have to work an entire week to pay for ought to be something worth seeking God's direction about. Let's look at a few big-ticket items that could eat up an entire week of pay or more:
- Rent or mortgage $_____
- Car or truck note $_____
- Insurance $_____
- Light bill $_____
- Other $_____
- Other $_____

There are 52 weeks in a year. That's 52 potential paychecks for a person who is paid weekly. For the individual purchasing one big-ticket item a month, over the course of a year, we can subtract at least 12 weeks of pay. This might explain why it seems as if we're broke! For anything that absorbs two weekly paychecks each month, such as a car note, the mortgage or rent, we can subtract an automatic 24 weeks of paychecks from the 52 we could get in a year!

We must have Godly direction and wisdom, if we are going to see wealth's intended purpose, and that is to help establish a covenant between God and His people. We must not chase wealth, nor chase God solely to acquire it. We should chase God to have His rule established in each of our lives. We should run after the rich righteousness that comes from a right relationship with our God.

... and his righteousness ...

We must make the kingdom of God our primary concern, because where Christ rules He also makes things right. We must seek Christ's way of doing things and apply

His principles in our daily lives. The enemy knows money matters to us, and he also knows money is a part of the method, by which God establishes His covenant with His people. Therefore, the enemy tries to trick us by encouraging us to reach for things on our own – things that would have been provided by the Father, if we had only taken the time to pay close attention to the King and the Kingdom. The Father continually makes a way out of no way, delivers us from bad situations and helps us recover from bad financial choices. This fact alone should confirm that God intended to bless us with what we need and desire all along.

... and all these things shall be added unto you.

A life filled with subtractions and not additions should be a hint that something is wrong spiritually. The saints must stop buying *stuff* just because the credit is available or the salesman says, "It was meant for you!" Remember, our first step before a purchase is prayer! Then, we should wait for a response from God. There are some foods that we have no business asking God to bless, because they are unhealthy. It works the same way with material purchases. Ask the Lord, "Is this item for me?" or "Is this my season to have this?" If the answer to those questions is no, we need to ask God for the grace to walk away. Many saints are scared that God is not good at addition, but the Bible is brimming with testimonies that show us we can trust God to add to our lives. As a matter of fact, He loves to add to the lives of His people! God gets great joy in blessing His children, who he loves boundlessly. God loves a cheerful giver and He gives cheerfully to His children. However, we must be mindful that with every blessing comes responsibility and accountability. Our Father will not put any more on us than we can bear, and that includes gifts, blessings and the things that we desire. Let's prove to Him that He matters more to us than things. At their best, things are only accessories in life. God is the true source to life and He alone makes life worth living. If we change our attitudes about Him, we change what we can get from Him. Believers who are growing, maturing and faithful are more likely to see the Father bestow great blessings, riches and wealth.

Verse 34. Take therefore no thought for the morrow: for the morrow shall take thought for the things of itself. Sufficient unto the day is the evil thereof.

We should never emerge from the day's troubles and try to pull in the cares of the next day. Each day has its own share of troubles. Tomorrow will have an adequate supply of drama, issues, challenges, trials, disappointments and trouble. When you overspend today, just know that you are adding to tomorrow's trouble. God will help us with whatever hard times arise in our lives. He specializes in helping us when we need Him the most. If we would only recognize that we need help before we make financial decisions, and acknowledge God knows what is best, we would discover we can travel the road to financial success with ease. Wiser decisions today can eliminate the possibility of worry tomorrow. Make spiritual, moral and financial decisions today that will not result in regrets tomorrow!

LESSON 24

THE MAGNITUDE OF MY LITTLE, AS A RIGHTEOUS MAN!
Psalm 37:16-19

    This lesson compares the wealth of the righteous with the wealth of the wicked. When it comes to wealth, riches and possessions, value does not lie in how much a person has, how expensive their possessions are, or even how impressive those possessions are. True significance lies in how the wealthy obtained what they have, what they are doing with those possessions, and how they are honoring and worshipping God with the things that they have. Take notice: Have they made a god out of material things? We must strive to never become high-minded or put our trust in material things. When it comes to possessions, what separates the righteous from the wicked oftentimes is the object of our attention and affection, our actions, our attitude and our adoration. Despite what we are blessed with in this life, the attention of the righteous ought to be turned toward God. Our hearts' affection should always be to commune with God. Our actions should show that we are pressing our way to God. Our attitude ought to be one of gratefulness for the things that we've received from God, and furthermore, that we are more grateful for the privilege of knowing God and being known by God. Our greatest adoration ought to be the presence, power and promises of God.

    Verse 16. A little that a righteous man hath is better than the riches of many wicked.

    A righteous person's little is not always less in the kingdom of God, and a wicked person's more is not always better, nor does it leave them better off than the child of God. A righteous person always has more, even when it appears he or she has less. It may be hard to believe the person, who is right with God, because of his or her faith in Jesus the Christ, always has more than the wicked. Even if we could tally up what the righteous have and then what the wicked have, though it may appear the wicked have more, the Word of God declares the righteous have more on their side. The scale will always tip toward the righteous, because no one can count the value of favor! We can count *on* the favor of God, but we can't count how much favor is worth or how much favor a righteous person has with God.

    Let's take another look at the scripture. The Word says, *A little that a righteous man hath is better than the riches of many wicked.* God's gifts supersede any other. It is unfortunate that the enemy of our faith can blind believers to the fact that we have the advantage, or the better portion. Many of God's children refer to their time in the world as "the good ol' days," but what they don't realize is these days are the best days! Those days in the world did not bring any glory to God or do us any good. Not one of those "good ol' days" in the world will count in the end. Only what we do for Christ will last and count in the end. The righteous have may be little, but it is better than what the wicked possess, because we obtained what we have with a good conscience. We don't have to be afraid, when law enforcement passes by. The blessings of the Lord are always better than any gifts or rewards the devil confers for doing wrong.

"A little that a righteous man hath" does not mean the righteous will always have little. The point the Spirit of God is making is that no matter what the believer has, it is always better than the riches of a wicked man. Even when it looks like the wicked have more, rest assured that it is an allusion, a façade, a fake. God graces His children with more than we can fit into a garage, put in our pockets or purses and hang in our clothes closets. Our Father gives us what we can handle.

Verse 17. For the arms of the wicked shall be broken: but the Lord upholdeth the righteous.

In this verse, "arms" refers to the power and strength of the wicked, which ultimately shall be broken. No matter how much power the evil possess to gain prosperity or seemingly get an advantage in this life, that power eventually will end. The fleeting success of the wicked is on a timetable of ruin, while a commitment from the Lord securely upholds the righteous. A righteous man may experience great success or temporary failure. However, he knows the future is brighter than the past, because of God's involvement. It is God who gives us the power to get wealth, and God's ways of acquiring wealth bring no shame or sorrow upon us, our future or the kingdom. Satan also gives people the power to get wealth, and his way urges people to get ahead through immoral and unethical methods. Even when Satan's way of prosperity brings about outward success, people find out in the end that the high cost of detangling themselves from resulting mess was not worth the money that was made. The wicked have no problem with using either way to get ahead, but the righteous know that there is but one choice – and that's God's way!

Verse 18. The Lord knoweth the days of the upright: and their inheritance shall be for ever.

One commentary says God is acquainted with all of our circumstances, sufferings, and our ability to bear them. Simply stated, God knows all that we are going through and He knows what we have to go through to get to the other side of prosperity. Tough times are often the training grounds wherein we learn how to live in a land of plenty. Therefore, if God does not take us out of the tough times, it's probable that He wants to take us through them so we walk away with a testimony. No one goes to the Olympics, as an athlete, without first having to go through the trials, tribulations and training necessary to shape a winner. God is making us winners in the area of money management. As a matter of fact, God is making us more than conquerors, when it comes to being money savvy. Before God finishes with us, we should know about investing, interest rates, the stock market, bonds, CDs and seizing great financial opportunities.

... And their inheritance shall be for ever.

As the children of God, we have to know that we have an inheritance in God! An inheritance is of no value to the person, who does not know how to get it or use it. In God, we have an inheritance that we can tap into in this life and the life to come. After Christ died on the cross and was raised from the grave on the third day, the will was probated and is now in full force! We can receive our share of the inheritance as children of God! Let's look at several verses in Psalm 37, which sheds light on our inheritance:

(v. 9) *"... but those that wait upon the Lord, they shall inherit the earth."*

(v. 11) *"But the meek shall inherit the earth; and shall delight themselves in the abundance of peace."*

(v. 18) *"The Lord knoweth the days of the upright: and their inheritance shall be for ever.*

(v. 22) *"For such as be blessed of him shall inherit the earth; and they that be cursed of him shall be cut off."*

(v. 29) *"The righteous shall inherit the land, and dwell therein."*

(v. 34) *"Wait on the Lord, and keep his way, and he shall exalt thee to inherit the land; when the wicked are cut off, thou shalt see it."*

This Psalm gives us a deeper understanding of why David, its author, was a worshipper. In that day, men wrote as they were inspired by God. David has a revelation of God and of the faithfulness of God. It is this type revelation of God that helps us worship even when things are going badly. Worshippers with a revelation of God understand that no matter what they go through, the worst trials are just teaching tools that show us we can trust Him. So, the financially frustrating places God has allowed us to be in were really opportunities to prove that He can and He will provide no matter where we are! When the training process is complete, God, in His wisdom, shows us He will always bring us out and put us in a place of prosperity. In that place of abundance, people would never believe what we came through had God not given us a testimony.

Notice each person to whom the promise of an inheritance from God is made. Verse 9 says those who wait upon the Lord will receive the inheritance; in verse, 11 it's the meek; verse 18 says the inheritance of the upright shall be forever; in verse, 22 it's those who are blessed of Him; verse 29 says the righteous shall inherit the land and dwell therein; and verse 34 says wait on the Lord, and keep His way, and He shall exalt thee to inherit the land.

Despite what we have in our hands today, we must always know we are rich, because of the inheritance that we received from God through Christ. How do we know that we have an inheritance? Just check the Word! We know we have an inheritance, because God said it! If you need a picture of who receives an inheritance, remember it's those people who wait upon the Lord; those who are meek; the upright; the blessed of

Him; the righteous, and those who wait upon the Lord and keep His way. It is God who makes us upright and righteous through Christ's righteousness, which is credited unto us, because of our faith in Him as Lord and Savior, and our acceptance of Christ's finished work on the cross of Calvary.

Verse 19. They shall not be ashamed in the evil time: and in the days of famine they shall be satisfied.

God will never allow those of us who have put our trust in Him to be ashamed of having believed that He would see us through. This does not mean God won't allow people to laugh at us, but it does mean that when the dust settles, the children of God will always get the last laugh, even if it's on our way to glory. Sometimes, in our immaturity, we are afraid to step out on faith, especially when it comes to financial matters and demonstrating that we trust God to provide. Paying God what He is owed should never evoke fear, especially in mature children of God. Because God always keeps His promises, He will never allow us to out-give Him. We should always pray before we give, asking for the confidence to give with the blessed assurance that He can be trusted to give us more than we give to Him.

When we give, it is also important to remind ourselves – and every demon and devil – that we are *already* blessed and *already* rich. This is because we have an inheritance from God! In order to overcome our fears when it comes to being faithful in our finances, we must speak into the atmosphere the faithfulness of God to meet all of our needs, and then speak into our own spirits that we are joint heirs with Christ. We should be joyful in our giving, especially in light of the fact that what we have is a small portion of the inheritance of the saints – and more is still to come! We have to grow into some of the blessings God has in store for us. Many of those blessings are too big for us to handle now. Because we are growing in grace, in knowledge and in favor with God and man, we eventually will receive all that our Father has for us!

... and in the days of famine they shall be satisfied.

God is going to make even our worst days great days, because He will ensure that His children are satisfied in the days of famine. If God ensures that the needs of His children are met in a famine, just imagine how we are going to fare in the season of prosperity! God wants to bless His people. So, the seasons do not matter and famines do not interrupt the flow of grace and goodness toward those who wait for Him, who are meek and humble, who are upright, and who keep His way, while they are waiting.

In May 1965, the Rolling Stones recorded their hit song *I Can't Get No Satisfaction*. A bit of the lyrics are *"I can't get no satisfaction ... I can't get no satisfaction ... 'Cause I try and I try and I try and I try... I can't get no... I can't get no ..."* Well, the saints will never have to sing that song! We have the revelation of God's commitment to meet our every need. God is saying that even in a famine His children will be satisfied in every area and in every direction they turn as they are led of the Lord. Gas is high, but God is giving us satisfaction! Grocery prices have gone up, but God is giving us satisfaction! Property taxes are going up, but God is giving us satisfaction! The saints may have to write a new song, declaring in the atmosphere, "I can't get no dissatisfaction, because God is working it out, God is working it out, God is working it out! We can't help but get satisfaction!" So, don't get frustrated by the announcement of a famine. Let your faith sing out that God is going to satisfy your every need.

LESSON 25

MY WAY IS GOD'S WAY!
Psalm 37:21-26

This study delves further into the comparison between the wealth of the righteous and the wealth of the wicked. In Psalm 37, David shows another example of the differences between the two. God stands firm on His judgment of the wicked, *"for the arms of the wicked shall be broken: but the Lord upholdeth the righteous," (Psalm 37:17)*. Yes, we want to see every dog have his day, but we must remember that God is the author and finisher of our lives. He is the one to determine, when it is time for something to end – not us. God has His own timetable.

You can tell a lot about a person's character by the way he or she handles money. The wicked person steals under the guise of borrowing. The righteous person gives generously to the needy. Wicked people, therefore, focus on themselves, while righteous people look to the welfare of others (Life Application). God bless those volunteers, philanthropists and others who want to ensure that the needy will always have a blessed and loving life.

This lesson illuminates how our wicked ways have lead us down a path of trouble and how our righteous ways have brought unspeakable joy to our lives. How can we be better Christians, or brothers and sisters in Christ, if we are scheming to take money from others? How can we expect to be rewarded for our good deeds, if we are habitual takers and thrifty givers? There are plenty of questions to ask ourselves, but in this lesson we will focus on what we can do to protect ourselves and others from the works of wicked people and our own wicked ways.

Verse 21. The wicked borroweth, and payeth not again: but the righteous sheweth mercy, and giveth..

In this verse, we see a consistent difference in the attitudes of the righteous and the wicked when it comes to money. Let's look at the ungodly attitude:
- To the wicked, paying debt is not a priority.
- The wicked person promises to repay as just a way of procuring a loan.
- The wicked person will repay, if he or she does not find something "more important" to do with the money owed.
- The wicked person is not bothered if he or she never pays a "brotha" back.

Now, the attitude of the righteous:
- The righteous understand that borrowing comes with an obligation to repay.
- The righteous understand that having credit means being trusted to be credible.
- The righteous will not only pay back what's owed, but will also give.

- For the righteous, giving is a part of living. One has not started to live, if he or she has not begun to give.
- The righteous understand the importance of giving, without expecting anything in return.
- If the righteous person is not repaid, he or she knows someone with an unlimited account who will repay him or her for giving in love.
- The righteous not only give – they give generously.

I am sure many believers can identify with these characteristics. We have to understand that every decision we make regarding our finances will ultimately show, where our hearts are toward God. A person with Godly intentions can be a great blessing to anyone in need. We pray to be the lender and not the borrower, so we have to practice that daily. You don't have to have a huge bank account to bless someone. Just show favor to someone in need and let God guide you in your decisions.

Verse 22. For such as be blessed of him shall inherit the earth; and they that be cursed of him shall be cut off.

When we show favor to others, we demonstrate God's love for His children. Through our actions, we demonstrate that we are truly brothers and sisters in Christ. As such, we purpose to treat those in need as family. A person who gives to the poor, and does so sincerely, will find that his righteousness does not have an expiration date. Nobody can establish expiration except God; sorry Visa and American Express! We throw so much money away daily. Yet, we are quick to talk about being strapped for cash. How many times have we walked into a store, bought more than we needed and then walked past someone asking for a donation for a worthy cause? Of course, there are deceitful people who ask for donations to fund scams, but how many legitimate causes have we ignored, because we didn't have any "spare change"?

We have established that believers have an inheritance with God. Now, let's take this a little further. God wants us to inherit the earth, but what is it on earth that He wants us to inherit? In order for everything to work in life, something has to be responsible for something else. Where do you fall in the line of responsibility? Are you like the servant with the five talents, or the servant with two talents, whose reward was to be made ruler over many because of their faithfulness over little, or are you the servant with one talent who is scared to use money, choosing instead to hide it for a rainy day? Will you make sure there is something to inherit on the earth? Decisions are made daily that will affect your financial status. What are you doing to offset those decisions? We must understand that in the process of receiving, there is an opposite process of giving. What are we doing with our time, talents and other resources to ensure that someone is being provided help to make it through the day? What you consider a blessing may be a breakthrough for someone else.

In the simplest terms, those who do not believe and will not under any circumstances let God guide them in their ways will be dropped like a bad habit.

Remember, an inheritance doesn't have to be tangible. It can be intangible, and so, last longer than any material object.

In Zechariah chapter 5, the prophet talks about a "flying scroll" (representative of God's curse) that is seen moving across the land. One side of the scroll proclaims every thief shall be banished. The other side says everyone who swears falsely will be banished. God declares that He will send out the scroll and destroy the thief, the swearer and the houses that they have built. Don't be in that group, because you haven't repaid your debts or you have schemed people out of their money. There is too much to lose.

Verses 23-24. The steps of a good man are ordered by the Lord: and he delighted in his way. Though he fall, he shall not be utterly cast down: for the Lord upholdeth him with his hand.

The person in whom God delights is one who follows God, trusts Him and tries to do His will. We have a Father, who is waiting for us to make a good decision. So, He can give us something else to praise Him about! When it comes to money, it is no different. God is watching how we handle what we have, and when He sees us make a good decision, He will give us another blessing. Remember, the blessing will not always be tangible, but it will be a blessing nonetheless.

The path to financial success does not include the lottery, casinos in Las Vegas or Gulfport, the dog track at Monticello or the late-night poker game at your friend's house. We are on a daily walk, but who determines our steps? In I Samuel 2:9, God says *"he will keep the feet of his saints, and the wicked shall be silent in the darkness; for by strength shall no man prevail."* Regardless of how good you are at picking numbers or predicting the stock market, by placing trust in those methods, you are placing your feet on unsteady ground. Place your feet on God's Word, and before long that mud you feel yourself walking around in will become solid ground. God watches over and makes firm every step that a believer takes. If you want God to direct your way, seek His advice before you step out. Let God in on your decision-making. You will find yourself praying to God after a not-so-good decision, so pray to Him on the front end!

Some may say, "Well, I have made some not-so-good decisions before, so what do I do to prevent it from happening again?" It is easy to say that we should learn from our mistakes and not repeat them, but we are prone to err, because of our nature. Thankfully, God will provide a way out. Creditors will tell you bankruptcy is a way out. God will provide a way out. Banks will tell you "no" based on your credit score. God will provide a way out. Regardless of what man tells you, God will provide a way. Proverbs 24:16 says, *"for a just man falleth seven times, and riseth up again: but the wicked shall fall into mischief."* Those who gained their wealth through wicked deeds will be spinning in turmoil, while they watch you high-step on the path of righteousness. Your breakthrough is coming – you just have to believe in God and make sure your ways are in accordance with His plan and purpose for you.

Verse 25. I have been young, and now am old; yet have I not seen the righteous forsaken, nor his seed begging bread.

What have you seen in your lifetime that is a testimony or word of wisdom for someone else? We have made financial mistakes and told our friends and family members, but what about a stranger? What about that person who is traveling down the same road that you are?

In this verse, the term "young" refers to the innocent or inexperienced at handling things. "Old" is the part of life in which we understand the lessons learned from our mistakes. Wisdom is a by-product of this. Some of us will spend money, before it reaches our hands. We don't know how to act, when we have a little bit left over, and yet, our responsibilities remain. You may say, "There is no way I'm going to stay at home while an event is going on! I can ball like everybody else!" You spend thousands on tires, rims and a system, but barely can afford to put $20 in the gas tank. You have a cell phone, but the bill goes to your mother's house, because you don't have your own place. That's youth. Time after time, we see examples of how people waste money and think it will always be there for them.

Some of us have done the same in our day, but then the light bulb came on. After hearing people tell us to stop being foolish with our money, God whispered (or shouted) and grabbed our attention. In whatever way God chose to do it, He helped us to see that wasting money was a disaster waiting to happen. Maybe some of you visited that disaster and found yourself in a recovery mode that has lasted for years. If you fall into this category, let me ask, have you died from it? No. God saw fit that you were to make it and live another day. Look at those difficult times, as learning lessons and preparation to teach the next learner.

When we see a Christian brother or sister suffering, we can respond in one of three ways:
1. We can say, as Job's friends did, that the afflicted person brought this on himself.
2. We can say that this is a test to help the poor develop more patience and trust in God.
3. We can help the person in need.

David would only approve of the last option. Although many governments have programs designed to help those in need, we cannot ignore the poor and needy within our reach. What is wrong with donating to a person or group in need? Don't let stereotypes, biases or prejudices prevent you from missing a blessing! Of course, don't be naïve, but be discerning and ask God for guidance in your giving.

Verse 26. He is ever merciful, and lendeth; and his seed is blessed.

When you do something to help others, it should be out of love and concern for their needs. Those who give to have their names printed in a newspaper or to receive the biggest-giver prize will find problems along the way and will get discouraged easily, when nobody recognizes their contributions. The heart of the wicked will never outshine the heart of the righteous. No one can count the treasures we have, because it is not kept in a bank account, cannot be searched on the Internet and won't be found in any church documentation.

A righteous person teaches his seed to do good deeds and passes along traits that are invaluable. The lessons you have learned should be passed on to your seed, so they won't make the same mistakes you did. Explain to them about debt-to-credit ratio, the pros and cons of consolidating loans, how to shop for a bargain instead of buying the first thing that they see, and most of all, giving tithes and offerings before everything else.

Most people desire their children to live and be better than they were. We have seen that in our lifetime. Some of us have more televisions in our houses than rooms to fit them in. Some have more cars and clothes than they can drive or wear at one time. However, what are we leaving behind for our seed? Are we setting them up for success or ultimate failure? Learning about bad credit at 18 years of age is not a good introduction into life. Using your baby girl's name, to get the lights turned on, is not financial wizardry. As a race different from any other, we have failed at teaching our children the importance of attaining financial success, because we ourselves have failed to learn the system. We cannot blame it on another race, because we can read and comprehend for ourselves.

The wicked will not prosper and the righteous will prevail. Remember, Joseph didn't suffer in the famine. Isaac dug wells in waterless areas. Don't get bogged down in the haves and have-nots. Concentrate on God. When He has His way in your life, you will not be disappointed.

LESSON 26

GOD'S STRANGE WAYS OF GETTING ME MONEY TO MAKE THE ENDS MEET!
Matthew 17:24-27 (Amplified)

This lesson focuses on times in life when we are not sure how we are going to meet financial obligations, and how not meeting those obligations leaves room for negative conversation about believers. Life does not always afford us the advantage of knowing how a person got to where they are financially, or even why a person struggles to make ends meet. This text teaches us that Christ can show us how to meet our obligations. He knows the location of resources that can get His people through tough times. After studying this text, you may be challenged to pray, "Christ teach me how to fish my money out of the fish's mouth!"

Verse 24. When they arrived in Capernaum, the collectors of the half shekel [the temple tax] went up to Peter and said, Does not your Teacher pay the half shekel?

Peter, a native of Capernaum, is back in town after a trip with the Lord. He is approached by tax collectors, who ask whether Jesus honors the law by paying the temple tax. The temple tax was instituted by God during the days of Moses, as the children of Israel journeyed through the wilderness on their way to the Promised Land. In Exodus 30:11-16, God institutes the temple tax, which mandated that all Jewish males age 20 and older help pay for public sacrifices and the expenses and upkeep of the temple. When Israel finally settled in Jerusalem, the temple tax was not only used for the upkeep of the temple, but also for the care of the upkeep of the holy city. Jerusalem was considered part of the temple property. The amount of money required for paying the temple tax was known by several names: the half shekel, two drachma, and denarii. The temple tax, which was collected annually, was the equivalent of two days' wages for the average Jewish male. The temple tax is not to be confused with the Roman tax, which the publicans collected and were oftentimes accused of charging.

...the collectors of the half shekel [the temple tax] went up to Peter and said, Does not your Teacher pay the half shekel?

The collectors of the temple tax were just like most religious leaders of the day. They had a problem with Jesus and sought opportunities to say something negative about the Lord, just as our enemies today look for anything with which to slight the people of God. Neglecting the temple tax would have been a great conversation piece for the enemies of Christ. No doubt they would eagerly purport that Jesus did not support the temple and the upkeep of it. They'd contend that Jesus did not have the means or the resources to take care of His financial obligation to the temple. We can just imagine their snide accusations. "What real man over twenty can't handle or won't handle his spiritual obligation to pay the temple tax?" And he calls himself a spiritual leader!"

The household of faith must always be careful around these types of critics, because the temptation is always there to join in their ignorance or become influenced by their venom. If we are not careful, we can begin thinking or speaking evil about the very ones who God has ordained and assigned to usher in the fullness of His glory. The collectors come to Peter (the follower, the student, and the disciple) and question him about his Master instead of going straight to the source. Some people's sole intent is to slant our opinions of our spiritual leaders. If the collectors really wanted to know if Jesus honored the law and paid His temple taxes, they could have looked at his record or gone straight to Jesus.

...does your Teacher pay the half shekel?

The collectors' entire reason for questioning Peter is to cause him to question Jesus and His leadership. If the enemy can get us to question Christ and our spiritual leaders, he knows that he can ultimately get us to question our faith and our allegiance. Satanic suggestion can cause you to doubt your spiritual leader's teaching and leadership. The enemy's hope is that we ask, "Should I follow the Christ's teachings, or are there some things I can decide for myself?" and then, choose the wrong answer.

Verse 25. He answered, Yes. And when he came home, Jesus spoke to him [about it] first, saying, What do you think, Simon? From whom do earthly rulers collect duties or tribute – from their own sons or from others not of their own families?

If we are going to follow Christ, we must learn to follow Him closely as we will be called upon to answer questions about Him. Without Jesus being there, Peter was able to correctly answer the critics' question about his Christ. Without any stumbling in his speech, Peter answered, "Yes!" Peter's answer raises the question, "How well do we know Christ?" Peter answers with conviction, and by now we should be able to stand up for Christ with the same conviction and credibility. When life and the world questions God's ability to handle financial issues, we should be able to answer with certainty. When is the last time you had to give an answer about the Christ and His trustworthiness, when it comes to financial affairs? Were you able to answer like Peter – with great boldness and belief that Christ can be trusted with money issues?

It is so disheartening to see people, who sing about Jesus, talk about Jesus, preach about Jesus and pray to Jesus, act as though they cannot trust Jesus when they are in need financially. We should be able to declare, even in the face of doubters and skeptics, "Yes, we can depend on Jesus to take care of every financial responsibility and commitment that has to be met!" Saints of God have got to stop being scared to answer that question on Sunday morning during the tithes and offerings part of worship. The children of God have got to get to that place were we can proclaim Christ's faithfulness with finances, whether we get paid weekly, bimonthly or once a month. Peter does not have to look around or scratch his head – when it comes to Jesus and His ability to meet His financial obligation, Peter declares, "Yes!"

...And when he came home, Jesus spoke to him [about it] first, saying, What do you think, Simon?

Jesus already knew that the world had questioned Peter, but Christ also knew that Peter did not doubt His faithfulness. Before Peter could speak to Jesus about the collectors' question, Jesus raises the issue. The Master teaches us to stick with what we know to be true about Him. God has already put the right answers to money dilemmas in His children. We have just got to learn to lean on the truth that already lives in us through the Holy Ghost. Jesus makes Simon think, and He asks us to think, too. We as children of God must no longer allow the enemy to intimidate us about God and money. We already have the right answer; we just hate having to think! If we just consider what God did to save us, that alone should be the evidence we need to prove that there is no good thing that He will withhold from us. God gave us His best when He gave us His Son, and He gave us His Son even, when we were at odds with God.

...From whom do earthly rulers collect duties or tribute – from their own sons or from others not of their own family?

Christ poses a question to Simon Peter, knowing that he already has the right answer. We, too, can arrive at the right answer if we would THINK! Our problem is that when it comes to money, we don't want to think. If we find ourselves in need of more money then there is coming in, all we have to do is think! There will always be a deficit, past-due bills, overdraft charges, garnishment and/or bad credit when income is less than what is paid out! The person who lounges in the house, preferring not to get a part-time job, and continues to spend outside of his or her means is someone who does not want to think!

Verse 26. And when Peter said, From other people not of their own family, Jesus said to him, Then the sons are exempt.

Jesus broadens the question of temple taxes to all taxes. Either way, Christ says, the kings of the earth do not pay taxes, nor do kings charge their children taxes. Christ is conveying to Peter that He is exempt from paying taxes because He is the King's Son. If the tax is the temple tax, and Christ, the Son of God, is royalty, then he would not be required to pay the tax.

Verse 27. However, in order not to give offense and cause them to stumble [that is, to cause them to judge unfavorably and unjustly] go down to the sea and throw in a hook. Take the first fish that comes up, and when you open its mouth you will find there a shekel.

Take it and give it to them to pay the temple tax for Me and for yourself. Though He had the freedom, as the Son of God to wave the temple tax, Jesus chose not to be a stumbling block to others' faith. Some people look for reasons to not believe. There are times, when we must be the bigger person and make sure that others are not injured by our freedom. The Greek word for "give offense" is *skandalizo,* meaning "cause to stumble."[5] The tax collectors were looking for something negative to say about the Savior, and He knew that nonpayment would become the topic of negative conversation. His critics would have had a field day talking about what they would see as a failure to abide by the law.

The children of God must be responsible for what our lives communicate to people, who are watching the kingdom through us. Though we have failed at times in life, we must be mindful that the only kingdom some people will see is the kingdom that lives in us. How the saints handle financial issues can be a great stumbling to many in the world, especially to those who believe they will be repaid, if they loan something to a child of God. Followers of God are granted credit, even by those in the world. Having credit does not mean that we, the people of God, are to get everything that we want now. If we do not have the means to pay, we should not use the credit to borrow. Borrowing on credit sends a message that we can't pay the whole amount now, but we can and will pay over a period of time. However, if we cannot pay for what we desire now, or see how we can pay a portion over a period of time, purchasing on credit is not an option. Credit without the ability to pay, as promised, is BAD CREDIT! The household of faith has become a stumbling block to the world. There was a day, when a Christian could obtain some things based solely on their word. Bad credit signifies more than a lack of purchasing power. Bad credit also indicates bad stewardship, and if we are not careful, we will mar the world's willingness to trust the word of Christians in the future.

...go down to the sea and throw in a hook. Take the first fish that comes up, and when you open its mouth you will find there a shekel.

God does have strange ways of helping His people meet their needs and obligations. Sometimes, His method requires us to get up, go, and do something! The Lord provided the money to pay the temple tax, but Peter had a part to play. The way was already made. If Peter had stayed home and sat on this Divine strategy for financial success, he, like many of us, would have missed out on the blessings of God. Divine strategy for financial freedom does not always make sense to the saints. Our understanding is not a prerequisite for following God's direction. Peter did not have to comprehend the instruction to get up, go, and do what the Savior commanded. The text shows us that God has some unlikely ways of meeting the needs of His people. We won't always be able to figure out how God's financial plan is going to get us out of the hole we are in, but the key is to accept - and do - whatever He says.

Many people would prefer that the Lord just hand over money, but the Lord requires that we fish in faith. Who would have ever thought that there would be money in the fish's mouth? God! That is why we must learn to listen to God and then follow His plan. When we follow God's unlikely ways of financing our future, we will discover that there is more than enough for us. There will be enough for the kingdom and others. Keep your heart open for God's unlikely ways of making ends meet. It's in the fish's mouth!

---

[5] Life Application Bible Commentary

LESSON 27

GOOD MONEY MANAGEMENT MATTERS!
Luke 16:1-9

This lesson stresses the importance of good management skills. We'll examine how negligence in business affairs can cause us to lose positions in this life and in the world to come. God wants His people to be business savvy and know how to manage whatever blessings He bestows. The Creator entrusts the children of God with less when we engage in unhealthy spending habits, constantly make poor financial decisions, are slothful in correcting bad management skills, and show disinterest in learning the intricacies of business, such as interest rates and credit ratings. The Body of Christ should always be thinking of honorable ways to make money, create jobs, empower the community and invest wisely. Simply stated, we as Kingdom Kids must become more entrepreneurial in our outlook on life. There are so many signs that, as a whole, the children of God do not value investments, credit, money management and financial prudence as we should.

Verse 1. ALSO [JESUS] said to the disciples, There was a certain rich man who had a manager of his estate, and accusations [against this man] were brought to him, that he was squandering his [master's] possessions.

In this text, the rich man is a depiction of God. The manager of the estate represents the children of God. It is always important to know who the owner is, and equally as important to know our role and our responsibilities as managers. The text does not spell out the specifics of what the manager supervises. What we do know is that he is given the privilege of managing someone else's affairs. It is a privilege to manage, supervise or oversee the possessions of others. When we are entrusted with someone else's goods, possessions, business, company, services or production, there is an expectation that value will be gained or added, because of the wisdom, skills, expertise and hard work we bring to the relationship. As managers, if we do not add value to the company, increase productivity, decrease waste and help the company to operate with a profit, we run the risk of getting fired. That is what happens to the manager in the text. Remember, Jesus tells this story to show His disciples the importance of managing well, whatever it is that they are entrusted with.

... and accusations [against this man] were brought to him, that he was squandering his [master's] possessions.

The manager was charged with wasting, mismanaging or mishandling his master's money. His offense was that he was not utilizing the master's possessions to the best of his ability. This is the accusation against the people of God. As a whole, the Body of Christ has failed to cause whatever we are entrusted with to grow and we've missed opportunities to make the best out of every blessing. We must exercise prudence, when it comes to purchasing and wisdom when it comes to saving. This is an assignment that many in the household of faith fail daily. Putting more thought into how we handle every dime that we are entrusted with must become a priority. As kingdom citizens, we must be able to account for our money. We cannot continue to say, "I don't know where my money went!" The person, who does not know where his or her money went, will discover, it probably did not go very far! There is always someone on the corner waving a vessel with an opening into which we can drop money. When we have little to no wisdom when it comes to spending, giving can beget trouble.

Many people of God have been accused of not being able to keep their hands off one paycheck. Believers must start managing their money and living on a level that leaves some left over, no matter their amount of income. As children, if we ate everything on our plates and then asked for more, we were called greedy! To devour every paycheck, within a year and not have any money left is greed on an adult level! The manager in the text is accused of squandering his master's possessions. A staggering misconception in the life of the believer is that once the tithe is paid, the rest is ours to do whatever we will. That mindset is directly linked to the fact we do not realize that we are accountable to God for the money that remains after the tithe. We need divine direction for the portion that is left over; it's the largest part of the whole!

Verse 2. And he called him and said to him, What is this that I hear about you? Turn in the account of your management [of my affairs]...

The owner required the manager to reconcile the books and give a report or account of his stewardship. It's a sad commentary that if many saints were asked to reconcile the books, they'd discover money management has mattered so little that the books would be found lacking – if there were any books at all! Most people do not keep receipts and have no record of whom they have and have not paid. Many saints have no idea how much they owe on a loan, the balance on the loan, or even the original loan amount! When the object is to get something, it does not matter what it cost us. When the object is to be found faithful over the possessions of God, the receipts, the balance, the interest, the cost, and all other financial issues will matter! Modern believers have got to get beyond the question, "How much is the monthly payment?" To the flawed mind, the length of the loan, the price of the purchase, the interest rate, and nothing else matters, so long as the monthly payment fits into the next few month's ability to pay.

... for you can be [my] manager no longer.

If Jesus is implying that this story is in line with what God requires of His people, then we are at risk of getting fired. The owner releases the manager, because of his poor handling of his possessions. The manager offers no excuses. There are no legitimate excuses for how poorly we have managed our lives, our time, our opportunities, our blessings, our responsibilities, or our resources. Maybe that is why we seem to keep getting the short end of the stick! Could it be that when we do nothing with the long end of the stick, the next stick we are handed is a bit shortened, and then, finally, we're given no stick at all? When it appears that we do not know how to handle what we're given, we run the risk of losing out completely.

Verse 3. And the manager of the estate said to himself, What shall I do, seeing that my master is taking the management away from me? I am not able to dig, and I am ashamed to beg.

The only reason the manager had his position was because of the favor shown to him by the master, and the master's belief in his ability to do the job. The manager has no one to blame for his dismissal, but himself. Somewhere, in the process of his assignment, he became distracted, lazy, careless, or just lost sight of his priorities. The manager's misfortune could happen to all of us. We can easily lose sight of what is most important.

For the believer who does not believe money management is important, my prayer is that this text will grab your attention. The church and the kingdom could benefit from people, who have good money management skills and good credit. People who are not over-extended, possess business savvy, are investment conscious, and are not at the mercy of predatory creditors are an asset to the kingdom. It is difficult to give money to the church and the causes of Christ, when your pockets are empty, because of bad financial choices and immature spending. Believers who have money and a heart to give enrich the church and the kingdom of God.

We can tell that the manager is resourceful, because the text says he decides to do something after losing his position. The manager rules out two options: manual labor and begging. Golf great Tiger Woods once divulged a secret to his successful career. Most people who play golf tee off and look across the green toward the hole, or the goal. Tiger Woods said a successful tee off starts in his mind. He begins at sinking the ball and works his way backward to the point of tee off. Take a cue from Tiger; visualize where you want to end up and work your way backward. When starting anything, you must know the goal, and then make decisions from the start based upon where you want to end up. Normally, we just make decisions, as we go. Until, we finally end up in some unforeseen place. If the manager had made decisions with the end in mind, he would not have been at this place – facing unemployment and the possibly of doing work that does not fit him, or a life of begging on the corner. The very decisions that we are making are taking us in the direction of a place we do not want to end up.

Verse 4. I am come to know what I will do, so that they [my master's debtors] may accept and welcome me into their houses when I am put out of the management.

The manager thinks through how he is going to live after life, as an overseer for his master. Some saints are close to retirement and have not given any thought to how they are going to make, it after their tenure with the company. Though we are told and taught to put our future in the Lord's hands, we shouldn't wreck our possibilities! The manager resolves how he's going to get out of the mess he is in. He has planned for the future, *after* realizing tough times might be coming his way. We would not have to react to tough times as much as we do if we would just plan – and then work the plan! Tough times are potentially coming the manager's way, because he stopped working the plan. Formulate a plan to get out of debt (credit cards, apartment rental, title-loan debt, furniture rental, etc.) – and then work the plan!

Verse 5. So he summoned his master's debtors one by one, and he said to the first, How much do you owe my master?

The manager is about to build some relationships with businessmen, who understand debt, debt cancellation and debt consolidation. He first begins to gather information. We should know how much we owe and how much we are owed. People who value money and are good managers know the answers to those questions. Poor money managers have no clue. Just because, we say we value money does not really mean that we do. Actions speak louder than words.

Verse 6. He said, A hundred measures [about 900 gallons] of oil. And he said to him, Take back your written acknowledgement of obligation, and sit down quickly and write fifty [about 450 gallons].

At the moment, the manager still has his job, and therefore has the right to renegotiate the bill of the master's customer. In an effort to find favor, the manager cancels a portion of the customer's bill; more specifically, he cuts the bill in half. This is not an uncommon practice in the business world today. When a company has a client who is unable to pay his or her debt, many times after the debt has gone to collections and then court, the case is labeled a bad debt and a collections company is paid to collect, as much of the debt as possible. This type of debt is normally collected at a rate of 25 to 50 cents on each dollar, if paid in full within a certain period. This appears to be the type of deal the manager makes with the customer in the text.

Verse 7. After that he said to another, And how much do you owe? He said, A hundred measures [about 900 bushels] of wheat. He said to him, Take back your written acknowledgement of obligation, and write eighty [about 700 bushels].

Neither customer denies owing the man's master, but rather each customer sees an opportunity to be forgiven for some of the debt that is owed. For both customers, speedy payment will result in a reduction of debt. Some of the debt might have been interest and fees that accrued for the services that had been received. Whatever the make-up of the debts, the costs could be drastically reduced if the bills were paid in full immediately.

Verse 8. And his master praised the dishonest (unjust) manager for acting shrewdly and prudently; for the sons of this age are shrewder and more prudent and wiser in [relation to] their own generation [to their own age and kind] than are the sons of light.

This verse is both a revelation and an indictment of the Body of Christ. The verse points to the fact that we should be wiser than the world. The children of God ought to be wiser, because all wisdom comes from God. The way the saints often handle money suggests we do not operate in the financial arena with much wisdom. The master praised the manager for thinking and acting on sound financial principles, eliminating the possibility of his having to live as a beggar or take a job that did not fit his future. The sons of this world are said to be shrewder, more prudent and wiser that the sons of light, or the children of God. While the children of light are waiting on God, the children of this world are utilizing the ideas and skills of their father, who is the father of all lies and darkness. Through the compartment of the soul called imagination, God gives creative ideas on how to be successful and how to make things happen, but the saints have confused imagination with pipe dreaming. As a result, many have missed out on great God-given ways of making money and making money work.

LESSON 28

FINANCIAL FAITHFULNESS = TRUST WITH MORE KINGDOM TREASURES
Luke 16:9-12 (Amplified)

This lesson examines how Godly money management has a direct connection to the responsibilities, rewards and reception that we will receive when this earthly life is over. For many saints, the idea of heaven and dwelling with Christ evokes images of how wonderful life will be. Few people, however, make the connection that our financial decisions on earth have eternal consequences. The way we handle our money on earth is so significant that it determines the portion God will give us in the end. If we are poor managers of the wealth, property, resources and inheritance God gives us, it will cost us in this life and in the life to come.

Certainly, at some point, we all have thought that poor financial management just costs us now, or at worst, about seven years. In the earthly economy, if a person mismanages his or her blessings and financial responsibilities, the person may enter a seven-year period in which he or she will not be able to acquire things on credit. If credit is approved, interest rates are high and more security is required. In this time frame, an individual with bad credit is not able to solicit help from normal lending institutions. Therefore, they may have to deal with individuals and companies, who prey on people in this situation. People whose credit has been damaged by paying late, not paying at all, or using credit for more than their means allow will always have to pay more for the goods and services they receive. The children of God are to believe in the power of prayer. After praying, we still have to pay our bills! Good money management practices, along with prayer and wisdom about what and when to purchase, can take each child of God a mighty long way. Knowing how to handle what we have in our hands now, will determine how much God will be put in our hands in the future.

Verse 9. And I tell you, make friends for yourselves by means of unrighteous mammon (deceitful riches, money, possessions), so that when it fails, they [those you have favored] may receive and welcome you into the everlasting habitations (dwellings).

Jesus tells His disciples to do what the unjust servant, who poorly managed his master's money did, when he realized his job was about to end. The servant built relationships through the wise handling of his master's money – money that he was entrusted to handle. Verses 6 and 7 tell us the servant forgave some of the clients' debt, knowing they would be grateful for his gracious treatment though money was owed. The servant used the debt owed to his master, as a bartering tool. The manager knew the people with whom his master did business. The manager also knew that forgiving 50 percent of one businessman's debt and 22 percent of the other's debt would incur their appreciation and favor.

The text shows us the importance of using money to build lasting relationships with those who can and will help, when we need it most. Simply building relationships is not enough. It is not beneficial to connect to those, who are only going to glean from your money and resources, and then forget you.

It's vital to understand the importance of building relationships with people we live with on the earth, even though those relationships are temporal. We have allowed financial matters to damage many of our relationships, and though some were never meant to last forever, they might have lasted longer, if we were more honest about money and committed to paying people back. Repaying the people we owe has to be a priority and not an option, especially when we have expressly said we would do so. We cannot go shopping with money that we owe others, just because it's Easter or Christmas! If paying people back is not a priority, we should not be in the business of borrowing. Otherwise, we are at risk of ruining good relationships that we will need down the road. Jesus says the greatest investment me can make is to use our money to build relationships with those who can help us now and in the future.

I remember a candy called "Now and Later", from my childhood. The colorful candy came in a packet of several individually wrapped pieces. Those of us who learned to share a piece of the candy with others "now" found favor "later", when our friends or siblings remembered our earlier kindness. What goes around comes around! God will not let us share with Him now and not remember and reward us later. No one likes to associate with stingy and selfish people, and neither does God. God is looking for individuals, with whom He can share now and later, but He does not want to do all of the sharing, nor does He want to be the only one glad to share! In verse 8, Jesus called the manager shrewd and prudent for using his resources and financial wisdom to build relationships that would benefit him in the future.

... And I tell you, make friends for yourselves by means of unrighteous mammon...

Please do not allow your handling of money to make enemies. Simply saying, "I haven't forgotten that I owe you" does not satisfy a debt. More than likely, the person to whom you are indebted has not forgotten you owe him or her either, and could probably do a lot more with the money than the acknowledgement that you owe it. Jesus calls the money "unrighteous mammon", because money and possessions can be deceitful and misleading. Some people believe they are blessed, because they have money, wealth, possessions and property. However, if having money and property causes you to act arrogantly and prevents you from trusting in the Lord, then that money is not a blessing – it's a curse!

... So that when it fails, [those you have favored] may receive and welcome you into the everlasting habitations (dwellings).

No matter how much money does for us, no matter what it buys for us or where it allows us to go, sooner or later money will fail. Money can buy a lot of things, but it cannot secure health, salvation, everlasting life, forgiveness, peace, rest, joy, love, or a right relationship with the Lord. Money can rent a man or a woman, but it cannot buy their heart. Money can rent a fishing boat, but it cannot buy a real friend to accompany you on that fishing trip. When money is used wisely and demonstrates that God matters to us, it can help in the investment of a relationship that will last throughout all eternity. Our money cannot buy God's love, but it can be a testament to the fact that we love God. It is our love that we give in exchange for a better relationship with the Lord.

Verse 10. He who is faithful in a very little [thing] is faithful also in much, and he who is dishonest and unjust in a very little [thing] is dishonest and unjust also in much.

No matter how much money we have accumulated (that includes all that we own and which we've taken out loans to obtain), we still are entrusted with very little in comparison to what God has in store for those who love Him. If we are not faithful with the little paychecks we get on a weekly, bimonthly or monthly basis, how can we expect God to graciously give us more? As children of God, our MORE is determined by how well we manage what we already have and not on the length of our prayers for MORE. Maybe, our prayers ought to be for the Lord to endow us with MORE management skills and MORE wisdom to manage the wealth He grants to us, rather than praying for money and more stuff.

The Word says those who are faithful over the little things in life will be faithful with the much they are entrusted with. Conversely, those who are not faithful over little are not likely to be faithful over much. God is grading us and many of the saints are failing the test that gives us access to MORE! Take a moment to consider what you are doing with the little you've been entrust with – time, health, marriage, children, ministry, a job, promotion, paychecks, credit, bills and, most importantly, a relationship with the Lord (prayer, studying, reading, sermon preparation, teaching preparation, witnessing, worship and personal development). One misconception in the faith is that God grades faithfulness solely based on sexual morality, alcohol and drug abstinence, tobacco intolerance and no-profanity pronouncements, but that is not simply true! Though believers certainly ought to abstain from these things, they in no way comprise the complete list! Included on the long list of things God wants His children to be found faithful in is money management! Many of the "really spiritual" people, who talk about living right, never mention not sinning against God in the area of financial responsibility! God views late payments and not paying bills at all, as being unjust and dishonest in the little things. Since God is doing the grading, it behooves the saints to study and ace the test of stewardship!

Verse 11. Therefore if you have not been faithful in the [case of] unrighteous mammon (deceitful riches, money, possessions), who will entrust to you the true riches?

Jesus makes it plain: Who do you think is going to trust you with what matters the most, if you cannot be faithful, honest, and mature with their less important stuff *(The Heard Translation)*? For the person who asks God, "Why haven't you blessed me with more?" The answer comes back from God, "When are going to be trustworthy with what you already have?" Jesus paints a picture of a God, who has much more to give, but first

He watches how we handle what we have before determining, if we can be trusted with His greatest treasures.

Consider this scenario: A person establishes a relationship with a banker and is permitted to borrow $10,000. When he receives the loan check, the borrower expresses his overwhelming appreciation for the loan and makes promises to repay the loan in a timely fashion. Time passes and the borrower fails to make payments on time. The banker makes phone calls and sends letter after letter to advise the borrower that loan payments are past due. The borrower chooses not to respond. Do you think this individual has a great shot at getting another loan at the bank? Perhaps, the loan goes into collection and the borrower still does not repay the loan. Do you think he can approach the banker to borrow more money? Worse still, what if in a year's time the banker sees this individual driving a new car, and yet, the banker is aware that not one penny of the $10,000 loan has been repaid? Do you think the banker would roll out the red carpet for this individual?

Verse 12. And if you have not proved faithful in that which belongs to another [whether God or man], who will give you that which is your own [that is, the true riches].

Think about the borrower in the aforementioned scenario. Now, imagine that a $100,000 management position opens at the bank, and as it happens, the borrower is by training and profession qualified for the position. The borrower interviews for the position with – you guessed it – the banker from whom he borrowed $10,000. Do you think he has a chance at getting the job? Of course not! God will not promote us or bless us with new positions and possessions, when we have not been faithful with the smaller responsibilities. The immature borrower could have been making $100,000 a year. Because he was negligent with $10,000, he spoiled his opportunity. The same God, whose name we tarnish in the business world by not being faithful in financial matters, is the same God we beseech for every position and possession we need.

... who will give you that which is your own [that is, the true riches].

According to Christ's parable, we will NEVER be trusted with our own until we can be faithful, mature and wise with someone else's riches. As we are waiting on God, God may be waiting on us to get our act together. You may not be able to correct the errors of your financial mistakes today, but you certainly can start the process! We should want to be entrusted with the true riches of God, but the Lord says it won't happen until we change our thinking, as it pertains to management. This is a difficult verse for the believer, who is tired of living in lack. Still, the Word is not going to change, because we are tired. We must admit there is self-improvement to be done. There is good news: The Word will change us, if we will let the Word get in us!

Let's live so that God will trust us with the true riches. Our being trusted with another level of anointing may hinge upon our faithfulness in financial matters. What true believer wouldn't hate to be operating in a lower level of anointing than is available? God trusts with more those who He can trust with the least. There may be more favor available to us than we are walking in, and we will never know the level of favor available to us until we first walk in maturity, when it comes to money matters. We don't know all that God has, but we do know God has more, and according to the Word of God, we can get it, if we become responsible managers of the blessings of God!

LESSON 29

EXPOSING WRONG ATTITUDES ABOUT WEALTH!
Matthew 19:21-24

This lesson focuses on exposing incorrect attitudes about wealth. If we were given the opportunity to pick between wealth and walking with God, which would we pick? It's easy to answer this question correctly, when you're seated in the sanctuary and feeling especially "spiritual." We face this choice frequently. The correct answer is not always the automatic answer when we are in other settings. In the legal setting, it is said that a trained lawyer can ask the same question several times and in several different ways to the same person and get several different answers. A skilled lawyer uses this tactic to reveal inconsistencies. Life has a way of asking us the same question in several different ways to reveal what we truly value as most important in life.

Matthew chapter 19 tells the story of a rich young ruler, who comes to Christ with an apparent desire to walk with the Lord. The rich young ruler has lived a righteous life – at least in his mind – and he believes there is nothing left to hinder him from walking with the Lord. Jesus exposes a deep-seated attachment to wealth that would hinder the young ruler from having full fellowship with God. In the spirit of the trained lawyer, allow me to pose the question in a different way: Is there anything you would not be willing to give up to walk with God? God is going to get the right answer out of us sooner or later, even if it takes repeatedly asking us the same question. The truth is none of us really wants to give up anything. However, when there is that one thing you just can't live without; this desire might cause you to live without the Lord.

Verse 21. Jesus saith unto him, if thou wilt be perfect, go and sell that thou hast, give to the poor, and thou shalt have treasure in heaven: and come and follow me.

Do not misconstrue the requirement for entering into the kingdom. No one has to sell all of their earthly possessions, before they can follow Christ. Christ's direction was aimed at exposing the heart of a young man, who thought he was perfect. Also, he believed his perfection could secure a place in the kingdom. This young man was not relying upon the grace or goodness of God to attain eternal life and enter the kingdom, but rather his own merit and goodness. The young man claims he has kept the law from his youth to that very day. Christ's requirement that he sell everything is a charge to get rid of his selfish spirit, rather than expend his surplus of savings. While people look at our outward appearance, we must always remember that God looks at our hearts. Christ saw the young man's heart. When Christ looks at the Heavenly Father's heart, He sees that the Father has not withheld any good thing from us, and everything the Father has He has willed it to us, His children. However, when Christ looks at the young man's heart and at our hearts, He sees that God does not matter to us as much as we matter to Him. God loves us so much that He gives us His BEST and His ALL, but God matters so little to us that we give Him freely only that which does not matter to us!

Again, is there anything that you would not give or give up to follow the Christ? Though Christ makes a tough request of the rich young ruler, we should not dispel the question so quickly. What if this was the requirement to enter the kingdom, would you be willing to give everything? Before you answer, remember, God never asks more of us than He gives Himself. No matter what we have, nothing is greater than God. A believer is not rich, without a right relationship with God through Christ. If we are not united with the Lord, we limit ourselves to poverty, perpetually holding onto wealth that will never be ours.

... and thou shalt have treasure in heaven: and come and follow me.

People, who rejected Christ all of their lives and have since passed away, would probably tell us that no matter what it costs or what you have to give up, it is worth the sacrifice to have Christ in your life! Jesus lets the young ruler know that he will receive something for his sacrifice – treasure in heaven. Is treasure in heaven enough to encourage us to give up all that we have on earth? If you were advising the young man, not at church but at home, the beauty salon or the barbershop, what would you tell him to do? Hopefully, your counsel would be righteous, regardless of the setting. Jesus never said the man would have to wait, until he got to heaven to receive his treasure. When we have the wrong attitude about money, all we can see is what we have and what we can count right now. According to Jesus, the man would have unlimited resources in heaven, if only he would break away from the bondage of money and the illusion of control. Many saints forego treasures in heaven for the fleeting comfort of money to buy cable, a cell phone, jewelry, rims, clothing, trendy hairstyles and the like on earth. The treasures that await those who love the Lord are greater than purses and pockets can hold!

... and come and follow me.

Even if the young ruler had to wait until he arrived in heaven to get all God had in store for him, the privilege of walking with Christ alone would have been worth the wait. No one walks with God and is not made the better, the richer and the wiser because of it. We cannot walk with God and not have a lifetime of conversation to explore.

Verse 22. But when the young man heard that saying, he went away sorrowful: for he had great possessions.

This is a classic picture of many people who sit in pulpits and pews. We do not always see the value of a right relationship with God. The young man acts as if he has more than what God would give Him. He never thought to ask Christ what he would receive, if he willingly gave up his wealth. The man, just as we often do, did a quick mathematical assessment and concluded he had more without God than he would have with God. It is sad, but some saints just cannot add, and that's the primary reason we rob God. We only want to pay the tithe to the penny. We never graciously give an offering, let alone periodically sow a seed that says we are blessed and grateful, because we know the origin of the blessings.

... he went away sorrowful ...

The man did not just walk away – he walked away grieved, distressed (Amplified Version) and very sad (New Living Translation). This same man must meet God one day face to face. How will he explain that he walked away from Christ, because he did not think God was worth the sacrifice? How will he justify his actions in light of the wondrous truth that when he needed a Savior, God deemed him (and us) worthy? The man walked away from Christ that day as if to say, "When you have a sale call me, because what you are selling isn't worth what I am willing to pay." No matter what the man had, God has more! No matter what we have, God has much more! God considers us worthy of all that He has, but when we continuously walk away, we send a message to God that we don't think He is worth a sacrifice on our part. One hundred years from now, what we have in our possession today will not matter. What will matter is what we did with and for Christ. Only Christ can make us rich in righteousness. Therefore, we cannot just walk away from Him! No one who has ever chosen Christ reached the end and regretted it. Yet, there are those who will reach the end and regret rejecting Him.

Verse 23. Then Jesus said unto his disciples, Verily I say unto you, That a rich man shall hardly enter into the kingdom of heaven.

The person whose ambition is to be rich has to be careful that the riches do not take the place of God. Some people prefer to place their confidence in their wealth, but God requires that we place our trust and confidence in Him. Riches make it difficult for some people to fully rely upon God. There is always a temptation to believe money can handle every situation. Thus, people begin to believe in their money instead of believing in God.

Pursuing God is a great investment. Having access to the kingdom and the King is a benefit of that great investment. Having an intimate relationship with the Lord is a benefit of that great investment. Anyone who would give us ALL would never be satisfied with us giving our LEAST. Anyone who makes us PRIMARY would never be satisfied with us making him or her SECONDARY! The individual who esteems riches higher than a relationship with God will more than likely always have more riches than he or she will ever have of God. No matter how poor a person is in riches, he or she will always experience an unfathomable level of poverty without God! When pleasing God is our priority, we will always receive more of Him, which leads to a richer life!

What is your attitude or demeanor after God asks something of you? Are you sour, because you would rather not honor the Lord's request? If so, it's probable that your possessions or gifts have too great a place in your heart. The Lord is looking for a people willing to bless Him, before He asks. So often, the Lord blesses us before we ask, and then in His giving grants us more than we asked for. Consider how many blessings pass by wealthy individuals, who have a poor attitude, when it comes to giving the Lord access to what they have. That type of attitude has kept many out of the kingdom of heaven. The freedom, the privileges, the power, the validation, the blessings, the grace, the mercies, the love, the forgiveness, the help, and the victories are all aborted, when we exempt ourselves from entering into the Kingdom of Heaven, by choosing things over God! The fact is, all of these benefits are ours NOW! So, while the rich person appears rich, the righteous person is truly rich. The key is to learn how to access what we have, because we are already in the Kingdom!

Verse 24. And again I say unto you, It is easier for a camel to go through the eye of a needle, than for a rich man to enter into the kingdom of God.

There are two lessons we can glean from this verse and, more specifically, the metaphor of a camel passing through the eye of a needle. This was a proverbial statement. One that people in Jesus' day would fully understand as a statement signifying the difficulty of something happening. Jesus does not say it is impossible for a rich man to enter into heaven. What He does say is it is easier for a camel to get through the eye of a needle, thereby illustrating that money makes it difficult for some people to put God in His rightful place in their lives. In the pursuit of money, some people work all the time and claim they have no time for God, church, Christian teaching, or even Christian fellowship. Those same individuals likely have no money to show for all of their labor, and usually little to no money given unto the Lord or His church. Some people will chase a dollar at any cost, including damage to their spiritual life, their spiritual growth, their beliefs and their spiritual connection to Christ. That type pursuit hampers a person's ability to have a real relationship with God, because the focus is on everything but God. This kind of person offers excuses, as to why he or she has no time for God or His house. The person whose life is filled with the pursuit of prosperity makes it difficult to be used of God, because their time is wholly used by the god of GREED!

In this passage, Jesus also uses "the eye of a needle" in reference to the entranceway of a city. In order to keep raiders out, who might invade a city on camelback, cities often would have an arch in the gate's opening. Usually a city's perimeter would be fenced or walled and an arch over the gate would prevent camels from quickly moving in. Anyone coming into the city on a camel would have to get the camel to drop its load, coax the animal to its knees and help it bend low through the gate. That is how we are to enter the kingdom of God: Drop our load, get on our knees and get as low as we can go to enter in. Too many try to come into the kingdom of God with a high-and-mighty attitude. There is but one King in the Kingdom of God. The rest of us should be grateful to enter in! Though there are many who are saved from the wrath to come, many have not gained full access into the Kingdom, because of their attitudes about money. We want to be saved, but we don't want to drop the load. For some folks, money is too important and God is not important enough. If we can change our attitudes about the money we have and the money we are to receive, we can change the amount of money that will be available unto us through the Father. God wants to bless those among His children, who know He is more important than having things. Those who have a hidden heart that hates to bless God and always want God to wait, until they get theirs first, will always be at a disadvantage. Don't walk away! Instead, we must decide to yield, in order to gain access to everything at the Lord's disposal!

LESSON 30

THE WISDOM AND WEALTH CONNECTION!
Proverbs 8:12-19

This lesson explores the connection and chemistry between wisdom and wealth. Proverbs chapter 8 explains that the child of God risks aborting the flow of wealth in his or her life, when he or she chooses not to embrace wisdom. There are three main ways of obtaining wisdom: the fear of the Lord, which is the beginning of wisdom; learning from God and Godly people over the course of life; and praying to the Lord to grant wisdom. The text teaches that the person, who rejects wisdom, is also rejecting wealth; the mishandling of wisdom and wisdom-increasing opportunities is comparable to lessening wealth potential and the amount of money one could be privileged to handle.

Learning about investing in stocks, bonds, mutual funds, retirement accounts, CDs, money market accounts and savings accounts must become a priority for believers. The children of God should take the time to learn at least one new thing about investing on a monthly basis, and then look at how those money management skills can be put to work. The children of God also should be responsible for teaching wise money principles and practices to all generations. Wisdom speaks through the entire chapter of Proverbs 8, conveying to us the importance and the value of having her (Wisdom) in our lives.

Verse 12. I wisdom dwell with prudence ...

In this text, Wisdom speaks about herself. We learn that she dwells (or lives) with prudence. Prudence is practical wisdom that enables a person to not be deceived by satanic strategies. "Prudence directs one where to advance, where to stop, where to yield, where to oppose, when to be silent, when to speak, what to follow, what to shun, and how to be on guard against the subtleties of Satan, the world, and the flesh."[6] Because the household of faith is always under attack – often in the area of finances – the children of God need wisdom coupled with prudence. If they are honest, most believers will tell you they do not know how to effectively manage money, invest money, save money or spend money. The enemy has led many saints to believe there are some things they *must* have for the house, though truthfully there is no money saved or even available to spend. Many people do not shop with prudence. Stores entice shoppers with items called "whatnots," small trinkets and statues and figurines of angels, couples, animals and the like. When we are not judicious in our purchases, these whatnots add up to more money sitting on shelves than we have in the bank!

It is amazing how many saints mature in their relationships, refusing to allow people to take advantage of them any longer. People who have become wiser do not easily give up their prize possessions and recognize when they are about to be used.

---

[6] Jamieson, Fausset, and Brown Commentary

Unfortunately, these same believers can walk into a store and easily be duped into yielding their pockets and purses for items that have no real ability to satisfy. Wisdom says stop being used, especially when you know better.

... and find out knowledge of witty inventions.

God empowers His people with the divine knowledge necessary to successfully manage money and have a plan to prosper. The prudence God gives is really wisdom applied in practice. Are you struggling financially? Ask yourself one question: How prudent have I been in my purchases this week? We really do not need many of the items we purchase. Most add no value to our lives or financial future.

Witty inventions include practical insight, tact and the know-how to make sure we are making the most of opportunities, seasons and resources. We have everything we need to be financially solvent and successful. Our problem is we do not use the skills given to us, through wisdom that comes from a right relationship with the Father.

Verse 13. The fear of the Lord is to hate evil: pride, arrogancy, and the evil way, and the froward mouth ...

The word "fear" in this verse means to reverence. When we reverence the Lord we begin to hate evil. Hating evil is the beginning of loving good. This verse lists some of the evil that is to be hated by the people of God. Not all, but much of our spending is birthed out of evil. When we see what the Word labels as evil – pride, arrogance, the evil way (corruption, evil behavior) and the forward tongue (deceit, bragging) – it is clear that much of our spending puts us in direct offense to God. Much of our spending is not based out of need, nor is it out of real want. Many of our purchases are rooted in satisfying our ego, pride, arrogance, and our attempt to keep up with others who themselves are consuming out of their ego, pride, arrogance or a desire to keep up with others, who from the looks of their possessions, seem to be doing just a little better.

... do I hate.

Wisdom lets us know that she hates evil. In life, there are signs that we may not be as mature as we should. One of those red flags is when we find ourselves feeding that which Wisdom hates. If you've ever taken a trip to the zoo, you may have seen a signs that says, "Please don't feed the monkeys!" Pride, arrogance, corruption, evil behavior, bragging, deceit and boasting are all monkeys that need to be caged – if not killed – and least of all fed! Every saint I know has at least one monkey that the enemy wants to feed. Shopping to satisfy or feed pride and arrogance, usually results in our shelling out more money than we should. Habitual spending, of this kind, leaves us much poorer than we would have been had we caged that evil desire to spend.

Verse 14. Counsel is mine, and sound wisdom: I am understanding, I have strength.

Just imagine how much farther along you would be financially, if you would just shop with wisdom. Back in the days of our youth, many times our parents would take us along on shopping trips. Sometimes, we were instructed to roll down the car windows and stay inside. We would politely call after our parents to bring us something back from the store. Laws do not allow us to leave children in our cars these days, but now parents are leaving wisdom in the car with the windows rolled up! We take our children in the stores and neither adult nor child exercises self control or wisdom. So, we find ourselves overspending and in a financial mess.

Let's delve a little further. Consider this statement: "Direction how to act in all circumstances and on all occasions must come from wisdom: The foolish man can give no counsel, cannot show another how he is to act in the various changes and chances of life."[7] Wisdom is counsel, and without wisdom a person does not know in which direction to travel and neither will he or she know how to direct anyone else. On the whole, we are not operating in wisdom, when it comes to financial management. This is why many families fall into financial ruin. Good money management is not just about adding and subtracting; it has more to do with knowing what to spend and when to save. Wisdom brings with it the ability to understand the importance of paying people on time and managing our money, so that we can pay those whom we owe. People who manage money poorly want their debtors to simply understand. Those who possess wisdom when it comes to wealth know that it is the borrower, who must first understand. We must understand what we can and cannot afford. We must understand seasons and the times. Some seasons are not for spending, but rather saving. Some seasons are not just for saving, but also investing. Finally, there are some seasons for purchasing. Yet, we have to have the wisdom to understand, if it is the best season to purchase a particular item. When wisdom and wealth are coexisting and cooperating, we are likely to be strong and financially solvent. Remember, if you lack the wisdom to govern your wealth, you can acquire it: Pray for wisdom, reverence God and His ways, or learn from the lessons of others and your own life to become a wiser steward.

Verse 15. By me kings reign, and princes decree judgment.

Wisdom is not only a necessity and a requirement for the common person. Sovereign leaders also need wisdom to rule effectively. The world's economy has shown us what happens when people are not making decisions based on and directed by wisdom. Unlike Wall Street, the common person might not be able to rely on the government for a bailout, so it is crucial to make Godly decisions. We are charged to get more wisdom, because simply put, we cannot make the sound decisions that ensure a better, brighter future without it. Wisdom helps kings rule over immense lands and handle weighty financial decisions. If wisdom can help a king effectively manage a kingdom, imagine how much more successful we would be as we consistently operated in wisdom. When a prince makes a decree, it directly affects the lives of those under his rule. There are children, spouses, churches, communities, charities and many others depending upon us to make the right decisions about the money that we are privileged to

---

[7] Adam's Clarke Commentary

manage. Consequently, if we do not manage well the money that is assigned to us, everything else will suffer, because we cannot give what we do not have!

Verse 16. By me princes rule, and nobles, even all the judges of the earth.

As stated before, the decisions of people in authority are often final and have a direct effect on the lives of others. This is also the case with the people of God. Our decisions are lasting and affect not only our futures, but also those of others who have no part in our decision-making. We must no longer let down future generations by continuing to pass on faulty money management practices. We have to decide whether we are going to prosper and be in good health or continue to rob Peter to pay Paul. The tradition we pass on to the next generation will depend upon us and our commitment to wiser living.

Verse 17. I love them that love me; and those that seek me early shall find me.

It is never too late to seek God's direction, though many of God's people have waited, until late in the day, to seek wisdom. We must begin teaching younger generations to seek wisdom early. The text does not suggest wisdom will not be found, when it is not sought early. The hidden truth behind the pursuit of wisdom is that the earlier you seek it, the earlier it will be found! By the time most saints seek wisdom in the area of wealth, they already have mismanaged and wasted wealth, credit, resources and opportunities! We must seek wisdom before we get our hands on the wealth, so we will know what to do with the wealth when we get it. Wisdom sought early helps eliminate the propensity to be wasteful with wealth that we will need. Wisdom is not hiding from us, but if we do not look for wisdom, we won't find it. By the time, we have the sense to seek it and find it the damage is likely already done.

Let's look at an example of seeking wisdom early. An individual who wants to purchase a home (we all should aspire to be homeowners) would be wise to obtain homeownership counseling. Many saints, who desire to own homes, forego counseling that often highlights the importance of a good payment history, managing credit, keeping receipts, property upkeep, wise furnishing of the house, home improvement, involvement in a neighborhood watch and much more. If you have never owned a home, wisdom would behoove you to learn from those who have and seek training from experts. Conversely, the unwise home shopper just wants to amass enough money to make a down payment and move in, because he or she believes that's all there is to it.

I love them that love me ...

Wisdom shows love to those who love wisdom enough to pursue her. When wisdom loves you and shows that love, life is much better and much sweeter. Sadly, many people's lives are bitter, because they have fallen out with wisdom. We must spend time learning and growing in every area we choose to venture into. Even if you choose not to venture into a particular area, gain wisdom for the friend or loved one, who may choose that road.

Verse 18. Riches and honor are with me; yea, durable riches and righteousness.

Wisdom carries with her great advantages. Here, we see that riches and honor are constant companions of wisdom. We miss out on so much, because we do not choose to be wise or to gain wisdom in the arenas in which we work. We will work with money, so long as we are upon the earth. Durable or lasting riches are with people who operate in wisdom. Wealth is fleeting for those who are not as committed to wisdom as they should be.

Verse 19. My fruit is better than gold, yea, than fine gold; and revenue than choice silver.

The revenue or return on investing in wisdom is greater than the revenue gained by investing in gold or silver. The rate of return on an investment in wisdom has a consistently higher and continual rate of return than we could ever get in the market of selling even fine gold. Let's commit to increasing in wisdom in every way possible so we can handle wealth more efficiently. Get a financial tutor. Pray fervently for the wisdom to manage wealth. Reverence God more with the wealth you receive and see what happens to the wealth you have! God has more for the wealth-wise believer!

LESSON 31

DOING RIGHT BY THOSE WE'VE DONE WRONG!
Luke 19:5-9

Today's lesson deals with righting the financial wrongs we have done toward others, especially when we know the Holy Spirit has called us to be accountable in every area of our lives, including financial faithfulness. Many believers buy into the fallacy that moving, or changing an address or phone number to avoid paying a bill is favor! In truth, it's dodging responsibility. The gentleman in the text, however, does not try to dodge his financial responsibility. As a matter of fact, when this man meets Christ, he is moved to pay everyone he owes, including those whom he has defrauded. He agrees to pay those individuals four times what he owes! It is not Christ who brings up the subject of repayment. This man's conviction concerning his new relationship with Christ brings about the change.

The Word of God speaks to the issue of owing people. Romans 13:18 says *owe no man any thing, but to love one another: for he that loveth another hath fulfilled the law (KJV)*. The Amplified Translation of the Bible says *keep out of debt and owe no man anything except to love one another.* It is important to manage our debt, so we can pay our bills, and pay them on time. When we fail to pay bills on time, we run the risk of hindering people we owe from coming into the Kingdom. Bad debt – and a bad example – can discourage others and dim our witness. When we fail to pay our debts, it appears to the outside world that we are dishonest and cannot be trusted. Therefore, we have to be mindful of the image that we are painting of the kingdom, the King and the King's kids. We should never want our behavior to be a stumbling block.

Verses 5. And when Jesus came to the place, he looked up, and saw him ...

As we read the text, we see Jesus is passing through the city of Jericho. Verse one introduces us to a rich man named Zacchaeus. This man has heard that Jesus was passing by and he wants to get a glimpse of the Master. Verse two tells us Zacchaeus is the chief tax collector. Therefore, a man of position, possessions and wealth. Zacchaeus is not just a tax collector or a person with a miniscule government job. As the chief tax collector, his position nor his possessions prevent him from wanting to see Jesus. This should speak to the children of God. One of the problems among believers is that wealth, things and the desire to have them can easily get in the way of the pursuit of Christ. This text shows a man who has wealth. Yet, he pressed to see Christ. Things will not consistently satisfy. This is why we need Jesus in our lives.

Because Zacchaeus has the right attitude about meeting Christ despite his wealth and powerful position, he is on track to become even wealthier. We open ourselves to true wealth, when Christ has a place of priority in each of our lives. Out of all of those who were standing, watching and waiting, Jesus looked up into a sycamore tree and noticed the very man, who seemingly was trying the hardest to get a glimpse of Him. Zacchaeus is not trying to be seen – he is trying to see. It is hard to go unnoticed by God, when you are willing to go out of your way to find Him. Zacchaeus does not get the Lord's attention, because he is rich. He gets Christ's attention, because he is willing to go through desperate measures to see the Lord.

... and said unto him, Zacchaeus, make haste, and come down; for today I must abide at thy house.

Isn't it interesting that Jesus knew who Zacchaeus was? Christ knew his name and He knows each of us by name. Jesus tells Zacchaeus to hurry and climb down from the tree, because He is going to visit his home that very day. Can you imagine a rich man with power and position climbing into a tree, because he heard the Christ was going to pass by? Imagine his desperation, as he decided to do whatever it takes – even if it means looking silly – to see the Master. It was not the size of Zacchaeus' house, but his heart that compelled Christ to visit his home. The Master is only impressed with a genuine heart. We can move God to walk anywhere with us, when we have the right heart toward Him. People who make knowing God, meeting God, seeing God, praising God, blessing God and honoring God a priority have a magnet-like spirit that draws God, as He continues to draw people unto Himself. God allows us to walk with Him, as he travels with us.

Verse 6. And he made haste, and came down, and received him joyfully.

We do not know what was on Zacchaeus' schedule that day. After Jesus' announcement, Zacchaeus – without a word of objection – hurried out of the tree to prepare to spend time with the Lord. Modern-day saints act as if God needs to call our secretaries and schedule an appointment to meet with us! We couldn't possibly break our schedules! We are busy people and we've already committed our time. Many saints will not enjoy the time that Zacchaeus had with God, because their schedules are too full. If it were left to many saints, God would not have an appointment until next week sometime. Even then, they'd want to know how much time God would need for this "meeting!"

There are provisions that always come with the Lord's presence. If you are struggling to fully realize those provisions, learn to commit more time in His presence. Time spent preaching, teaching, rehearsing, or having meetings does not qualify. What makes the difference is intimate time spent talking with the Lord and getting to know Him for ourselves. We need to spend more time with the Lord just loving on Him, asking for nothing, but giving Him all of the love, adoration, honor, glory and praise we can muster.

Verse 7. And when they saw it, they all murmured, saying, That he was gone to be guest with a man that is a sinner.

There will always be critics, who place believers in disparaging categories, because of what they perceive was said or done. Nevertheless, it does not matter what people say about you. What is most important is whom they see with you. Christ with you and you with Him – that is what matters most.

Verse 8. And Zacchaeus stood, and said unto the Lord; Behold, Lord, the half of my goods, I give to the poor; and if I have taken any thing from any man by false accusation, I will restore him fourfold.

This is what happens in the life of an individual, who has had a meeting with the Christ. We no longer want to cheat people, steal from people, beat people out of their money, be dishonest about paying people back, or devise ways to take advantage of people. As believers, we have a responsibility to be above board in all of our business dealings. Although, we like to talk about the more apparent sins of others, we must classify the failure to repay others and the lack of financially accountability to God as sin. For these sins, we must repent. According to the biblical record, Christ never told Zacchaeus that he needed to give away his money, as he told the rich young ruler in Matthew chapter 19. Helping the poor ought to be the desire of the people of God. If we say we love God and people, and yet, there is no record that we helped anyone, though we had an ample supply of blessings, that does not speak well of our Christian faith. It is said that giving was a new experience for Zacchaeus, because he was only accustomed to taking. Something happens to a heart that has been touched by Christ. When Christ crosses your path, He stirs within a desire to not always want to be on the receiving end. Christ's influence causes a person to delight in being on the giving end, too!

... Behold, Lord, the half of my goods, I give to the poor ...

Zacchaeus voluntarily gives half of his wealth to the poor. On the whole, modern saints would rather give to people, who do not need it. Then, we ignore or sell to those in need even though they are less fortunate. An individual who has never been moved to give to the poor has never been around God. Such an individual truly does not know God. God cares for and is concerned about the welfare of people. There is very little God in a person who has never lifted a finger to help another. Christ did not ask Zacchaeus to give, nor did He squeeze money from him. Just spending time with the Lord made Zacchaeus decide he had too much not to be a blessing! After one meeting with Christ, Zacchaeus gave away half of what he had.

... and if I have taken any thing from any man by false accusation, I will restore him fourfold.

Simply put, if Christ has not gotten to our pockets it is probably, because we have not allowed Him to reach our hearts. When Christ has reached our hearts, we have no problem blessing someone else. Some would have an easier time comprehending Zacchaeus repaying those people, whom he wronged by overcharging their taxes. But giving half of one's possessions to those in need? This seems unbelievable! Most saints today could not give half their wealth away, let alone give away their wealth and repay those they have wronged! This is why we cause people to wonder, if we have really been with the Lord.

... and if I have taken any thing from any man by false accusation, I will restore him fourfold.

Zacchaeus' office gave him the latitude to be excessive in his extracting of taxes from the Jews. It was rumored in that day that people were being overcharged on their taxes. Though Zacchaeus' curiosity prompted him to climb into a tree and above the crowd to see the Lord, his decision to repay those he wronged moved him to a higher place in righteousness. The law of the day mandated that anyone found guilty, by the court of wrongdoing, would pay four times as much as was defrauded. The law also stated that if a person – outside of the court – confessed to defrauding someone, the guilty party could simply restore what was taken and tack 20 percent interest to the amount. Zacchaeus penalized himself more harshly than the law required. It is indicative of a child of God, who has wronged someone to not only offer restitution, but also help the person who has been hurt financially to become better than he or she was before meeting a believer. If this lesson is hard to grasp, it might mean that you could benefit from more meetings with the Lord! Defrauding, taking advantage of others, cheating and borrowing with no intent to return is difficult, and I dare say, painful, for those who have truly been touched by Christ. The amount of money Zacchaeus is willing to give up and then repay demonstrates his remorse for the role he has played in taking advantage of others.

Verse 9. And Jesus said unto him, This day is salvation come to this house, forasmuch as he also is a son of Abraham.

Jesus, Himself, acknowledges that this man has experienced the salvation of God. Jesus says the change is evident in the way Zacchaeus is handling the money in his possession. I pray that the saints will always desire to be above board, when it comes to being trusted by others. Never make a financial commitment you are unsure you will be able to keep. It is more important to be honorable than it is to amass money. Money will always come to those who are honorable. However, if it is your aim to obtain money without honor, chances are your ability to acquire that wealth soon will run out. Zacchaeus should not be the last believer, who chooses not to defraud others. He should not be the last who is willing to give to the poor and offer restitution for the wrongs he has done. When Zacchaeus left with Jesus, the people were calling him a sinner. When he emerges from his home after spending time with the Lord, people had to admit something wonderful happened in his life! We are the children of the faithful – Abraham!

LESSON 32

MY PROSPERITY MAY BE HIDDEN IN MY PRAYER!
Job 42:7–13

This lesson focuses on God's ability to restore to prosperity those among His people, who once were thriving, but by misfortune or an attack of the enemy fell into hardship or lack. Loving the Lord and being called according to His purpose does not preclude believers from hard times, dark days and problems. The life of Job teaches us to never lose faith, never give up our integrity, and never allow our circumstances to change how we see our Creator. Through his struggles, Job shows us that even in our suffering we must watch what we say; surround ourselves with compassionate Christians; worship even when we do not know why bad things are happening; and last of all, forgive friends who have hurt us.

In the two opening chapters of the book of Job, we watch a very successful and prosperous man lose 7,000 sheep, 3,000 camels, 500 yoke of oxen, 500 female donkeys, most of his servants, all 10 of his children and his health. As we look at the life struggles of Job, we also learn there is nothing that we cannot live without – except GOD! No individual is ready to live with anything he or she cannot live without – except GOD! Even when a child of God is stripped to nothing, his or her life is still worth living, because of God. Things do not make life worth living. A relationship with the Lord is what truly makes life worth living.

This lesson will show that there also are hindrances to the believers' prosperity. Though waste, mismanagement, unwise spending, and a lack of financial restraint can be hindrances to prosperity, Job discovers unforgiveness can stop the flow of blessings in each of our lives.

Verse 7. And it was so, that after the Lord had spoken these words unto Job, the Lord said to Eliphaz the Temanite, my wrath is kindled against thee, and against thy two friends: for you have not spoken of me the thing that is right, as my servant Job hath.

In the last chapter of the book of Job, God finally speaks directly to those among Job's friends who have been speaking, so fluidly and frequently on His behalf. After listening to the words of Job's friends, one would think that they have a direct pipeline to God! If God is offended by the unrighteous talk of Job's circle of friends, surely He is livid with us over the sin of our mouths. Believers must acknowledge we can sin with our mouths, just as easily as we can sin with our hands. God brings an indictment against the friends of Job: Unlike Job, they do not speak the things of God.

... my wrath is kindled against thee, and against thy two friends...

God's wrath, or anger, has been stoked, because of these three. Believers must never crush people, when they are down, out or up! Saints should not spend their time giving unwise and unauthorized commentary about the lives of others. God's anger burns against those, who hurt others with harsh, cruel, judgmental, mean-spirited and unkind comments. God calls the other two men friends of Eliphaz. Notice that not one is called a friend of God or a friend of Job. This ill-speaking trio almost managed to do what Satan and Job's wife could not: to break Job's spirit and frustrate his faith in God through negative words.

Verse 8. Therefore take unto you now seven bullocks and seven rams, and go to my servant Job, and offer up for yourselves a burnt offering; and my servant Job shall pray for you: for him will I accept: lest I deal with you after your folly, in that ye have not spoken of me the thing which is right, like my servant Job.

God instructs the trio to take seven bulls and seven rams to Job's home and offer them, as a sacrificial offering for their sins. Seven is the number for divine completion. If Job's three friends are going to completely repent and obtain complete forgiveness for running their mouths, sinning against God and crushing Job's confidence in God, they must offer the bulls and the rams at Job's home – not at the temple or a church. This offering has to be done the way God requires it. The Lord says Job then will act as priest, praying over them and their offering, so they might be forgiven.

... for him will I accept ...

Sins can block the flow of God's blessings. If we are going to unstop the blockage, we must be willing to pay the price and give an offering of repentance. This is the essence of a burnt offering. It is an offering, gift or price a person paid in that day for their sins to be forgiven. And though Christ has come and died on Calvary, there are times that God still requires the equivalent of a burnt offering. It would behoove the people of God, in an effort to experience the full freedom of the forgiveness of God, to make a sacrifice.

Verse 9. So Eliphaz the Temanite and Bildad the Shuhite and Zophar the Naamathite went, and did according as the Lord commanded them: the Lord also accepted Job.

People who want to walk in the fullness of God also must be willing to do all that God has commanded. It is apparent that these three men realized God was sincere in His anger. Therefore, they had no desire for God to deal with them according to their foolish ways. Job's three friends did exactly as the Lord required, turning Job's home into a sanctuary and Job himself into their priest.

Many times, we are not as blessed as we should be, because things around us are out of order. However, they are fully in our control to set in order. These three men did as the Lord commanded. Fulfilling God's command had to be tough for these three. Not long ago, they were accusing Job of suffering, as a result of some secret sin. They declared that God would never allow a righteous person to suffer so horribly. Now, the very person they talked about has become the very person they need to get deliverance. Job prayed for them and the Lord accepted Job's prayer on behalf of his friends.

Verse 10. And the Lord turned the captivity of Job, when he prayed for his friends ...

The hidden truth behind Job's breakthrough is that it came not when Job prayed for himself, but rather when he prayed for those who had hurt him! Their deliverance broke the grip of sickness and poverty in Job's life! Job implored God for His friends even though he was hurting. It was understood that God would only hear the prayer of Job on his friends' behalf. If Job could not move God to have mercy upon them, most assuredly their menu their menu would consist entirely of misery..

Consider this question: What would have happened, if Job had been too hurt to pray for those who hurt him? If Job did not pray for the friends whose words almost crushed him, they would not have received their deliverance. If these three friends were not delivered, Job would not have received his breakthrough. Job's breakthrough was tied up in their deliverance, and their deliverance was tied up in Job's prayer! While Job was praying for them, God was turning things around for him! We do not always know the importance of our prayers, nor do we always get to see how our prayers are affecting the chain of events in our lives. It is not always when we pray for ourselves that we see the salvation of the Lord. If you really want to see God working things out for your good, love God enough to release people from their mistakes and trespasses. Love God enough to pray for the naysayers, as if they were still the best of friends.

In this text, we see that God brought restoration to every area in which Job was bound – financially, emotionally, spiritually, socially, physically, politically, and mentally. Job may never have fathomed that his prayer of forgiveness would matter so much that it would cause God to turn things around so suddenly for him. The unwillingness to forgive can be a blockage to blessings no matter how faithful, spiritual and credible we may be. No matter how badly we want our blessings, the lack of forgiveness will not allow them to flow freely to us. When Job sincerely and fervently prayed for the folks who hurt him, Job opened the airway for blessings to flow again to his house. The saints must live a life with no grudges, bitterness, hatred, unforgiveness or unrelinquished pain, especially if we want all the blessings that God has for us.

... also the Lord gave Job twice as much as he had before.

Not only did God turn things around for Job and bless him, but Job also received DOUBLE for all of his TROUBLE! Rather than complaining about our troubles, we should speak double! God would double ours, if we could handle it! God gave Job double, because Job has shown that he could be faithful with much or with little, and that he could worship no matter how much he has. This was not some return on an earthly investment. The text teaches that *the Lord gave Job twice as much as he had before.* If people thought Job was wealthy the first time around, just look at him now! God does not just fill Job's cup to the brim; He gives Job new cups and fills each of them up until they run over! This is why we should never underestimate God and His faithfulness to come through for us. God is not slack concerning His promises and He does not delay, nor is God slow to act. God is extraordinarily patient with us and He does not want any of us to perish. He wants all to come to repentance.

When Job prayed – as requested by his friends and required by God – Job opened up something in the heavens! We too will open up the heavens, when we willingly obey, forgive and pray for former friends from whom we have separated, because of injury. Let me reiterate: Job does not get a breakthrough because, he prays for himself. It only comes when he prays for his friends. Open up new doors of mercy and new windows of heaven, by praying fervently, faithfully and frequently for those who have hurt you.

Verse 11. Then came there unto him all his brethren, and all his sisters, and all that had been of his acquaintance before, and did eat bread with him in his house: and they bemoaned him, and comforted him over all the evil that the Lord had brought upon him: every man also gave him a piece of money, and every one an earring of gold.

The text does not reveal that Job has brothers and sisters until we read of him praying for his friends. When Job prayed for his friends, God released everything good and perfect, as gifts unto him. Unforgiveness not only blocks the flow of financial resources, but it also blocks the flow of family, friends and others, who would potentially bless us. Look at the text. People are showing up from everywhere! When God turned the captivity of Job, everything turned for the good! Just look at the atmosphere. Family and friends are at Job's house and they are eating and fellowshipping. Light and life have returned to Job's house!

... and did eat bread with him in his house ...

Job has his appetite back again. God can restore everything! God will restore everything! God is restoring everything! New excitement is in Job's house and in his life. That is the beauty of waiting upon the Lord. He will and He is lifting our heads again! The very man who talked about dying is eating! He wants to live again! Never allow hard times and the dark days to break your spirit and cause you to want to give up on life and give up on God! Job's family and acquaintances show up in chapter 42 and they do for him what his original friends were never able to do. They sympathized with him and they comforted him. Job's greatest comfort, however, came from the hand of God moving in unbelievable ways in his life. Not only did the Lord bless him, but the Lord also touched the hearts of all the people, who came to see about him.

Verse 12. So the Lord blessed the latter end of Job more than his beginning: for he had fourteen thousand sheep, six thousand camels, a thousand yoke of oxen, and a thousand she asses.

The Word shares that the latter shall be greater and we see this happening in the life of Job. Many were impressed with all that God gave him in the first chapter. Now to see that everything has doubled for Job – it's breathtaking! We do not know how the

Lord is going to bless us, nor do we know all the great things the Lord is doing for us right now. We shall reap, if we do not faint, get tired, get weary or give up! Some might wonder why God would God give Job so much more in the latter days. The answer from the Lord is that Job has proven he can handle the blessings! My prayer is that all believers grow in the Lord, so much so that all will be able to handle the blessings He wants to bestow upon his people. There are many, who are always looking backward. For the children of the Most High God who do not allow the spirit of a grudge or unforgiveness to linger, God has more in store! The faith of the saints must be rooted in the knowledge that God can and God will. The latter will be greater than the former!

Verse 13. He also had seven sons and three daughters.

God gives Job new life and allows him to experience new and unexpected blessings. The 10 children of Job who die in the first chapter appear to have been of adult age. Though some may have never expected Job to have more children, chapter 42 brings new life, new blessings and new opportunities. Are you open to living again? Sometimes, tragedies come in our lives and we begin to think that the best days are behind us. I encourage you to believe you have not begun to see your best days! Live through your setbacks and your disappointments and know that the latter shall be greater than the former, because the Lord said it!

LESSON 33

MAKING IT THROUGH A FAMINE!
1 King 17:8-16

Today's lesson is about posturing yourself to succeed during seasons of scarcity. It is not always God's desire that we go through famines, but it is always God's will that we *grow* through the famines that we face in life. The Word of God has many examples and recorded testimonies of people, who learned to live through tough times and became the better, because of what they went through. Not every believer will be exempted from the harsh realities of living through poverty, famines, scarcity, droughts and hard times. Just as the widow woman in this lesson discovers, there are things that we would never know the Lord could do had he not allowed us to go and grow through trials. God does not want His people to live in famine; He wants them to live through famine! In doing so, we learn that God is faithful and we should never be afraid to sow in seasons of scarcity.

At this point in history, we as Americans have found ourselves closer to a famine than we have been in a while. No matter whether the economist label it –a recession, an economic slowdown or financial bailout – we are called to go and grow through these difficult financial times. However, this is not the time to decide to rob God or be stingy toward Him. This is the time to hear God's voice and completely respond to God's commands.

Verse 8 & 9. And the word of the Lord came unto him, saying. Arise, get thee to Zarephath, which belongeth to Zidon, and dwell there: behold, I have commanded a widow woman there to sustain thee.

At the time of the text, everyone is going through the famine. There has been neither rain nor dew for a long period of time. Though Elijah is the prophet of God, he too has to go and grow through the famine. God tells Elijah his next step is to go to Zarephath and remain there. God has spoken to a widow woman there and commanded that she sustain the man of God.

One key to living successfully in and through a famine is having the determination to live a purposeful and pointed life. Many of the decisions we make are made with no consideration or real purpose in mind. In a famine, one cannot afford to waste anything, including money, resources, time, opportunities, relationships and strategy. Living a pointed life means to live life with divine direction. We should not simply exist, without a goal in sight. We need to be headed in the direction that the Lord is sending us. Many saints are wasting gas and time in relationships with people, who will not help, on the road to destiny. God gives Elijah specific directions, as to where he is to go. Only when we consistently trust in the Lord and do not lean on what we think will God direct our paths. This is not the season for guessing. We need the guidance of the Holy Ghost. When we follow the directions of the divine, we find stability even in seasons of scarcity. Elijah will not want or lack, even in this season. The Lord is leading him, as shepherd leads his sheep. We must pray for direction on how to spend, shop, sow and save.

Verse 10. So he arose and went to Zarephath. And when he came to the gate of the city, behold the widow woman was there gathering of sticks: and he called to her, and said, Fetch me, I pray thee, a little water in a vessel, that I may drink.

Without any recorded doubt, hesitation or delay, Elijah shifted in the direction of the divine. As the Lord said, the widow woman to whom he is sent is at the gate of the city. The famine had taken its toll on the poor widow. Elijah found her gathering sticks to build a fire, in order to cook her last meal. Sometimes, our faith is not ready to run with the plans of God. It's at those moments that God will give our faith the jumpstart it needs to get us going. Have you ever dealt with a stick shift vehicle that wouldn't start? More than likely, all it needed was a good jumpstart. Elijah asked the widow woman for some water. This was her jumpstart. Elijah ignited her faith by asking her to do what her faith could handle. Sometimes, the things God asks of us are just a fraction of what He wants from us, but if He can get our faith rolling, we ultimately discover that God has much more in store! Sometimes, God will ask or compel us to give a certain amount in the offering. This nudging is just a jumpstart to stir up our faith and get us on track with God. Do not ignore these opportunities, especially when you know it is the Lord, who is speaking to you about giving.

Verse 11. As she was going to fetch it he called to her, and said, Bring me, I pray thee, a morsel of bread in thine hand.

The man of God is now requiring more of her faith. It did not take much faith to give the man of God water, but now he is asking for something that she does not have much of – bread! For the purpose of teaching, bread in this text could refer to money, sustenance, material possessions, food, clothing, shelter or anything needed for human survival. What is your response to God when He asks you to give what you seemingly do not have enough of? The man of God took the formalities out of the request, by telling the widow that the bread does not have to be on a plate or in a dish. He instructed her to simply put the bread in her hands and bring it to him.

The text raises a poignant question: Whose hands are holding your bread? We have got to get our bread – money, sustenance and material possessions – out of our hands and into the hands of the Lord. God has sent the prophet, by the widow woman's home to expose the true location of her bread. It is easy to say that you trust in the Lord, but do your actions confirm that profession? Where is your bread? The widow's husband is dead; therefore, she is the sole provider for her household. Nevertheless, if she works her faith and feeds the man of God, her bread will move from her hands, through the hands of the man of God, and into the hands of the Lord. This is the best place for all of our provisions. Our spirits much be challenged to tithe, sow and give sacrificially to the Lord. Our bread belongs in the hands of the Lord.

Verse 12. And she said, As the Lord thy God liveth, I have not a cake, but a handful of meal in a barrel, and a little oil in a cruse…

The widow woman tells the man of God that she does not have a loaf baked in the house. One of the enemy's tactics against believers in the household of faith is to cloud our reception, so that we hear more being asked of us than really was requested. God does not want her entire loaf, and neither does the man of God. Elijah is asking that she share what she has. The enemy of our faith wants us to believe that what is asked of us is too great, but God never asks for more than what He has given us. God never asks for more than what we have the ability to do.

…and behold, I am gathering two sticks, that I might go in and dress it for me and my son, that we may eat it, and die.

The widow woman was too desperate to deny the Lord's request. Many believers today face that same desperation. She needed God to move in mercy on her behalf, and so do we! If she did not heed the Lord's direction and give to the man of God, she and her son would have eaten their last supper. There are times when we reach the end of our ropes. Here, we conclude that we might as well go with God and trust what He says, because what we have is not enough to sustain us. What the widow had was not enough to live on but just enough to die with! Unless, we are ready to face death, we must learn what we can live without. Here, the widow woman is talking about dying. Yet, God has sent Elijah, so that she and her son can live! We have got to learn how to live, and living starts with giving the Lord whatever He wills, wants, demands or desires! Though the widow thought she and her son were about to die, God was about to teach her how to grow in a famine.

Verse 13. And Elijah said unto her, Fear not; go and do as thou hast said: but make thereof a little cake first, and bring it unto me, and after make for thee and for thy son.

To the carnal mind, the prophet's request may seem extremely selfish. The widow woman has told Elijah her financial condition. In spite of this, he still wants her to make him something to eat! It's this type of seemingly, self-serving request that prompts people to speak badly of a preacher or parishioner in the barbershop or beauty salon. Immature saints would say that Elijah is taking advantage of the woman and looking out for himself – not the widow and her son. The truth is the man of God is acting in her best interest, by not letting her off the hook with a feeble excuse of not having much. People who let us off the hook of our Christian responsibilities to God are not doing us a favor. All the woman really had was a seed. It was Elijah's responsibility not to allow the woman to eat her seed and die! She was about to kill herself and her future. She had to sow the seed to save her and her seed's seed (to save the future generations). How often are we eating seed that could save us and our future generations?

…and Elijah said unto her, fear not…

The prophet tells the widow to take control of her fear. She has to stop fearing the famine and being too scared to trust God in her scarcity. We all need godly people in our lives who will not allow us to be afraid to take God at His word, when times are tough. Fear can be arresting. It can stop us in our tracks. Therefore, we must overcome all fear that inhibits us from relying upon God and His faithfulness.

...but make thereof a little cake first, and bring it unto me...

Elijah tells the widow that she can make all the plans she desires for herself and her son, but first thing's first – she must tend to the man of God. In verse 9, the widow woman was commanded to sustain the man of God. Therefore, Elijah is not asking her to do anything that God had not already spoken with her about! God knew her financial condition. Sending the man of God was not intended to be a burden, but a blessing. We will not see God's blessings until we learn to live with a gracious spirit, and get out of our minds and spirits the notion that giving is a burden. The man of God was only telling the widow to do what God has already instructed her to do FIRST! The way to make it in a famine is to do what we know the Lord has commanded us to do.

Verse 14. For thus saith the Lord God of Israel, the barrel of meal shall not waste, neither shall the cruse of oil fail, until the day that the Lord sendeth rain upon the earth.

The Word that God sends to the widow woman is that what you have will not fail you, nor will it run out, if you do not waste the meal and the oil on satisfying only your own appetite. We run out of bread, because we waste it all on ourselves. Any bread belonging to the Lord that we choose to use to satisfy our own greed is wasted bread. That kind of consumption may fill us up for a moment, but it will not last a season. The saints have got to take a stand – NO MORE WASTED BREAD! That which belongs to the Lord must go to the Lord. That which the widow woman thinks will be her last meal will *last,* until God sends down rain or new provisions – if she obeys the man of God. We must rest in the assurance that what most people think is our last will last throughout the duration of a famine, because we honored the Lord!

Verse 15. And she went and did according to the saying of Elijah: and she, and he, and her house, did eat many days.

Elijah's arrival was not a burden, but a blessing, because Elijah brought the blessings of God with him. When the widow woman met Elijah she was gathering sticks to make a fire and cook her last meal. However, because she obeyed God's voice and put God first, God worked a miracle, so that there was more than enough for the widow woman and her son. She could feed the man of God and still have enough for many days! When we keep the bread in our hands, we opt out of the miracle-working plans of God. God's blessings will blow the minds of those, who make Him a priority. Victory is not just about saying it. It's also about consistently doing it, and doing it with a happy heart!

Verse 16. And the barrel of meal wasted not, neither did the cruse of oil fail, according to the word of the Lord, which he spake by Elijah.

This text first attests to the fact that God does put His word in the mouths of men and woman and, secondly, that it is crucial to have a close connection to God so that we can discern between the word of man and the Word of the Lord. In whatever manner God chooses to send His Word, we must commit to doing something with it. Everything that God said to the prophet and to the widow woman came to fruition. The widow woman did not get to see the full manifestation of the Word of God, until the famine was over. It is believed that God never filled the barrel, but every time she turned the barrel up for meal, there was always enough to make a meal. While she had the barrel tipped to pour meal out of the top, God was shooting more meal in the barrel from the bottom! The potential of the barrel did not fail, because the widow walked in faith. She never would have known how much meal was in the barrel, if she had not obeyed. There was more potential in that barrel than she could see, when the prophet first asked for a little bread from her hand. When she was willing, gave graciously and with purpose, the widow found out that God had more in store for her! God will provide your bread!

We've wasted meal, because we would not give unto the Lord, and, therefore, missed the opportunity to see what God was willing to do. We waste meal, when we don't live by faith. God has set aside meal for us, but we never gain access to it, because we fail to trust God enough to give in seasons of uncertainty. God never reveals the full provision He has for us, thus the need to live by faith! The cruse of oil never ran out. God does things that we cannot explain. Oftentimes, He requires a certain measure of faith on our part in order for us to grasp His mysteries. The amazing thing is that unbeknownst to us, God is keeping oil in the cruse and meal in the barrel! God does things in such a great manner that we often do not notice them, until He reveals them unto us. We should want meal that we did not buy with money, but rather acquired with faith. We should want to taste the meal that the Master makes and provides for believers who are willing to trust Him – even in the tough times. The text does not directly speak to it, but I believe we can surmise that the meal lasted long after Elijah left the widow's home. The meal did not run out, until it rained. When the man of God left the house, the Lord kept on providing! The Lord will make a way somehow, and He wants His people to receive it, believe it and achieve it.

LESSON 34

GIVING THAT COMES BACK WHEN IT LOOKS LIKE IT'S ONLY GOING OUT!
Ecclesiastes 11:1-6

This lesson focuses on the necessity of giving, sharing, being benevolent and sowing. This passage of scripture assures the children of God that whatever kindness, money, help, support or love we measure in the name of the Lord has a way of coming back to us – guaranteed! Not everything we give comes back in the same form in which it was given. Moreover, no one will ever give in the perfect spirit of Christ or to the degree of purity in His motive, which was and is genuine love. There are times in the life of every believer when he or she is discouraged in the area of giving, because of a lack of gratitude shown by the recipient. Many times in life, people fail to show appreciation for the sacrifices you make. As children of God, we must hold on to the knowledge that our genuine gifts will never go unnoticed by God, nor will they go unrewarded by the Father of Light, in whom there is no variableness or signs of changing.

A heart to help, a spirit to sow and a will to give are included among the attributes or characteristics we as believers inherit from our Heavenly Father. We should give without expecting anything in return from the recipients of our gifts. We should never give without expecting something great in return from the Father. This lesson highlights the fact that God always has a way of returning favor to people, who are willing to extend favor to others. God treats every gift given from our hearts to bless others as an investment, which means there is always, at the very least, a divine return on the money we give and the seeds of kindness that we plant. Even in instances in which people borrow from us and never pay us back, if we give or loan to others out of our love for God, He makes sure that in His own way and in His own time we never lose for loving in the same manner that He loves.

During tough economic times, benevolence is often a challenge. If we can look out for others who may be less fortunate than we are, we will find out the Lord will look out for us! Too many children of God are living so high on the hog that they struggle to care or commit help to anyone but themselves! When the saints are in the midst of recession, it is important to be content with living frugally and with more self-control. When we are judicious with finances in tough economic times, we afford ourselves more room for benevolence. Living on less might mean washing your own car; being conscious of wasteful spending, such as exceeding the minute limits on your cellular phone, or allowing the children to over-text on their phones; reining in the eating out; buying big-ticket items, such as televisions and cars when the old ones work just fine; and gambling on the lottery with money you can't really afford to lose.

Verse 1. Cast thy bread upon the waters: for thou shalt find it after many days.

Some people don't know what to do with money, and then there are others who know only to spend money, and spend it in areas that bring no return or lasting value. We must move from bad money management, wasteful spending and the unwise handling of money with which we have been entrusted.

The book of Ecclesiastes was written by Solomon, the son of David and Bathsheba, and it is believed, the wisest man to have ever lived. In this passage, Solomon tells us that God admonishes us to cast our bread – our money and resources – on the water. When we share with others, who are going through tough times, we are making an investment in our own future. Never look at your giving as a waste. People, who give liberally to help meet the needs of the misfortunate, will always get a God return on the seeds that were sown. A God return is much greater than a good return! It must be noted that we might not see the return on our benevolence the same day we sow our seeds. This lapse in time is a problem for many saints. Most would not mind giving or helping others out, if they could see the great return within a couple of days! The text reads *for thou shalt find it after many days.* A God return on the help we give is guaranteed! Never be afraid to trust in God's promise that as we help others He is going to make sure that He helps us.

We have established that God is gracious to those, who are gracious to the poor, the helpless, the widow, the orphan, the stranger, the needy and the down and out. There will always be tricksters who prey upon the compassion of the saints, but that should never deter us from mirroring the love of God. God will bless those, who cast their bread on the waters, even if they were deceived. The New Living Translation says *"send your grain across the seas, and in time, profits will flow back to you."* One's ability to say to God, "I believe that these seeds that I have sown will be an investment in me, my family and my future," is an indicator of maturity in the household of faith!

Though America has its seasons of economic uncertainty, we must admit that many Americans would not trade places with many of those, who live in third world countries. Though poverty exists in America, it is not the level of poverty we see in places such as Africa, India and Haiti. Many people are familiar with the expression "Charity starts at home." The Body of Christ indeed should show love at home to the least, the last and the left out, but we also should let that love spread to foreign lands. The church should want to give in such a way that compels God to add something special to the bread that returns to us, even if it's just a little butter!

Verse 2. Give a portion to seven, and also to eight; for thou knowest not what evil shall be upon the earth.

Wise benevolence is akin to diversifying investments, within a stock market. Those who invest in stock are taught not to put everything in one stock. By taking that precaution, in the event that the stock drops considerably, the investor will not lose all of his or her money. Believers also must diversify their investments into the lives of those, who are hurting. Some people want to be the sole beneficiary of a person's benevolence. We should help people, but not cripple them. When our giving paralyzes individuals from trying – with the grace of God – to get on their feet, our help has become a hindrance. When people stop looking to God and look only to us to help them get out of the mess that they are in, our help has become a hindrance. Solomon advises us to spread out our charity. The help you offer to a person in need should give him or her enough lift to get up and move forward. Giving the right amount of help, without habitually enabling, allow you to move on and help someone else.

Furthermore, Jesus himself teaches about the value of going the second mile. However, when people expect us to carry them so far that the second mile turns into 20 miles, it's likely time to spread the generosity elsewhere. The New Living Translation says *"But divide your investments among many places, for you don't know what risks might lie ahead."* This is why many believers donate to charitable organizations, giving beyond the tithe, talent and time they give to a local church. The Boys & Girls Clubs of America, the United Way, the National Association for the Advancement of Colored People (NAACP) and countless others are worthy of support. Nonprofit organizations care for specific needs, within the community and the world. When we cast our bread on the waters and diversify our giving through philanthropy, we help nonprofit organizations to be a blessing to people in dire need. The Word of God calls contributions to these types of groups an INVESTMENT! The best day on the stock market could not reward us as the Lord does, when we cast our bread on the waters.

Verse 3. If the clouds be full of rain, they empty themselves upon the earth; and if the tree fall toward the south, or toward the north, in the place where the tree falleth, there it shall be.

There are some things in life that we can be sure of, and one of them is that when the clouds are heavy, rain will fall. People, who have studied the weather, can look up at the clouds and determine if rain will fall. Most amateur cloud-watchers can announce it is going to rain only, when the water is literally about to drop on their heads! We expect a tree that has fallen to stay where it lands. No one is shocked, when the tree does not periodically move around and then return to its resting place. And neither should we be shocked about receiving a God-sized return, when we invest or sow into those who are poor, aging, hurting or helpless, or give to agencies that specialize in helping others. There are some things we simply should know about extending kindness that reflects our Creator. One way or another, kindness always comes back to the sender. Giving and extending God's love through giving is like a boomerang. If you release it, it will come back to you – so expect it!

Verse 4. He that observeth the wind shall not sow; and he that regardeth the clouds shall not reap.

Simply stated, we've just got to do it! We cannot always wait for the perfect time to give or to sow, because more than likely, the perfect time will never present itself. To that end, we must realize the perfect opportunity to sow is when God moves on our hearts, and not when we have a certain amount of money. The perfect opportunity arises when God speaks to us and tells us to obey – and we know it is His voice! The perfect time to share and sow into the lives of others is when God opens a window of opportunity and, through His peace, we receive the green light to proceed! We as believers can all admit that we have missed great opportunities to be a blessing and be blessed in return, because we *"observed the wind or regarded the clouds."* God often lists all the reasons we should help, be kind or be benevolent. We in turn look at all the reasons why we cannot at that time. The Amplified Translation of the Bible says *"he who observes the wind [and waits for all conditions to be favorable] will not sow, and he who regards the clouds will not reap."* There always will be a reason to say "Not now. Not today." There always will be something else that *needs* to be done first. The key is to realize there probably will never be a perfect time, but there is always a perfect opportunity to do good unto others. Again, the perfect opportunity is when the Holy Spirit moves you to get involved, to give, or to do your part.

The New Living Translation of the Bible states: *"Farmers who wait for perfect weather never plant, and if they watch every cloud, they never harvest."* Can you imagine a farmer waiting on perfect weather to plant? If a farmer had to wait for perfect weather, seeds would never be planted! A farmer could start planting in the morning, and because of extenuating circumstances, have to stop later in the day. The efficient farmer looks for the moment, when he can get back into the field, whether it is later that evening or early the next morning. Then, there are times when the farmer just has to plant in the midst of imperfect weather. Oftentimes, we are not as determined as the farmer. We fail to realize everything is riding on us having seeds sown in the field. The farmer is determined to plant the seeds, because he knows the harvest is contingent upon the seeds being in the soil – not in the sack. The modern church has got to get its seeds out of the sack and properly sown into the soil of what our Master said! We have got to stop making excuses and make it happen!

Verse 5. As thou knowest not what is the way of the spirit, nor how the bones do grow in the womb of her that is with child: even so thou knowest not the works of God who maketh all.

There are some things we just have to leave up to the Lord. We must commit to do our part, and then trust God to do his part. It is not our job to figure out how we are going to reap. It is our job to sow seeds and expect a harvest. Many times, believers do not support the church or its ministries, because they cannot see how giving will directly benefit them. We do not know how the Spirit of God is moving. Therefore, we have to get out of the way of the Spirit, by no longer living in doubt and disbelief. We have got to live a faith life and walk step by step in faith. Just as a baby's bones form in a mother's womb and neither she nor the father understand how they grow, we do not know the manner in which God will bless us for being financially faithful to the cause of the kingdom. We should, however, know that somehow He will make it happen! Most parents do not ask that God help them understand how the bones of a newborn grew in the womb. The parents simply learn to enjoy the blessing of a baby.

Verse 6. In the morning sow thy seed, and in the evening withhold not thine hand: for thou knowest not whether shall prosper, either this or that, or whether both shall be alike good.

It is critical to learn the necessity of generosity early in life. As we grow, we learn not to be hesitant to do good. We should teach our children not to spend everything on themselves, but to always be mindful of God and their responsibility to others.

LESSON 35

"FACING MY FINANCIAL FAILURES!"
Luke 15:12-20

This lesson addresses the importance of financial responsibility and sets forth the steps we as believers should take to set things in order when we have been financially irresponsible. The children of God operate in an earthly economy, and unlike the convenience of a weather forecast, we do not get a forecast for the daily or weekly financial climate. Oftentimes, we spend and make crucial decisions about saving – or not saving – without any consideration or information based on a financial forecast. Financial immaturity can be detrimental – and almost fatal – when we spend with the belief that we will always have more money than we will ever need. Effective money management prepares us for the lean years in life, and also can help us have more than enough to meet our needs – and the needs of others – during the lean years. As we examine the issue of financial responsibility through the well-known story of the prodigal son and it is told by Jesus, consider this question: Who is the person in your life who provides you with a candid financial forecast and helps you to see the best way to handle your money?

Verse 12. And the younger of them said to his father, Father, give me the portion of goods that falleth to me. And he divided unto them his living.

The younger son approaches his father and asks for the inheritance he would receive, when his father dies. Through his request, the young man conveys that he does not want to wait until the death of his father to get his share of his father's wealth; he wants to get his now and handle it the way he chooses. This text is a classical example of an individual who has money, but possesses neither money management skills nor wisdom on how to spend wealth wisely. Money is like a powerful and fast-moving car – it can get away from you if you are not careful.

So often, we are like the son in this text. We want more than we are really ready to handle. The father honors his son's request, and actually gives him more than what he deserves under normal circumstances. As was custom after the death of a father, the oldest son would receive two-thirds of the total of the father's wealth. The younger son would receive one-third of the father's total inheritance. But this father evenly divided his wealth and gave one portion to his son – an action that could have negatively affected the whole household. The younger son, whether ignorant of the potential repercussions of his request or indifferent toward them, shows he was only looking out for what he wanted.

When dealing with wealth and increasing or maintaining wealth, what we want is not always what's most important. Decisions have to be made based on what is best. If we make financial decisions based on what we want and not what is best, we risk putting a lot of people in danger! The father, the eldest son and the servants are at a greater danger, because of the younger son's desire to satisfy his wants rather than considering the greater good. We must always remind ourselves that what may be OK for now may not for the best later, and whatever is not best later is not OK for now. When making decisions about wealth, we must always consider more than ourselves. There are too many people who could be affected by our decisions for us to make choices about debt and income solely based on our own desires.

Verse 13. And not many days after the younger son gathered all together, and took his journey into a far country, and there wasted his substance with riotous living.

As soon as this young man received his portion of the father's fortune, he moved as far away as he could from anyone who would pull his son strings. The son moved away from direction, discretion and discipline. Many times, we move away from the voice of reason and restraint, especially when we have money and we want to do our own thing. The young man attempted to flee from the very one God had used to accumulate wealth and build an inheritance that could later be bestowed upon him and his brother. It appears that the father was in tune to the financial forecast, because the son had more than enough to last for a lifetime. Furthermore, the father had invested and acquired enough to last even into the next generation of his two sons! The father knew how to make money. When the son got his hands on the money his father made, he moved away from the one with the wisdom. He also surrounded himself with people who had no knowledge of how to make money. What they did know was how to spend it. There are people who have excellent salaries and excellent jobs at some of the finest companies in America. Many of those people are struggling just as badly as the person who is working a minimum wage job. It's been said that "It ain't what you make but what you do with what you make." Without his father's influence to guide him, the son lives – almost to his detriment – without restraint.

... and there wasted his substance with riotous living.

The son did nothing with the money he received from his father. The young man could not blame his money trouble on investments not coming through; he wasted it! He could not blame his financial trouble on money loaned, but not repaid. Scripture says he wasted it! It is a bad feeling to know that one is broke without cause for it. This young man could not blame anyone. He brought the trouble upon himself. He spent his money recklessly, loosely and without self-control. Just as it takes bad direction to get into bad debt, it will take good direction to get out. Most saints followed a poor path that led to poverty or a lack of prosperity. Believers must become fully persuaded to find a path that leads to prosperity.

Verse 14. And when he had spent all, there arose a mighty famine in that land, and he began to be in want.

Want always follows waste, and everyone who wastes will soon find himself or herself in want. The son spent all that he had. He did not save anything for a rainy day. It is important for parents to teach children how to manage money, and it is also important for children to have a teachable spirit and a willingness to learn how to be wise with monetary wealth. This is one of those seasons, in which, parents are forced to teach children about budgeting and paying bills. Some parents believe they are obligated to buy children all that they want and claim they need. Some wants are disguised as needs. It is imperative to know the difference.

We must be especially careful, when it comes to giving. Christmas during lean years is not the time to try and convince others you are not struggling. When it's time to tighten the belt and make smarter financial decisions, children must hear the truth. If the credit cards are maxed out and minimum payments are a struggle each month, it's all right to say, "We're not pulling names for gifts this year." Some families can hardly pay the light bill, and yet they feel cheated out of Christmas if gifts – many of which are unnecessary – are not exchanged. There are people today who find themselves in the same place, or one step behind, the reckless son. The manner in which you handle Thanksgiving, Christmas, or any occasion in which giving is expected may be a harbinger of whether your next step is the hog pen – so be careful!

Verse 15. And he went and joined himself to a citizen of that country; and he sent him into the fields to feed swine.

When we waste what we will really need, we find ourselves doing things we never would have done had we not made such bad decisions earlier. In order to make a dollar, get the rent paid, keep the lights on, or live a certain lifestyle, many people connect with people they never would have before. Hard times often unite strange bedfellows. Don't put yourself in a position in which you are forced to engage people who go against everything that you believe.

Jews did not touch or eat swine. Their convictions would not allow them to have anything to do with pork. Because the son squandered the wealth he received from his father, he put himself in a position in which he was abased enough to lower his standards. If we are honest, most believers will admit we have not always been wise with the wealth we have received from our Father. We too have found ourselves in compromising positions, because of needs that would have been correctly satisfied had we not wasted our wealth and our resources. Some saints have not only fed swine, but some have even dated pigs just to make ends meet! This is why we should not be quick to condemn, when we see individuals in pigpen situations. We must encourage those individuals and help them get out! There is a pigpen waiting for those who waste wealth, mismanage money and incorrectly control their income.

Verse 16. And he would fain have filled his belly with the husks that the swine did eat: and no man gave unto him.

The son has so lowered his standards that he almost wishes for what the pigs are eating! This is a sad place to dwell in, and there are many who recognize this place. Many believers have found themselves in a place, where the realization sets in that they have sunk to an all-time low. The son reached a level of such degradation that he considers living as the pigs live. The life of hogs would never satisfy him, nor was it meant to.

... and no man gave unto him.

Most people really don't want to find out who their true friends are. Most people have a lot of "friends" with whom they can shop, fish, bowl, talk on the phone, or even worship, but very few have true friends, who will be there through thick and thin. Out of all the people with whom the son shared his wealth, scripture says *and no man gave unto him.* There are people who will eat your food, run up your cell phone minutes and burn up your gas, but they are not necessarily the same people upon whom you can count when the chips are down.

Verse 17. And when he came to himself, he said, How many hired servants of my father's have bread enough and to spare, and I perish with hunger!

The son could not see the pigpen from the house, but thank God he could see the house from the pigpen! He remembered how great it was back at home – the place he rushed to leave; the place of wealth. The son remembered that his father had been so successful in business that even his servants were doing well and had more than enough!

He comes to the realization that he is starving, whereas his father's servants – at the very least – have leftovers. The servants have leftovers, because they remain connected to the father. Look around and take note of the people the Lord is using to make things happen. Learn from them rather than running away from them. Establishing a connection with those who are wise with their wealth can move you into a place of overflow. Conversely, disconnecting from connection to the wise with wealth can cause us to live in the overflow, and disconnecting from the Father, who understands finances, can and will cause you to struggle and live in scarcity. Too many saints live too far from the Father and from His instruction concerning wealth, increase and prosperity. Seek out God's guidance concerning giving and living. Sons will never have what servants have, when they live apart from their Father.

Verse 18. I will arise and go to my father, and will say to him, Father, I have sinned against heaven, and before thee.

Many members of the Body of Christ need to follow the son's example: Be honest, accept the realization and return to the Father. Many a believer has sinned in his or her heart concerning what he or she should give unto the Lord. Even if these individuals manage to present an offering, it is usually given with an unwilling heart – a sure indication that the giver has moved away from the Father's heart. Others tithe faithfully and yet, harbor ill will toward the Father, because in their mind, they do not owe the Father an offering. The possessions the son had before he left the house, belonged to the father. After he left the house what he lost really belonged to the father, as well. Many believers have the wrong attitude about what belongs to the Father, and that is partly why many struggle with tithing and sacrificial giving. Everything belongs to the Father. The lives we live belong to the Father. When we change our attitudes about giving, we will make our atmosphere conducive to blessings from the Father. If you struggle to give everything to the Father, it's time for introspection. There is a secret sin of selfishness. The Father gave us ALL, and He has no regrets! We as saints must posture our hearts to desire to give to God more, even if our giving is less than we desire it to be. The desire to give to the Father should always be greater than the ability of the moment. There should never be a moment in which we desire to give Him less than He requires!

Verse 19. And am no more worthy to be called thy son: make me as one of thy hired servants.

Fully aware of his failures, the young man was willing to become a servant in his father's house. Sometimes, our mistakes make us feel utterly unworthy. Nevertheless, despite our shortcomings, we must be assured that the Father is not looking for servants; He is seeking sons! God is not interested in you becoming a servant. He wants us to return to Him, as children and admit that our hearts have not always been right concerning His money, His blessings, His provisions, His resources and His prosperity! We must acknowledge that we were in the pigpen, because we wanted to handle His blessings our own way. Because of a failure to relinquish control, many are in debt over their heads, credit cards are maxed out, houses are facing foreclosure and cars are on the verge of being repossessed. That is the pigpen! Whatever comes, failure will never change our status with the Father!

Verse 20. And he arose, and came to his father. But when he was yet a great way off, his father saw him, and had compassion, and ran, and fell on his neck, and kissed him.

The son never would have known the extent of his father's love if he had remained in the pigpen. Believers have to rise from their respective pigpens, and the first step is heading back in the direction of the Father. The son was not going back home; he was going back to his father. Many believers want to go home, without first returning to the Father. The son's father stood watching and waiting for him, as does the Heavenly Father as He awaits our return. The father had mercy on his son and never mentioned his son's wayward behavior; only how much he missed him. Wouldn't it be wondrous if people could just see how loving, caring, compassionate and forgiving the Father is? The Heavenly Father, as the young man's father did, welcomes us back with love. The father ran to meet his son. With the stench of the pigpen still on his son, who did not have the benefit of a shower and a shave, the father embraces him and instructs the servants to bring the best robe. Others may have focused on the stench, but the father simply reveled in his son's return. Though we as believers have squandered the Father's wealth, we are still His sons and daughters. The Father wills to bless us, restore us and entrust us with His blessings again!

LESSON 36

DON'T PROMISE IF WE AREN'T WILLING TO PAY!
Ecclesiastes 5:1-2, 4-6

This lesson deals with the importance of keeping the commitments we as believers make to God and to others. It is easy to make a promise or a vow. The challenge comes in living up to a vow. Solomon, the son of King David and Bathsheba, gives us wise instruction on how to enter the house of God and also how to approach our commitments to God. For believers whose lives have been filled with nothing, but broken promises, the pain inflicted by those who at their best make promises and at their worst never keep them is evident. Oftentimes, when people get into trouble, they make noble promises that they should never have made, knowing they were not committed to doing everything in their power to keep the vow. If it will take a miracle for a vow to be fulfilled – unless God Himself has made a promise in advance to bring it to pass – one should not enter into such a vow.

When believers are known for broken promises and unperformed vows, it becomes difficult for people to trust the saints of God and others of the faith in the future. We are always representing the Father and the one thing we should not want to do is to make God look bad by overstating our commitments. In our youth, parents would often instruct us to stop "running your mouths!" If we don't mean it, we should not say it! If an individual completes an application for credit, no matter what type credit it is, the act is akin to making a promise. Every time money is borrowed and not repaid, that is akin to breaking a promise. Approved credit comes with an obligation to pay. Many Christians talk a good game and have no problem saying they can repay those to whom money is owed. However, they do have a problem, when the time comes to repay. Every time we are recorded as breaking a promise, all we are doing is assuring ourselves that the door of credit is not going to remain open for us. Broken financial promises do not occur only in the community and the business world. This type of behavior also spills over into the church and into one's relationship with the Lord.

Verse 1. Keep thy foot when thou goest to the house of God, and be more ready to hear, than to give the sacrifices of fools: for they consider not that they do evil.

Solomon challenges us to watch how we enter the house of God. He admonishes us to think about what we are doing, when we come to God and into His house. Biblical scholars connect this verse to the previous chapter, as a continuation of the warning against vanity or emptiness. Our feet bring balance or stability to our bodies. We must guard our spiritual feet to make sure the Body of Christ is balanced and stable. When coming to the house of God, the Word of God says we should be ready to hear. The Teacher's Bible Commentary says, *"Silence before God is a good policy. It is better for God to speak to us than for us to speak to God."* There is always a temptation to make promises to God that we are not spiritually or mentally committed enough to keep. Many have promised God that they were going to do better, but then, in truth, they actually behaved worse! The Lord will keep every commitment He has made to us, even though we struggle to keep almost every commitment that we make unto Him. Not only should we enter the house of God with silence, but we also should enter each day with silence to allow the Lord do the talking. The New Living Translation of the Bible says, *"As you enter the house of God, keep your ears open and your mouth shut. It is evil to make mindless offerings to God."* The sin is to promise and then not pay. Many believers readily make promises to God – sometimes in songs, sometimes in sermons, sometimes with an amen, and sometimes in testimonies – that they have no intention of keeping. The *sacrifices of fools* are the empty promises we make with our mouths. We must stop promising to give and begin the act of giving God the best of what we have and who we are.

Verse 2. Be not rash with thy mouth, and let not thine heart be hasty to utter any thing before God...

"The more the merrier" is a very familiar phrase. That philosophy certainly does not apply to what we should say unto the Lord. Saints should never make promises to God that have not been weighed in the heart and approved by the spirit. An old hymn sets forth these words: "A charge to keep I have and a God to glorify… to serve the present age my calling to fulfill, oh may it all my powers engaged to do my Master's will." When we are rash with our mouths and hasty in our hearts, we fail to think things through. Some vows never would have been made had we took the time to weigh the responsibility of the commitment and gauge the likelihood of pulling it off. As it pertains to money management, understanding the weight of a promise is vital. If we can easily break a promise to God, then, the promises we make to others and breaking them comes with even more ease. Every promise we enter into should be made, as if it were made unto the Lord. Have you ever made a vow that you knew would be impossible to keep at the moment you made it? Because your sights were set on what that promise would allow you to have, making the promise seemed like the right thing to do. Making an empty vow – a vow made with no intention to honor it –is never the right thing to do.

... for God is in heaven, and thou upon earth: therefore let thy words be few.

Many saints struggle with this admonition. They believe the only reason they have received some blessings is because of promises they made, albeit empty promises. No promise we can make moves God or tricks God into trusting us or giving unto us. God knows when we are lying and He knows when we are promising more than we can accomplish in our own strength. It is just by the Lord's mercy that we are not consumed, because of the string of vows that we have made and not kept. There are times when individuals with whom we make vows are fully aware of our big talk, but by the grace of God they help anyway! Big talk may get your foot in the door, but when you are more talk than integrity, you may fool some people some of the time, but you will not fool everyone all of the time. We as believers should want to be credible, so that if we have a need we can return – with a good record – to those who can offer aid. Big talk with no action normally results in a closed door.

Verse 4. When thou vowest a vow unto God, defer not to pay it; for he hath no pleasure in fools: pay that which thou hast vowed.

We should never delay in repaying God what we have promised. In fact, be swift to make good on promises you have made to God and others! It is God who moves on the hearts of people to be gracious to us. It is God's love that causes people to give us another chance. Do not waste precious opportunities to restore your credit by simply being honest and disciplined in repaying what you have promised. The reason many believers fail to repay what they owe God and others in a timely fashion is because they think they have the option to defer payment. In fact, they prefer to do so! These individuals would rather pay God and their debtors later instead of using the blessings God gave during the week to take care of their obligations. They would rather use God's blessings to buy a birthday present, buy a child a Spiderman or Incredible Hulk Halloween costume, treat themselves to dinner, or buy something nice for themselves, because they are "the only ones working." We must understand that we are working to pay off promises and debts. Once we have met those obligations, we can satisfy our simple or selfish desires. We as believers have no right to buy ourselves something or reward ourselves, when we have not first satisfied the people we owe, first and foremost God! Don't put off paying God! The Word says He hath no pleasure in fools. Simply stated, when we make a promise to God, we should not delay in following through on it.

... Pay that which thou hast vowed.

For those who made a promise to tithe if you secured a good job, start now to pay the tithe and give additionally toward the back pay that you owe. For those who promised to tithe and give unto the Lord, if He delivered you from trouble, begin to pay what you have promised. For those who promised to bless the Lord, if He healed you, do not delay in repaying the promise made unto the Lord. People who make promises and do not honor them end up with bad credit with the Creator! We should not want to have credit issues with the very One, who can open doors for us even when banks, credit unions, family and friends turn us down.

Verse 5. Better is it that thou shouldest not vow, than that thou shouldest vow and not pay.

Every day there are people who find themselves in court, facing litigation, because they are being sued for not paying as they had promised. Christians should never have to be taken to court, because Christians should pay their debts! Sometimes in life, there are unforeseen events and tragedies that hinder the children of God from fulfilling promises. However, oftentimes, the only hindrance we face is an inability to be disciplined. An undisciplined lifestyle is one of the leading causes of broken promises. If the saints were disciplined, debts would be paid, and if wise management principles were applied, money would even be left over! We cannot make enough money to compensate for undisciplined behavior. The Word of God says it is better not to vow than to not live up to promises. Any person who makes promises easily will eventually find him or herself overcommitted and unable to live up to those promises.

Rather than tell a lie, the old saints would often just say nothing. Whether we say it with our mouths or say it by signing our names on the dotted line, we are making a statement and making a promise. So, we can sign a lie, just as easily as, we say it with our mouths. Becoming a people of integrity is important. Often, we exercise integrity, when it comes to other areas in life. We must be just as committed to financial integrity. Unforeseen circumstances do not release us from our spiritual obligation to make God look good! It may mean that we have to get a part-time job for a season. As believers, our main concern should be keeping our commitment intact.

Verse 6. Suffer not thy mouth to cause thy flesh to sin; neither say thou before the angel, that it was an error: wherefore should God be angry at thy voice, and destroy the work of thine hands?

Let me reinforce – and we must remember this fact – that it is a sin to make promises and not keep them. From this day forward, make a decision to abstain from making empty promises about giving of our time and money, spending and serving. Rather than tell God what we are going to do – let's just do it! We must admit to God that we have sinned against Him, and acknowledge that the sin has been with our mouths. We must realize sin is sin. All sin is offensive to God. If you are going to show up only if the weather is ideal or if a co-worker doesn't make you mad; if the children steer clear of trouble at school; or if the price of gas drops, then say that! If you are not absolutely sure that you can commit to a promise, don't make the vow!

... neither say thou before the angel, that it was an error ...

We have heard the words "I am sorry" long enough. There must be a difference – starting today. The world does not take the word of the saints seriously, because we do not take seriously that which comes out of our mouths. We cannot keep reneging on what we promised to give unto the Lord. The Word of God says we are not to go back on our word by saying, "I didn't mean to say that!" Heaven is listening! God is listening! The angels are listening! The world is listening! Our children are listening! If this vast an audience is listening to the words that come out of our mouths, then it is critical that we learn to live up to what we say unto the Lord. Some of us have made great promises to God in times of distress and have failed to live up to them. There is a new day in America and a new day in each of us! Let's live up to every promise we have made to our Master!

The angels in this text are also referred to as temple messengers, priests or pastors. Even the promises, we make to God through angels, ministers and pastors should be honored! The Word makes it clear that the promises we make to angels are expected to be fulfilled, as if they were made with God directly. The text says God tires of and is even angered by all talk and no action. Many ministers are frustrated with ministry, because people want to count on the church and the minister, but very seldom can the minister and the church count on them.

... wherefore should God be angry at thy voice ...

As stated before, not honoring our word incurs the anger of God. We should want God to delight in hearing our voices. Those same voices can be offensive to Him, when they bear lies. If you promised to start spending time with Him, start and don't stop! We must ask God for the grace to accomplish every commitment for which He is holding us responsible. The passage of time does not mean that God has changed His mind. We must seek His face concerning every promise we have made to find out if He has released us from certain promises, or if He is yet requiring us to fulfill assignments.

... and destroy the work of thine hands?

God can render unsuccessful every event, every effort and every project in which we have played a part. We need God to bless the works of our hand. In His offense, He reserves the right not to do so. God has given us the key to repel the spirit of failure from the projects and plans that we have in Him. Repent for failed promises and trust that the Lord will be faithful and just to forgive and to cleanse you. He is able to give you a new start in Him.

LESSON 37

A WISE WAY TO LOOK AT WEALTH!
Ecclesiastes 5:10–14

    This lesson addresses the attitudes, affections and actions we develop in regard to wealth, and how the accumulation of wealth can be a hindrance and a help in the Body of Christ. There is a right way and wrong way to purse wealth. Oftentimes, the manner in which the children of God go after wealth leads to the detriment of our faith, our witness and our families. It is not the goal of this lesson to discourage the saints from acquiring wealth, nor is it to suggest that having wealth is a bad thing. The purpose of the lesson is to encourage the Christian to get wealth God's way. God is the One, who gives us the power to get wealth. Therefore, we must posture ourselves for wealth that results from simply being in a right relationship with the Lord and following His principles concerning prosperity.

    People are often blessed with good things and then proceed to handle those blessings badly. In doing so, people turn what was meant to be a blessing into a burden, or worse. For example, a depressed person can use food, which is enjoyable and necessary for life, as a comfort. Soon comfort can turn into overeating. No matter what the person is depressed about, the food never addresses or corrects the problem at the root of the depression. Eating to ease depression can lead to weight issues and the need for larger clothing. It is clear then that using a good thing for the wrong reasons can be costly. Excessive shopping, because of depression, is another example of a harmless action turned into a detrimental habit. Shopping does not solve the problem. It simply makes the person, who is discouraged feel better for the moment. Overindulgence does not solve problems; it creates more problems.

    Many saints believe their problems would be solved, if they just had more money. Christians, who believe this, often spend too much of their time pursuing goods rather than pursuing God. Simply put, many chase wealth rather than seeking God's wisdom. The value of having God in your life will always supersede the value of having material possessions, but the truth is we can have both God and goods! To have both, however, God must be sought first. Material things will never bring you complete satisfaction. Things are made to be enjoyed. Only God can satisfy. Saints must stop trying to obtain their identities through material things. We can only discover who we are in Christ. Things we purchase from stores will eventually wear and need to be replaced. There is no replacement or substitute for God. Everything that is man-made has an expiration date or shelf-life expectancy. What we derive from Christ, however, has eternity written all over it! The Christian must learn to enjoy a relationship with God and put things in their proper place. Christians who value goods more than God will never have much of either, because God will give to His children only what we are able to handle. If the Christian can be blessed and still value his or her relationship with the One who blesses higher than all else, then that believer is postured to be entrusted with more from the Father.

Verse 10. He that loveth silver shall not be satisfied with silver; nor he that loveth abundance with increase; this is also vanity.

As we've just learned, things will never bring full satisfaction in a person's life. We were never supposed to love silver. The Christian is admonished to love God and people, and simply enjoy the benefits of using silver. We were never supposed to feel as if we have to have silver or believe the possession of it adds value to our self-worth. We have allowed silver and other indicators of wealth to have too much importance in our lives. Silver – and wealth in general – will never satisfy, because it was never intended to do so. We must not spend all of our time trying to accumulate silver, gold or any other substance that will not bring true satisfaction to us in the end. Silver and abundance could never bring value to a person's life, because they are accessories in life! God and a right relationship with God bring value and self-worth to a person's life, because God is the source and the sustainer of life. I can recall an old saying in the church: *"If you meet me and forget me you have lost nothing, but if we meet Christ and forget Him you have lost everything!"* Things can accessorize our lives and people can add flavor to our lives, but only God adds value to a human's life. Things will make us feel good for a moment, and people will make us feel good for a season, but only God can give us a great feeling throughout eternity. The Word says silver and abundance are vanity or empty. If the Christian works all of his or her life to gain possessions, amassing silver cups, silver jewelry, silver rings and silver furnishings, at the end of the day, it's all for naught, if he or she does not have friends, family and faith!

Verse 11. When goods increase, they are increased that eat them: and what good is there to the owners thereof, saving the beholding of them with their eyes?

The Scripture says that when we acquire more, more people flock to us in an effort to get what we have. So often, we are surrounded by people when we are prospering. Many times those people are there solely to help consume the blessings that we have. Pro football player Michael Vick fell from grace in part, because he attempted to bring everyone with him to enjoy his prosperity. Michael Vick should have disconnected himself from a few old friends and family members, when he became successful. Successful people and people who are experiencing seasons of prosperity, often face the challenge of determining, which individuals to keep in their circles and which individuals to cut off. Financially successful Christians have to be very selective of the people allowed in their space and in their spirit. Have you ever noticed that the more money you have, the more people you have calling and hanging around you? People are willing to use you, until they use you up. When you are broke and begging, the same people often are nowhere to be found.

Delving further, the New Living Translation says this verse this way: *The more you have, the more people come to help you spend it. So what good is wealth – except perhaps to watch it slip through your fingers!* The tenor of the verse is that people will use us, if we let them. Some people are involved in sweetheart relationships, meaning the other person does not come around until they have need of something. The Christian has to be able to discern, if he or she is on the verge of being used. The Message Bible says

"The more loot you get, the more looters show up. And what fun is that – to be robbed in broad daylight?" Simply stated, stop letting people use you! Some people's friendship is too expensive! Some people's love is too expensive! Some relationships are at their best high-priced, polite prostitution! We, as believers, must know when we are being taken advantage of. We also must resist the desire to be liked or to be loved so badly that we allow people to rob us. Surround yourself with people who love you just for you.

Verse 12. The sleep of a labouring man is sweet, whether he eat little or much: but the abundance of the rich will not suffer him to sleep.

It is a gift from God to be satisfied with the blessings that come, as a reward for our honest efforts to provide and to prosper. Christians should give their best, work hard and give careful thought to how we provide a decent living for ourselves and for our families. When a Christian works hard with his or her hands and mind to accomplish goals and dreams, sleep should be sweet and come easily, at the end of the day. When we know we have given our best and we trust God for the rest, sleep will be great and peaceful. The Word says *godliness with contentment is great gain.* We as saints must learn to be content with where we are and what we have today in God. God does have more in store for His children, but that does not mean we are going to get it all before next weekend! The Message Bible says, *"Hard and honest work earns a good night sleep, whether supper is beans or steak. But a rich man's belly gives him insomnia."* Some people put too much emphasis on wealth and the accumulation of things. It is great to have wealth and it is wonderful to have things, but it is even greater to have the peace of mind that comes from peace with God.

In developing a relationship with God, a primary goal should be to develop an attitude of gratitude, when it comes to whatever blessings God bestows. Whether it is beans or steak, learn to say with sincerity, "Thank You!" Some Christians cannot say "thanks" unless the meal is a Red Lobster special! We have to be grateful for the McDonald's meal, too. Whatever God blesses us with and wherever God blesses us, we have to grow to be able to give Him the greatest praise even there!

... but the abundance of the rich will not suffer him to sleep.

The text also shows what happens to the person, who is never satisfied with blessings from the Lord. The ungrateful always want more without first pausing to enjoy and appreciate what they already have. The rich person who has a warped mindset concerning money and material things will not be able to sleep, because that person's greed fuels a constant desire to get more; so much so that they cannot rest, until the desire is satisfied. The rich man's bed is likely better and his pillows fluffier, but greed can keep him from enjoying the amenities he already possesses. People fueled by greed cannot enjoy life, because they are on an endless pursuit for more. When these individuals finally decide they have enough and sit down to enjoy their treasures, the journey ends, the ride is over and it's time to meet their Maker! We should work to have more, but we also should pause to celebrate the victories in life and enjoy what we already have accumulated.

Verse 13. There is a sore evil which I have seen under the sun, namely, riches kept for the owners thereof to their hurt.

The manner in which we pursue wealth can hurt us, especially when we put God aside for the sake of great gains. We should never allow the accumulation of things to hinder us from spending quality time with the Lord or setting aside time in the service of the Lord. The most important accomplishments we can have in life are to love God with all that we have; honor Him with the utmost humility, to live for God on a daily basis, and to do all that is within our power to please Him, by having a living faith in Him that never doubts His power. Some Christians hurt themselves, because they do not set aside time to spend with God. Some Christians are just too busy and too important for their own good! If we know more about politics, government, corporations, stocks and bonds, investing, fishing, golfing, boxing, basketball, football, professional athletics, the Obamas, or any other subject than we know about God, then we need to turn our attention to Him! If there is anything that a Christian should be able to articulate or discuss with great depth, it is Christ, the cross, the empty tomb and how to become a Christian.

God deserves our time. People who claim they cannot attend worship, because they are always working have a value system that is absolutely out of order! People believe they have to work to keep a job, work to keep a marriage, work to pass a tough class, and work to keep food on the table, nice clothes on their backs and a roof over their heads. For many, NO work is put into working out their soul's salvation with fear and trembling! Many Christians do not have great faith because they have not put in the work. Many Christians do not know much Word, because studying God's Word takes a lot of work! We hurt ourselves when money and what money can buy become the priority of our lives. No matter how much money a person has, he or she eventually will discover money cannot buy what is truly important. Money cannot buy more time, when death has come. Money cannot buy peace, when confusion runs rampant in the home. Money cannot buy a real friend, when we are feeling alone. Money cannot buy us love, when we find ourselves hated and ostracized by men. Money cannot buy salvation, when we come to the end. Money cannot justify us, when God and the world judge us for our wrongs. Money cannot buy us a relationship with God, when we stand before Him and He declares, "Depart from me you workers of iniquity!" Don't hurt yourself by putting too much stock in what money can do for you. Money is good but God is great!

Christians also hurt themselves by neglecting families in their pursuit of wealth. Family must always have a place in the heart of every believer. There are times when the Christian must choose family over the dollar. Don't miss your child's game in the name of making money. Your children will not always be children. Many people who pursue riches hurt their families by not being there, choosing instead to leave discipline up their children's teachers, principals, bus drivers, police officers, the church and a list of others. An undisciplined family will never handle wealth and prosperity correctly. To have great riches, but leave future generations unequipped to inherit the wealth is a great disappointment.

Verse 14. But those riches perish by evil travail; and he begetteth a son, and there is nothing in his hand.

So much can go wrong with investments. A person can spend his or her lifetime accumulating wealth, and with one wrong turn everything can go sour. People have lost their retirement funds in failing stock markets. Thousands of people lost their investments and retirement savings in Enron. We never really know how the world's economy will fare; that is why we invest in people and invest in the Kingdom. Our greatest investment should be in the Kingdom. Second, we should make our investment in our families and in people. Investing in people helps ensure that when trials come in life, those you help will be better equipped to handle them. Investing in the Kingdom ensures we will always have more, because seed has been sown. Investing in the Kingdom affords us a God guarantee that He will always make sure we get out more than what we put in. The stock market and Wall Street cannot make that type of promise!

LESSON 38

FACING FINANCIAL LOSSES WITH FAITH IN OUR FATHER!
Job 1:3, 9-17

    This study deals with learning to live with financial losses in life. There is always a danger in believing that we cannot live without the things that we have accumulated. Anything that we cannot learn to live without, we do not need the experience of living with. Financial losses are not always a punishment from God or even God's way of teaching us something. One of the recurring themes in the book of Job is that when nothing is left but God, God is still enough. The children of God must never become so comfortable with possessions that we allow them to take the place of the One in whom we are suppose to trust. Even when a child of God is stripped to nothing and is left with only his or her faith in God, we will see in this lesson that God is enough. We must never allow wealth or the conveniences of this life to trick us into believing that things are what make life worth living. Sometimes, Satan tries us, and the Lord allows it because, He knows those who have been born of His spirit can make it through any test. We will take a look at the life of Job, a man who lived in the land of Uz. We will see a man who is not only rich in finances, but who is also rich in faith and the truth. As a matter of fact, he is much richer in faith than he is in finances. Job is a special man, because out of all that he owns and the great successes in his business life, he has a great sense for faith and family. Job teaches us to be balanced as believers.

    Verse 3. He owned 7,000 sheep, 3000 camels, 500 teams of oxen, and five hundred female donkeys, and he employed many servants. He was, in fact, the richest person in that entire area.

    If we had to describe Job's wealth to people today, we would have to say that he was richer than the Rockefellers! Job had more money than the Kennedys and he was much wealthier than Sam Walton of the Wal-Mart enterprise! Bill Gates would observe Job's wealth in awe and Oprah would be considered a beggar in comparison! Scripture says Job was the wealthiest man in the region. The King James Version of the Bible says that he was the greatest man in the east. No person's wealth compared to what Job had amassed. A careful look at Job's financial portfolio shows 500 teams of oxen, which means Job had in his possession at least 1,000 oxen. Naturally, all of his sheep, camels, oxen and donkeys were reproducing more of their own kind. Thusly, Job's wealth increased even as it was counted! This is how to generate money and increase in the lives of God's people. As we gauge the wealth of the believer, the figure we arrive at is never totally correct, because investments should perpetually make money or increase in interest.

    Job is another Old Testament patriarch, who exhibits a keen sense for business and entrepreneurship. The laws of reproduction are in operation all around us. However, the saints are oftentimes not in a reproducing mindset. This is why it is not smart to spend every paycheck on things that we desire and not use some of the money we earn to make money reproduce or work for us. Job employed many servants, which means he hired people to help make money for him. The servants worked for a paycheck, but Job hired them, so they would help create wealth for himself and his seed. Job spent money on what made money for him: 7,000 sheep, 3,000 camels, 500 teams of oxen, 500 donkeys and the many servants employed. What have we spent money on this year that yielded a return on our investment? When we conduct this kind of financial assessment, we begin to see why many of God's people remain in poverty. Everyday items that we spend money on could be used to make money. Trucks can be used for hauling. Take the car and pick up a paper route. Use the computer to type resumes, letters or documents for others. Use that nice kitchen and those new appliances to bake and sell cakes and pies for the holiday season and other special occasions. Take those Black & Decker tools and use them to start a small handyman business.

Verse 9. Satan replied to the Lord, Yes, but Job has good reason to fear God.

The enemy suggests Job's respect and reverence for God are conditional and seasonal and have nothing to do with God. We should indeed reverence God, and that reverence should not be based on how things are going for us. Some people have no problem honoring God, as long as, God gives them want they want. Our reverence of God should be based on the revelation of who God is. People with a clear revelation of God ought to reverence God no matter where they are and what they are going through.

Verse 10. You have always put a wall of protection around him and his home and his property. You have made him prosper in everything he does. Look how rich he is!

Even Satan can see why Job has been so successful. It is important that we understand it is the Lord who helped Job succeed, and it is the Lord, who helps us succeed. Believers will be balanced only when we realize it is the Lord who gives us the power to get wealth. God then shields our prosperity with a wall of protection that cannot be penetrated without His permission.

You have always put a wall of protection around him and his home and his property ... Satan is alluding to the fact that, despite his attempts, he has not been able to get to Job! If the saints could really see the protection God provides, we would have no problem paying tithes and blessing the Lord! Every time Job's investments, property or wealth expand, God extends Job's invincibility through an invisible wall of protection. God's invincible wall prevents the enemy from penetrating our premises. An alarm company is not a fail-safe method of deterring theft. All an alarm company can do is call your house after someone has broken in and then alert the police or the fire department that something may be wrong. Too many saints have too many assets not to be protected with the blessed assurance of God!

You have made him prosper in everything he does. Look how rich he is. We should never let it go on record that Satan sees God's blessings in our lives clearer than fellow believers do. The enemy says he knows it is God who made Job to prosper. We must come to the realization that it is not our hard work, smart work, long hours, or our overtime hours that brought us to a place of blessing. It's the Lord's doing – and it is marvelous in our sight! It is the Lord, who is bringing us to our wealthy place. That is why we should never be afraid to bless the Lord, praise the Lord or sow unto the Lord. Job, whom the Lord made rich, was able to handle all that God wanted to bless him with. This may be why many people have only enough for today. In their state of immaturity, many people can only handle being given "this day our daily bread." Job was given more than he would have spent in his lifetime.

Verse 11. But reach out and take away everything he has, and he will surely curse you to your face!

Mature children of God should not want anything they cannot live without. If we lose a commodity held in that kind of regard, we risk falling out with God. Every blessing we have is a gift from the Lord. Though it may appear so to the immature eye, not everything we have is a blessing. Anything that takes our attention away from God is not a blessing. If what we have takes the place of God, it is not a blessing, but rather a curse. We, as Christians, should never allow the loss of things to make us act ugly! People who are truly grateful are grateful with or without. A pretentious person feigns gratefulness.

... and he will curse you to your face.

Many have said some ugly things to God in the face of their losses. To profess, "I don't know what I'm going to do!", after losing a job, is an ugly thing to say in the face of God. To exclaim, "I don't have anybody!", after the loss of a loved one, is also an ugly thing to say in the face of God. Satan is betting that we are going to curse God when things are not going right for us. Those who trust God must know that God has no interest in breaking us. It was the enemy's idea to take everything from Job. He wants to strip us of everything. Yet, even if God allows tragedy to befall us, we must remember that we are not responsible for what happens to us, only for how we respond to those circumstances. We don't know what God is going to allow. Our response and responsibility is to bless the Lord at all times.

Verse 12. "All right, you may test him," the Lord said to Satan. "Do whatever you want with everything he possesses, but don't harm him physically." So Satan left the Lord's presence.

Satan could not have tested Job, if the Lord had not allowed it. That spiritual principle remains. Satan cannot meddle with a child of God, without God's permission. God gave Satan permission to test Job. God knows what we are made of, even when Satan and we do not. God knows us and He knows what we can live without. Job lost everything, but he lived through it, and so can we! Oftentimes, we overrate the value of things and underrate the value of a right relationship with the sovereign Lord. Most of us do not know what we can live without, until we have to. No one likes living with losses, but the truth is we all can! Satan was given permission to ruin Job financially, ruin his credit and ruin his businesses, but Satan was not given permission to ruin Job! We must always be cognizant of the fact that possessions do not make us. Sometimes, we own and cherish things so long that we begin to allow those things to define who we are.

There is a second spiritual principle in this verse. When God grants the enemy access to His children, He alone will determine how far the enemy can go. Satan was permitted to ruin Job's wealth, but he could not disturb Job's health. When the enemy is allowed to shake our lives, we must keep in mind that he is only allowed to go so far. This verse shows us God is in control, even in bad times brought on by Satan. If God is in control, His people still should praise Him despite their circumstances. The season in which things are going wrong is the season that the saints must praise God for what is going well! We have to be expressly grateful for the things that seemingly are going wrong, but have not gone out of the realm of God's control! At no time was Job's situation out of God's control, and at no time are our financial troubles outside of God's power to restore control.

Verses 13-15. One day when Job's sons and daughters were feasting at the oldest brother's house, a messenger arrived at Job's home with this news: Your oxen were plowing, with the donkeys feeding beside them, when the Sabeans raided us. They stole all the animals and killed all the farmhands. I am the only one who escaped to tell you."

No one is immune from bad news. Once Job's bad news begins, it seems to flow continuously. However, every bit of news that reached Job's ears was first run by the ears of God. The same is true for us. Every ounce of trouble is checked, weighed and tested by God, before His children are levied with it. This verse suggests things were going well for Job on what appeared to be a normal day. Life indeed can change in a moment. If we did not fall out with the Father when we had possessions, we should not fall out with Him when our possessions are gone. God is actually good – with or without things! It is my prayer that bad news never comes to your house, but just in case it does, you will need a Father and an unwavering faith to get you through the tough times. Difficult days are the perfect time to affirm and to remind yourself that God can deliver you from whatever you are going through. Your faith can give you peace, while you are going through. America recently has seen a time in which bad economic news reached many homes. Many have lost their savings, retirement money has dwindled to nothing, familiar companies have shuttered their doors and foreclosures are prevalent. Still, none of this bad news is new news to the Father. The news did not reach God's house on the same day it reached Job's home. As a matter of fact, God had already discussed Job's testing and pre-determined how far it would go. There is nothing that is not under God's control, so there is no reason for us as believers to lose our cool!

Verse 16. While he was still speaking, another messenger arrived with this news: "The fire of God has fallen from heaven and burned up your sheep and all the shepherds. I am the only one who escaped to tell you."

Many believers have a history of falling apart, when bad news comes their way. What helps in times of bad news is the knowledge that there is good news at our disposal! First and foremost, God knows what's coming, before we do. Secondly, God would not allow the trouble to come, unless He had weighed the trial and was sure we could handle it. Thirdly, God is still in control, even when it is apparent that we are not! There are trials that cannot be reversed by people, but there is nothing God cannot work out!

Verse 17. While he was still speaking, a third messenger arrived with this news: "Three bands of Chaldean raiders have stolen your camels and killed your servants. I am the only one who escaped to tell you.

Job, like many of us who have been hedged or fenced in by God's protection, has never experienced bad news of this magnitude all at once. There is still more bad news to come about his children! It is not bad news that will thwart many a believer. It is the lack of faith and trust in the Father to deliver. Tough economic times call for a tough faith in a tremendous Father, who will not fail us, and who will always outperform our faith. When it appears that we have lost almost everything, the one thing the enemy cannot steal is our joy.

Job worshipped his way through economic and personal disaster and so must we. When Job had finished expressing his grief, he praised his way to a good place in God. God has been too good for us to wallow in trials, troubled, because we cannot see how God is going to make things better. Keep good news close to you at all times. Our lives are in God's hands and that is good news. We are covered in every disaster. People purchase insurance for the purpose of recovering and bouncing back from disasters in life. If we are in God's hands, we are in great hands. Our lives are never out of control, because our lives are in the hands of the Lord. Even when we cannot control what happens to us, we can rejoice in the fact that our God has all things under His control. It may not have appeared so, but God always had things under control in Job's life. Sometimes, we struggle with whether God has things under control. Remember, God's sovereignty is reality, even at times in our lives, when we don't see the manifestation of it. There is not a moment in our lives where God stresses about working all things together for our good.

LESSON 39

INTENTIONAL GIVING TO AN INTERESTING GOD!
Matthew 2:10-11

    This lesson focuses on giving with intent, with purpose and with meaning. When we give, oftentimes not much thought is put into our gifts. Our gifts to the kingdom ought to reflect an understanding of who and what we are sowing into. God is deliberate in His giving, and He never gives us more than we are able to handle. Blessings and burdens are proportioned, measured and distributed according to the ability of every saint. A wise man would not give his wife and his mother the same birthday gift. Even though both recipients are women, each relationship influences the type of gift that is bestowed. A woman's gift to her husband or boyfriend would probably differ greatly, from that which she would give her father. Again, relationship has a direct bearing on the gift.

    In every season of our lives, the gifts we give unto the Lord should reflect our revelation of who He is to us. Even if a man presented roses to his wife and mother on Valentine's Day, the spirit, the heart and the intent behind each gift is totally different. The heart ought to consider the spirit, the emotion and the reason behind each gift we give to the Lord. Though our monetary gifts may come out of the same pocket or purse, the purpose behind the gift is not always the same. Sometimes, we give for benevolent causes. On other occasions, we give because we owe a percentage of our income. There are times when we give in response to repentance. Sometimes, we give solely as an expression of gratitude for the goodness bestowed upon us. There are times when we are called to sow into the future or into a vision, and there are times when we are called to sow, as an act of faith and obedience.

    This text will highlight the journey of the wise men from the east, which traveled to Jerusalem to see the child born King of the Jews. By the time the wise men arrived in the holy city of Jerusalem, and to Bethlehem in particular, Jesus was a toddler between the ages of 3 and 4. While the wise men did not see Jesus in the manger, shepherds did have the privilege of seeing Jesus in that familiar scene soon after His birth. The issue worth extracting for the purpose of our learning is that the wise men did not come empty handed; they brought gifts to the Lord. Wise men, wise women, and wise youth – they never come to the Lord empty handed. The first Christmas was solely about God's gift of a savior to the world and a fallen humanity. In modern times, we have taken our attention off what the Father has given us. During the holiday season, many people shift their focus to what others are giving or what we "have" to give other people. Christmas heralds the fact God is a giver, He gives the best gifts, and God gives gifts we truly cannot live without. The wise men teach us the correct response to God's gift. We should accept what God has given unto us and then respond with a gift of our own. Our gifts should express that we recognize the value of the gift that has been given to us.

Verse 10. When they saw the star, they rejoiced with exceeding great joy.

The star guided the wise men to the place, where are Lord now lived. The wise men, excited to have finally arrived at the place where Christ was, expressed their joy in seeing the star. Over time, the star has come to carry astrological significance. We also know, as the old saying goes, that the wise men saw Christ, the bright and morning star and the star of our salvation. Men showing excitement about seeing the star is a long forgone site, but when humanity again begins to get excited about meeting Jesus, seeing Jesus, being in the presence of Jesus, touching Jesus, and being touched by Jesus, we will see a revival in our churches and communities like none that have come before! We should never become so apathetic about coming to the House of the Lord and worshipping together that we lose the excitement, joy and anticipation of meeting with the Christ and encountering His Spirit. Many saints need to ask the Lord to restore the joy they once held, when it came to going to the House of the Lord and connecting with Him. One of the gifts that we can give to the Lord is a joyful noise and a shout of triumph, especially when we have had to press to get to Christ and His house!

Verse 11. And when they were come into the house, they saw the young child with Mary his mother, and fell down, and worshipped him: and when they had opened their treasures, they presented unto him gifts; gold, and frankincense, and myrrh.

These men left home with a mind to give. Presenting an offering unto the King was a priority and a part of their purpose for leaving home. It is unfortunate that some people like to give – they just don't like giving unto the Lord. The wise men had a heart to give. The Word tells us people look at the outward appearance but, the Lord looks at the heart. Too often we have to be coerced to give in the house of the Lord. The truth is, those who are really in love with the Lord and what He is doing should have a made-up mind about giving in their houses of worship. Please notice that the wise men do not find the Christ in the manger; they find Him in a home. They do not find a baby, but rather a young child with His mother, Mary. Some saints believe attending church is enough. They believe they owe the Lord nothing more than their attendance.

... and fell down, and worshipped him.

The wise men gave the Christ homage, reverence and worship. They fell down, bowed and then they worshipped. Some saints want to worship, but they want their worship to be a substitute for giving. Intense worship is no replacement for giving unto the Lord of our treasure. There are people, who attend more than one worship service almost every Sunday but – other than a waved hand, a musical note, a lifted voice – they have no record of giving. The text tells us that it was after their bowing, after their worship that the wise men opened their treasures. Authentic worship ought to make us want to give gladly unto the Lord. Worshippers, who have no heart for giving, are as much an oxymoron as a healthy, beating heart devoid of blood. The old saying goes, "You can give without loving but you cannot love without giving!" Love is not inherent when a person gives to someone or something, but genuine love guarantees that giving will take place. God sees the heart of people who have the means to give, but choose not to. No matter how vehemently these individuals claim to love the Lord, the Lord knows that giving will always accompany genuine love. Wise men and wise people give unto the Lord of their treasures.

... and when they had opened their treasures, they presented unto him gifts; gold, and frankincense, and myrrh.

Wise men and wise women live with their treasures open the Lord. Too many saints today live with closed treasures, especially when it comes to the Kingdom. Just imagine how much joy it brings the Father to see His people following the example of the wise men, living with their treasures open before Him. Have you ever had a person turn his back to you, when he opens his wallet to give you money, as if to prevent you from seeing what he has? We must stop turning our backs on God, when we open our treasures. God already knows what we have – don't forget He gave it to us! It is out of our treasures that we give gifts unto Him. The wise men did not give Christ all of their treasure. They gave gifts out of their treasure. Don't let the enemy deceive you, and take care not to deceive yourself. Many people falsely believe God has access to their entire treasure. In truth, many have not opened their treasures to Him and others have given only a portion of their treasure.

Isn't it amazing that we are showered with gifts, when we celebrate our birthdays, but when it is time to honor Christ in the season in which we celebrate His birth, everyone receives gifts except for Him! Something is wrong with the psyche of saints, who can buy a gift in their child's name, take their child to a birthday party and present that gift. Yet, the same saints see nothing wrong with withholding gifts from Christ. The Body of Christ has to declare that this behavior is not acceptable. We should start shopping our hearts for the acceptable gift to give unto the Lord and the acceptable amount to put on the altar to say, "Happy birthday, Jesus!"

... gold, and frankincense, and myrrh.

Each of these gifts has significance and meaning. Gold is a gift usually given to a king. The wise men had met Herod, who ruled at the time of Christ's birth, but there is no record that they presented gifts to him. The Christ child, who they recognized as the King of the Jews, is presented with gold. There were religious leaders and others in Jerusalem, who had no clue that the King had been born. The Christian must always thank God for revelation and, most importantly, act upon revelation. Sometimes, God hides incredible potential in small things – babies, children, new beginnings, people, situations, churches, moments in time, and even our faith. Gold speaks to the kingship in Christ. Though He was a small child, the wise men's gift of gold that day expressed to God that they recognized the king, the ruler and the leader in Him! Sometimes, we are called to give out of the revelation of who we know Christ to be.

The wise men also gave frankincense unto the child Jesus. Frankincense is an aromatic gum resin taken from the Boswellia tree. When the substance is gathered and hardened it is used as an incense, fragrance or perfume. Frankincense is a gift one would give unto deity. At times, we are called to give unto the Lord simply because we receive the revelation that He is God. Anything and every situation that confirms He is God in us, God with us, and God for us should be celebrated with some form of giving that is acceptable unto Him! Praise has a way of giving off a sweet fragrance, when that praise is pure, sincere and freely given. Prayer is an excellent fragrance – one that God saves and stores. Their gift of frankincense had a sweet aroma. Gifts given grudgingly to the Lord also have an aroma. It is a foul odor in the nostrils of God. It is my prayer that when we come to the altar, our gifts are a sweet fragrance in the nostrils of God.

The third gift the wise men presented unto the Lord Jesus was myrrh. This was an especially unusual gift to give a child. Myrrh is an ingredient in the anointing oil used for embalming. This gift was given, because Jesus is not only God and King, but He, during the time He dwelled among humanity, was also man and subject to suffering and death. He was born to die so that we who place our trust in Him can live. The myrrh suggests His life has special significance in the plan of God the Father to save fallen humanity from sin. We must always keep in mind how much God really loves us. No gift that we give could ever amount to the gift of the Father's only begotten Son, and His Son gave us His life. What a mighty sacrifice! What an incredible sacrifice! We should tell everyone about this gift! Let us pray that all earth receives Him as King and that everyone prepares Him room.

Every gift the wise men gave to the child Jesus spoke of a facet of the revelation they had of Him. As God grants us revelations of His love and of His Christ, may we too respond with gifts that speak of the revelation of Christ and the preciousness of God's love toward us. We should give God the best. We should present Him with gifts that can be given to no one else – the gifts of our complete lives, our souls and our spirits! He is worthy of all we have to offer and so much more. Give a special gift that says, "I recognize who you are and who I am now, because of your birth, life and sacrifice."

CONCLUSION

Jesus Christ wasn't opposed to wealth or a high standard of living. He said, *"I have come that they may have life, and that they may have it more abundantly."* (John 10:10 NKJV). The Bible is a guidebook toward the abundant life He wants us to enjoy. Money is oftentimes an integral part of the right kind of success. Christian money-management is crucial to a believer's financial stewardship. Only through good stewardship and management will the believer know true success.

Often, people want to get something for nothing. They look for a shortcut to wealth and success. The luck of the lottery comes to only a few. This minority sometimes experiences more pain than pleasure.

While it has been said that the test of a man's character is how he spends his time and money, money makes a good servant but a poor master. This is why we need God, the One who has mastered all things, to help us manage money His way.

Though money is necessary, the love of money is the root of all evil, as the Word of God says. Money is certainly a necessary medium of exchange, but it doesn't have to be evil. Whether money is a good or bad influence depends on our approach to it. Money is entrusted into our care. This is a key to the correct way to think about money. Money comes into our hands for us to administer in love, faith and wisdom. May we seek God's help in this office of administration. Amen!

www.ingramcontent.com/pod-product-compliance
Ingram Content Group UK Ltd.
Pitfield, Milton Keynes, MK11 3LW, UK
UKHW050414240426
12048UKWH00020B/1501